Men with ADHD 10-in-1

The Ultimate Blueprint to Master Productivity, Control Your Environment, and Build Unshakable Routines for Home and Work

TABLE OF CONTENTS

PART 1: MEN WITH ADULT ADHD 5-IN-1

PART 2: ADHD ORGANIZATION AND CLEANING 5-IN-1

PART 1: MEN WITH ADULT ADHD 5-IN-1

Master Focus, Productivity, and Your Emotions with CBT Tools to Improve Executive Function, Organization, Time Management and Relationships

DEDICATION

To every man facing the daily challenges of Adult ADHD. May this book be a guide, a toolkit, and a testament to your inherent strength and limitless potential. Your journey matters.

FOREWORD BY CAROLINA ESTEVEZ, PSY.D.

Men with Adult ADHD 5-in-1: Master Focus, Productivity, and Your Emotions with CBT Tools to Improve Executive Function, Organization, Time Management and Relationships by Jaren Knox is an exceptional and empowering handbook for men facing the challenges of ADHD. This book addresses the unique challenges that men with attention, concentration, and memory concerns face every day—such as managing impulsivity, disorganization, emotional reactivity, and inconsistent focus—through practical and evidence-based Cognitive Behavioral

Therapy (CBT) tools.

What sets this book apart is its clear, relatable tone and structured approach to helping readers build executive functioning skills. The strategies for improving focus, time management, and emotional regulation are not only rooted in research, but are also highly actionable and tailored to real-life situations that adult men often encounter, both professionally and personally.

As a psychologist, I appreciate how the book balances skill-building with emotional insight, acknowledging the frustration, shame, and self-doubt that frequently accompany undiagnosed or untreated ADHD. The guidance on improving relationships and self-awareness helps clients reframe their struggles and feel empowered rather than defeated. I would wholeheartedly recommend this book to clients because it offers a sense of clarity and direction, and it can complement therapy sessions by reinforcing skills that are learned and practiced in sessions. For men seeking to take control of their ADHD and create lasting change, this book provides a practical roadmap that is both motivating and accessible.

INTRODUCTION

You've likely felt it: the relentless hum of a mind that won't quiet, the struggle to initiate tasks even when you know their importance, or the frustration of seeing your best intentions derailed by disorganization or a racing clock.

Perhaps you've been told to "just focus harder," "try to be more organized," or "get it together," all while feeling an unseen battle raging within. This internal landscape, often misunderstood and mislabeled, is the unique experience of Adult ADHD in men, and it can feel like trying to navigate a dense fog with a compass that spins wildly.

Building on that, this internal struggle is not just a personal feeling but a scientifically recognized condition with measurable impacts. For instance, studies show that men are more frequently diagnosed with ADHD than women, with one study finding the prevalence to be 5.4% in men versus 3.2% in women, although the gender gap narrows in adulthood (Montare Behavioral Health). This is often because men are more likely to exhibit the hyperactive and impulsive symptoms that lead to an earlier diagnosis.

The consequences of undiagnosed or unmanaged ADHD extend beyond daily frustrations and can significantly affect a man's quality of life and occupational and social functioning. Men with ADHD, for example, are at a higher risk for adverse outcomes in their daily lives. Research indicates that drivers with ADHD are more likely to have a license revoked, receive multiple traffic citations, and be involved in serious car crashes. One study from Sweden's Karolinska Institute found that men with ADHD who are not receiving treatment are up to 47% more likely to be involved in a car accident (Mark Salomone). Furthermore, the link between ADHD and the criminal justice system is striking. As many as 1 in 4 people in prison have been diagnosed with ADHD, which is more than eight times the rate in the general population (WebMD). This underscores the critical need to understand and manage this condition.

For too long, the narrative around ADHD has focused on childhood hyperactivity or the simplistic notion of "lacking attention." But for adult men, the manifestation is often far more nuanced: a complex interplay of executive function challenges, emotional dysregulation, and a pervasive sense of overwhelm that impacts careers, relationships, and self-esteem. You might excel in bursts of hyperfocus, only to crash into walls of procrastination. You may possess brilliant ideas, yet struggle to translate them into consistent action. And the emotional swings can feel isolating, leaving you feeling frustrated and alone.

A paradox lives in this struggle: the very strategies you've employed to control, fix, or suppress your ADHD symptoms may have inadvertently intensified them. The harder you've pushed for perfection, the more anxiety may have swelled. The more you've tried to force focus, the more your mind may have resisted. True mastery doesn't come from battling your brain, but from understanding it, honoring its unique wiring, and equipping it with the right tools.

This book is your comprehensive toolkit, a 5-in-1 guide meticulously crafted to address the core areas where men with Adult ADHD often seek greater mastery. Drawing on effective Cognitive Behavioral Therapy (CBT) principles, alongside practical, actionable strategies, we will navigate:

- **Executive Function:** Sharpening your planning, prioritization, and decision-making skills.
- **Focus:** Cultivating sustained attention and minimizing everyday distractions.
- **Productivity:** Transforming intentions into consistent output and achieving meaningful goals.
- **Emotional Regulation:** Understanding and managing intense emotions, irritability, and rejection sensitivity.
- **Organization, Time Management & Relationships:** Building practical systems for order, optimizing your schedule, and fostering stronger, more fulfilling connections.

Your journey towards a more focused, productive, emotionally balanced, and connected life begins now. You possess an incredible capacity for growth and adaptation. All you need is the right map and the right tools.

BOOK ONE

STRENGTHENING EXECUTIVE FUNCTION

THE BRAIN'S COMMAND CENTER

CHAPTER 1

UNDERSTANDING EXECUTIVE BRAIN FUNCTION IN MEN WITH ADHD

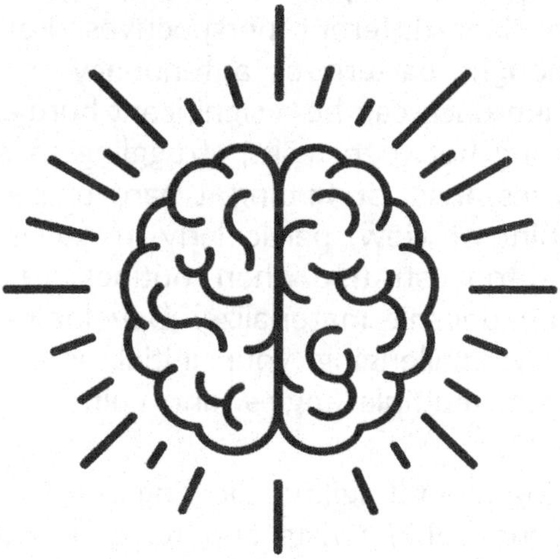

Imagine your brain as a highly sophisticated command center, constantly processing information, making decisions, and directing your actions. At the heart of this command center lies what scientists call executive function. Think of it as the air traffic controller of your mind, responsible for managing your thoughts, emotions, and behaviors to achieve your goals. It's what helps you plan your day, stay focused on a task, remember important details, and resist distractions. More formally, executive functions are a set of cognitive skills that include:

Working Memory: The ability to hold information in your mind and use it to complete a task. It's like your mental scratchpad. For men with ADHD, working memory can sometimes feel like a sieve, allowing crucial details to slip away. This isn't a deficit in intelligence but a difference in how the brain retains and manipulates information short-term. Challenges might manifest as forgetting what you were about to say mid-sentence, misplacing items immediately after using them, or struggling to follow multi-step instructions without constant reminders.

Enhancing working memory isn't about brute force memorization but developing strategies to offload cognitive burden, such as note-taking, using visual aids, or breaking down complex tasks into smaller, more manageable parts that require less simultaneous mental juggling. We'll delve into specific techniques, from active recall exercises to utilizing external memory aids, designed to solidify your mental "scratchpad" and make information more readily accessible when you need it most. These foundational working memory skills impact nearly every other executive function. Strengthening your working memory is a cornerstone of improved daily performance.

Flexible Thinking: The capacity to shift gears, adapt to new situations, and consider different perspectives. For many men with ADHD, a rigid thought pattern or a tendency to get "stuck" on a particular idea or approach can be a significant hurdle. This might mean difficulty transitioning between tasks, struggling to adjust plans when unexpected obstacles arise, or finding it hard to see a situation from someone else's point of view, particularly in social interactions. This inflexibility can lead to frustration when routines are disrupted or when a planned outcome doesn't materialize. Developing flexible thinking involves consciously challenging your initial assumptions, practicing problem-solving from multiple angles, and cultivating an openness to change.

It's about building mental agility, allowing you to pivot gracefully in response to life's inevitable twists and turns, whether it's a sudden change in work priorities or an unforeseen social engagement. We'll explore methods to deliberately practice cognitive flexibility, encouraging you to embrace novelty and reframe setbacks as opportunities for creative solutions.

Self-Control/Inhibition: The power to resist impulses, override automatic responses, and pause before acting. This executive function is often profoundly impacted in men with ADHD, leading to impulsive decisions, interruptions in conversation, or difficulty delaying gratification. Whether it's blurting out thoughts without considering the consequences, overspending on a whim, or getting drawn into immediate distractions instead of focusing on long-term goals, challenges in self-control can have wide-ranging implications. This isn't a moral or self-control related failure, but a neurobiological deficit in the brain's "stop" signals.

Learning to strengthen inhibitory control involves recognizing triggers for impulsive behavior, developing a pause-and-plan mechanism, and practicing mindful responses. We will cover strategies like the "STOP" technique (Stop, Think, Observe, Proceed) and cultivating a greater awareness of your internal states to allow for more deliberate, rather than reactive, choices. This enhanced ability to inhibit unwanted behaviors is critical for fostering healthier relationships, making sound financial decisions, and maintaining focus on important tasks.

Planning and Prioritization: The skill of organizing tasks, setting goals, and determining the most important steps. For men with ADHD, the process of breaking down large projects into manageable steps, estimating time accurately, and ranking tasks by urgency and importance can be overwhelming. This often results in a sense of paralysis, an inability to start, or a tendency to focus on less important, more engaging tasks while critical deadlines loom. The challenge isn't a lack of desire to plan but a difficulty in the sequential and hierarchical thinking required.

Effective planning involves understanding your energy cycles, creating realistic timelines, and utilizing visual tools to map out your objectives. We will introduce frameworks for robust planning, such as backward planning from a deadline, and various prioritization matrices (e.g., Eisenhower Matrix) that help cut through the noise and identify truly high-leverage activities. This mastery of planning transforms vague intentions into concrete action steps, providing a clear roadmap for achieving your ambitions.

Task Initiation: The ability to start tasks without excessive procrastination. This is a common and often agonizing hurdle for men with ADHD. Despite knowing what needs to be done, the gap between intention and action can feel immense, leading to significant delays and missed opportunities. This isn't laziness but often a struggle with perceived effort, fear of failure, or a lack of immediate reward. The "just start" advice often falls flat because the neurological mechanism for initiating action is affected.

We'll explore techniques to reduce the friction of starting, such as the "five-minute rule," body doubling, breaking tasks into minuscule "micro-steps," and building motivational cues. Understanding the specific barriers to initiation, be it overwhelm, perfectionism, or distraction, allows for targeted interventions that make starting feel less like climbing a mountain and more like stepping onto a gentle slope. Cultivating strong task initiation habits unlocks productivity and reduces the mental burden of uninitiated work or tasks awaiting action.

Organization: The systematic arrangement of information, thoughts, and physical items. A common challenge for men with ADHD is maintaining order in both their physical environment and their mental landscape. This can manifest as cluttered workspaces, disorganized digital files, chaotic schedules, or difficulty categorizing thoughts during problem-solving. Disorganization isn't merely untidiness; it's a significant drain on executive function, as constant searching for items or information consumes valuable mental energy and time.

We will explore practical strategies for creating intuitive organizational systems, from "a place for everything and everything in its place" for physical items to digital file management and effective note-taking methods for thoughts and information. The goal is to create external structures that support your internal executive functions, reducing cognitive load and freeing up mental resources for higher-level tasks. An organized system creates predictable pathways, minimizing distractions and maximizing efficiency.

Monitoring: The capacity to check your work, track your progress, and adjust as needed. This executive function involves self-awareness and continuous self-assessment. For men with ADHD, challenges in monitoring can lead to overlooking errors, misjudging the impact of their actions, or struggling to adapt strategies that aren't working. It's the "feedback loop" of the brain that helps you learn from experience and refine your approach. This might mean difficulty staying on track during a task, failing to notice when your attention drifts, or not recognizing when a conversation is going awry. Improving monitoring involves cultivating metacognition (thinking about your thinking) and implementing checkpoints throughout your tasks and day.

We will discuss methods for self-correction, reviewing progress against goals, and developing a heightened awareness of your own cognitive and emotional states. Effective monitoring transforms your experiences into valuable learning opportunities, enabling you to continuously refine your strategies and achieve consistent improvement.

For men with ADHD, the ability to self-monitor operates a bit differently. While the core machinery is all there, signals might sometimes get crossed, priorities might shift unexpectedly, or impulse control might take an unscheduled coffee break. Perhaps you've experienced the frustration of knowing exactly what you need to do but you struggle to start it or you've found yourself constantly side-tracked by incoming emails, notifications, or a sudden, compelling idea. Maybe keeping track of appointments feels like a constant battle, or organizing your workspace (physical or digital) seems insurmountable. These experiences are not uncommon and are deeply rooted in the neurobiology of ADHD, leading to a pervasive sense of being overwhelmed, constantly playing catch-up, and feeling as though your potential is hindered by internal resistance. The mental fatigue that accompanies these struggles is substantial, often leading to burnout and a cycle of self-criticism.

This isn't a sign of weakness or a lack of intelligence; it's simply how your brain is wired. Research shows that ADHD involves differences in brain structure and neurotransmitter activity, particularly in areas of the prefrontal cortex: the very region responsible for executive functions. Specifically, there are often variations in the density and function of dopamine and norepinephrine pathways, which are critical for regulating attention, motivation, reward, and impulse control.

These neurochemical differences can explain why tasks that require sustained effort, planning, or inhibition feel disproportionately challenging. You're not alone in this experience, and understanding why these challenges arise is the first crucial step toward addressing them. Recognizing ADHD as a neurodevelopmental difference, rather than a character flaw, is profoundly liberating. It shifts the narrative from "I'm not trying hard enough" to "My brain works differently, and I need specific tools to help it operate optimally." This understanding paves the way for self-compassion and effective strategy development.

We're going to dive into the intricate workings of the executive brain, specifically through the lens of adult ADHD in men. We'll explore how challenges in areas like working memory, attention, planning, task initiation, and self-regulation can impact daily life, from professional endeavors to personal relationships. From missed deadlines and forgotten errands to difficulty managing anger or sticking to a budget, the ripple effects of executive function differences can be profound and often lead to feelings of overwhelm, frustration, or even shame. Consider the professional sphere: a brilliant idea stalled by procrastination, a promotion missed due to disorganization, or strained collegial relationships from impulsive remarks.

In personal life, it could be the frustration of a partner over forgotten promises, the chaos of a perpetually messy home, or the guilt associated with unfulfilled intentions. This book aims to dismantle those feelings by providing clarity and actionable solutions, not by masking symptoms, but by building robust internal and external systems that support your unique brain wiring. We will move beyond merely identifying problems to proactively constructing a life that leverages your strengths and mitigates your challenges.

More importantly, we'll begin to lay the groundwork for a new understanding of your own brain, recognizing its unique strengths while identifying areas where targeted strategies can make a profound difference.

This isn't about "fixing" ADHD. It's a neurodevelopmental difference rooted in the brain's unique wiring and chemistry. While ADHD impacts everyone differently, its core lies in variations in how certain brain regions, particularly those in the prefrontal cortex (the brain's executive control center), communicate and how neurotransmitters like dopamine and norepinephrine are regulated. These neurotransmitters are crucial for attention, motivation, reward, and impulse control.

For individuals with ADHD, these systems may not function optimally, leading to the well-known challenges of the condition. Understanding this underlying neurobiology is crucial because it shifts the perspective from a moral failing to a recognition of a genuine neurological difference. This perspective empowers you to approach your challenges with curiosity and strategic thinking, rather than self-blame. It enables you to see your brain not as broken, but as a uniquely wired instrument that requires a specific instruction manual and maintenance schedule to perform at its best.

In the chapters to come, we'll break down each of these executive functions, offering practical, evidence-based strategies tailored specifically for the ADHD brain. You'll learn how to bolster your working memory, sharpen your attention, master the art of planning, overcome procrastination, and cultivate greater self-control. We will equip you with a comprehensive toolkit that includes Cognitive Behavioral Therapy (CBT) informed techniques, practical organizational hacks, and mindfulness practices, all designed to create sustainable change. Each strategy will be presented with clear explanations, relatable examples, and actionable steps you can implement immediately.

Get ready to embark on a journey that will empower you to become the architect of your own mind, transforming challenges into opportunities for growth and success. This journey is not about eradicating ADHD, but about building a life where your neurodiversity becomes a source of unique strengths and adaptive capabilities. The command center of your mind and behaviors is yours to master and lead, and with the right tools, you will navigate it with unprecedented clarity and control.

CHAPTER 2

ENHANCING WORKING MEMORY AND ATTENTION

In the grand scheme of your brain's command center, working memory and attention are two of the most critical operators. They work in tandem, constantly interacting to help you process information, stay on task, and make sense of the world around you. For men with ADHD, these two functions often present unique challenges, and developing specific strategies to enhance them can dramatically improve daily functioning and reduce frustration.

This chapter will illuminate the intricate interplay between working memory and attention, offering actionable, evidence-based techniques to sharpen these vital cognitive skills. Understanding their individual mechanisms and how they are impacted by ADHD is the first step toward reclaiming control over your mental focus and capacity. We will delve into the latest research insights, translating complex neuroscience into practical, everyday applications that resonate with the experiences of adult men navigating ADHD. The goal is not just to manage symptoms but to cultivate robust cognitive habits that foster greater efficiency, clarity, and confidence in all aspects of your life.

The Power of Working Memory: Your Brain's Mental Scratchpad

Think of working memory as your brain's temporary holding area: a mental scratchpad where you actively hold and manipulate information for a short period. It's what you use when someone gives you a phone number and you hold it in your mind just long enough to dial it, or when you're following a recipe and remembering the ingredients you've already added. It's crucial for understanding complex instructions, solving problems, and even following conversations. Without a robust working memory, even simple daily tasks can become arduous, leading to errors, forgotten details, and a pervasive sense of being overwhelmed. Consider the cumulative effect of constantly having to re-read instructions, re-ask questions, or retrace your steps; this cognitive friction drains energy and erodes confidence.

For men with ADHD, this "mental scratchpad" is often prone to glitches. It's not that the capacity isn't there, but rather that the information might not "stick" long enough or might be easily overwritten by new stimuli. This isn't a deficit in intelligence or effort, but a characteristic of how the ADHD brain processes and retains transient information, often due to differences in neural pathways involving neurotransmitters like dopamine and norepinephrine that are vital for information processing and retention.

For men with ADHD, a common experience is that this mental scratchpad can feel more like a sieve. Information goes in, but it often slips out before it can be fully processed or stored. This can manifest as:

- **Difficulty remembering instructions**: You hear them, but they vanish moments later. You might nod along, fully intending to comply, only to find the specific details have evaporated when you go to execute the task. This can lead to frustration from supervisors, colleagues, or partners who may misinterpret this as disinterest or incompetence. The internal experience, however, is one of acute blankness, a "tip-of-the-tongue" sensation for information that was just presented.

- **Struggling to follow multi-step tasks**: You get lost halfway through. Imagine trying to assemble furniture from a detailed diagram or cook a complex meal; each step seems to overwrite the previous one, forcing you to constantly refer back to the instructions, which itself becomes a taxing act on working memory. This often leads to incomplete projects, errors, and significant time overruns.
- **Losing your train of thought in conversations**: You forget what you were going to say or what the other person just said. This can make reciprocal conversations feel like a high-wire act, leading to awkward pauses, accidental interruptions, or the inability to contribute meaningfully to a discussion. It impacts social connections and professional interactions, as others may perceive you as inattentive or disengaged.
- **Challenges with mental math or complex reasoning**: Holding numbers or ideas in mind feels overwhelming. Simple calculations, comparing options, or synthesizing information from multiple sources can become a Herculean effort if you cannot reliably hold the necessary data in your short-term mental buffer. This impacts decision-making, problem-solving, and your ability to engage in strategic thinking.

These manifestations are not indicators of your overall intellectual capacity but rather signal specific points of friction within your working memory system. The good news is that just as you can train a muscle, you can implement strategies to bolster your working memory, compensating for inherent differences and building more robust systems for information retention and retrieval.

Strategies to Bolster Your Working Memory

Externalize Everything: Your brain isn't the best place for storage. Get the information out! Use notebooks, sticky notes, whiteboards, or digital tools (apps like Evernote, Google Keep, or Trello) to capture ideas, to-do lists, and crucial information immediately. The act of writing or typing helps solidify the information, and having it externalized frees up your working memory for active processing.

This is perhaps the single most impactful strategy for working memory challenges. Instead of relying on your internal "scratchpad," which is prone to erasure, create an external, durable one. This means immediately jotting down ideas that pop into your head, capturing instructions verbatim, documenting decisions, and maintaining comprehensive to-do lists. The specific tool doesn't matter as much as the habit of consistent, immediate externalization. For physical items, consider a dedicated inbox for documents, a hook for keys, or a consistent spot for your wallet. The less your working memory has to hold onto, the more capacity it has for the active processing required for problem-solving and immediate tasks. This also reduces anxiety, as you no longer have to fear forgetting something important.

Break It Down: Complex tasks overwhelm working memory. Deconstruct large projects into smaller, manageable steps. If you have to remember five things, break them into five separate, smaller "chunks" that are easier to hold. This strategy is critical for avoiding cognitive overload. When faced with a large project like "organize the garage" or "prepare for the annual review," the sheer scope can paralyze working memory, making it impossible to even begin. Instead, break it down: "clear a 2x2 foot section of the garage," "gather last year's performance review," or "outline the main points of my contribution."

Each smaller step requires less simultaneous mental effort and feels more approachable. For instructions, ask for them to be given one or two steps at a time, or immediately write down each step as it's provided. This reduces the burden on your mental scratchpad, allowing you to focus on executing one "chunk" before moving to the next.

Visualize It: If you're trying to remember a sequence or a list, try to create a mental image or a story connecting the items. For example, if you need to buy milk, bread, and eggs, picture a cow drinking milk, eating bread, and laying eggs. The more vivid and unusual, the better. Our brains are incredibly adept at remembering images and stories. By transforming abstract information (like a list of items or a sequence of instructions) into a concrete, often absurd, mental picture, you're tapping into a more primal and resilient memory system. This is why memory champions use elaborate "memory palaces."

While you don't need to build a palace for your grocery list, a simple, vivid visualization can significantly improve recall. If you have to remember a series of steps for a procedure, imagine yourself performing them, perhaps with exaggerated or humorous movements. This active mental engagement encodes the information more deeply than passive listening.

Use Repetition and Elaboration: When you receive new information, repeat it aloud or to yourself. Then, try to elaborate on it or connect it to something you already know. For instance, if you're introduced to "John Smith," you might think, "John Smith, like the explorer." This active processing helps solidify the memory. This technique leverages the principle that active engagement with information strengthens its neural pathways. Simply hearing something isn't enough; you need to process it. Repeating it aloud (or sub-vocally) forces your brain to re-encode the information. Elaboration takes it a step further: by linking new information to existing knowledge, you're creating a richer, more interconnected neural network, making the new information easier to retrieve. For example, if learning a new concept at work, try to explain it in your own words or think about how it applies to a past project. This deep processing transforms shallow, transient memories into more robust, accessible ones.

Minimize Cognitive Load: Reduce the number of things your working memory has to manage simultaneously. Close unnecessary tabs on your computer, put your phone away, and dedicate yourself to one task at a time when possible. Fewer inputs mean more capacity for the task at hand. In our hyper-connected world, we are constantly bombarded with stimuli. Each open tab, each notification, each background conversation is vying for a slice of your limited working memory.

For the ADHD brain, which already struggles with filtering, this constant barrage creates significant cognitive noise. By proactively reducing inputs, you create a clearer mental workspace. This might involve closing all but essential applications when working, designating specific "no-interruption" times, or even physically turning away from distracting environments. The goal is to funnel your mental resources into a single stream, allowing your working memory to operate at its full, albeit unique, capacity without being fragmented by competing demands.

"Chunking" Information: Group related pieces of information together. Phone numbers (e.g., 555-123-4567) are a classic example of chunking. Apply this principle to lists, concepts, or instructions. Instead of remembering seven individual digits for a phone number, we remember two chunks (a three-digit and a four-digit sequence, or three sets of three or four digits). This dramatically reduces the burden on working memory.

Apply this to other areas: if you have a list of errands, group them by location (e.g., "bank, post office, grocery store" as one "chunk" for the main street). If you're studying a topic, group related sub-topics together. This strategy makes large amounts of information more digestible and manageable for your working memory, transforming what feels like an endless stream of data into discrete, memorable units.

The effectiveness of this technique, known as "chunking," is a cornerstone of cognitive psychology, first popularized by George A. Miller in his 1956 paper, "The Magical Number Seven, Plus or Minus Two." Subsequent research has confirmed that chunking helps bypass the limited capacity of working memory by organizing information into meaningful groups. For example, a 2021 study on high school students found that those who used chunking to divide information into two or three groups were able to memorize and recall information significantly more effectively than those who were given the same information all at once (ResearchGate).

This ability to recode smaller units into a single, familiar chunk reduces cognitive load and frees up capacity for other information, leading to better overall retention and recall.

Sharpening Attention: Focusing Your Mental Spotlight

Attention is your mental spotlight, determining where your brain's resources are directed. It allows you to select relevant information and filter out distractions. For men with ADHD, this spotlight often behaves more like a disco ball, flitting rapidly from one stimulus to another, making it difficult to sustain focus on a single task, even one you find interesting. This isn't a lack of desire to focus, but a challenge in regulating the intensity and duration of the mental spotlight. The brain's filtering mechanisms, particularly in the prefrontal cortex, may struggle to prioritize relevant stimuli over irrelevant ones, leading to an almost equal weighting of all incoming information. This can be exhausting and lead to fragmented experiences, as your mind constantly pulls you in different directions. The insidious part of attention difficulties is that they often go unnoticed until a significant consequence (a missed deadline, a misunderstood instruction, an incomplete task) brings them to light.

This can lead to:

- **Difficulty initiating tasks**: The sheer volume of potential distractions makes starting hard. The very act of beginning a task requires a commitment of attention, but if your spotlight is constantly scanning for the next shiny object, it's hard to settle it on the task at hand. The decision paralysis stemming from a myriad of competing stimuli can be debilitating.
- **Frequent mind-wandering**: Your thoughts drift away from the task at hand. Even when you do manage to start, your internal

landscape can be just as distracting as the external one. One thought leads to another, pulling your attention away from your intended focus, often without you even realizing it until minutes later.

- **Easily distracted by external stimuli**: A sound, a notification, or something visual pulls your attention away. The ADHD brain can be exquisitely sensitive to novel stimuli. A siren outside, a phone vibrating, a person walking by; any of these can hijack your attention, pulling you away from what you're doing, sometimes for extended periods as you re-engage with the new stimulus.
- **Hyperfocus on less important tasks**: You might get intensely absorbed in something tangential while ignoring critical priorities. Paradoxically, the ADHD brain can also exhibit "hyperfocus," an intense absorption in a task that is often intrinsically interesting. While this sounds like a superpower, it becomes problematic when directed at non-priority tasks (e.g., meticulously organizing your sock drawer when a major work report is due). This is a form of attention dysregulation, not controlled focus.

Cultivating sustained attention requires intentional effort and the creation of an environment, both physical and mental, that supports focus. It's about training your mental spotlight to stay aimed, even when faced with compelling diversions.

Strategies to Cultivate Sustained Attention:

Create an "Attention Zone": Designate a specific physical space (even if it's just a corner of a room) that you associate only with focused work. Keep it tidy, free from distractions, and minimize visual clutter. This primes your brain to enter a state of focus when you're in that zone. The power of environmental cues cannot be overstated. By creating a dedicated "attention zone," you're building a psychological association between that space and focused activity.

This means no eating, no social media Browse, and ideally, no unrelated conversations in this specific area. The fewer competing associations that space has, the stronger its power to cue focus. Optimize lighting, minimize noise (noise-cancelling headphones can be a game-changer), and ensure comfortable ergonomics. This physical boundary helps create a mental one, signalling to your brain that "this is where deep work happens."

Time Blocking and the Pomodoro Technique: Allocate specific blocks of time for focused work (e.g., 25-minute intervals). During these blocks, commit to working on only one task, eliminating all distractions. The Pomodoro Technique, developed by Francesco Cirillo in the late 1980s, involves 25 minutes of focused work followed by a 5-minute break. This structured approach trains your attention span. A study in *Time and Society* found that implementing the Pomodoro technique in a digital marketing company helped employees work more efficiently and improve their work-life balance (Pedersen et al., 2024). Time blocking means assigning specific tasks to specific time slots in your calendar. This prevents decision fatigue and provides a clear agenda.

The Pomodoro Technique breaks work into manageable sprints, leveraging the idea that sustained, intense focus is difficult beyond certain durations. The short breaks prevent burnout and allow for a mental reset. The structure provides external scaffolding for your attention, making the daunting prospect of "working all day" into a series of achievable, short focus bursts. During your focused "Pomodoros," put your phone on silent, close irrelevant tabs, and commit fully to the chosen task.

Single-Tasking: Resist the urge to multitask. While it might feel productive, switching between tasks rapidly depletes your attention and working memory. Focus on completing one thing before moving to the next. Multitasking is a myth for deep, meaningful work. What we perceive as multitasking is actually rapid task-switching, which incurs a "switching cost." Each time you jump from one task to another, your brain has to reorient itself, load relevant information into working memory, and discard the previous context. This process is inefficient and incredibly draining for the ADHD brain. Commit to true single-tasking: pick one item, and dedicate your full attention to it until it's complete or until your designated focus time ends. This practice dramatically improves the quality of your output and reduces the feeling of mental fragmentation.

Scheduled Distraction Breaks: Instead of fighting distractions, acknowledge them and schedule time for them. If a nagging thought or a desire to check social media arises, make a quick note of it and promise yourself you'll address it during your next scheduled break.

Trying to suppress every distracting thought or urge often backfires, increasing their intensity. Instead, use a "parking lot" approach: keep a notepad handy, and when a non-task-related thought pops up ("I need to call X," "Did I send that email?"), quickly jot it down and tell yourself you'll address it during your next scheduled break.

This validates the thought without letting it derail your current focus. Similarly, schedule specific times for checking email, social media, or news, rather than allowing them to constantly interrupt your flow. This creates boundaries for your attention, putting you in control rather than being at the mercy of external stimuli.

Active Listening and Engagement: In conversations, practice active listening by repeating or summarizing what the other person has said. This forces your attention to remain engaged and helps prevent mind-wandering.

For men with ADHD, conversations can be particularly challenging due to the interplay of working memory and attention. Active listening is a powerful antidote. When you actively summarize or reflect what the other person has said, you're not just proving you heard them; you're forcing your brain to process, encode, and momentarily hold their words in your working memory.

This acts as an "attention anchor," keeping your mental spotlight firmly on the conversation. It also ensures comprehension and builds stronger rapport. Practice asking clarifying questions, making eye contact, and resisting the urge to formulate your response while the other person is still speaking.

"Attention Anchors": Use subtle physical or sensory cues to bring your attention back. This could be a deep breath, focusing on your posture, or a specific object on your desk. When you notice your mind drifting, use your anchor to gently pull it back to the task. Attention anchors are mindful cues you can use to gently redirect your focus when you detect mind-wandering. A deep breath is a classic example: when your mind starts to drift, simply take a slow, deliberate inhale and exhale, bringing your awareness back to your body and then to the task.

You might choose a specific object on your desk, such as a pen, or a paperweight, to glance at and use as a visual cue to re-center. Alternatively, simply re-adjusting your posture can serve as a physical reminder to re-engage.

The key is to develop a consistent, simple anchor that you can deploy quickly and unobtrusively to bring your mental spotlight back to where you want it. This builds self-awareness and self-regulation.

Minimize Notifications: Turn off non-essential notifications on your phone and computer. Each chime or pop-up is a direct assault on your attention. Notifications are designed to hijack your attention.

For the ADHD brain, which is already prone to being externally distracted, they are particularly disruptive. Take ruthless control over your notifications. Turn off all non-essential alerts on your phone, tablet, and computer. For work-related apps, customize settings to only receive critical alerts.

Consider using "Do Not Disturb" modes during focused work periods. The fewer artificial "pings" your environment generates, the easier it will be for your brain to sustain its focus.

This simple act can dramatically reduce cognitive fragmentation and the constant urge to check your devices, freeing up significant mental bandwidth.

By understanding the distinct roles of working memory and attention, and by actively implementing these strategies, you can begin to strengthen these foundational executive functions.

It's a process of intentional training, much like building a muscle. The more you practice, the more resilient and effective your mental command center will become, setting the stage for greater control over your daily tasks and overall success. This journey requires patience and self-compassion.

There will be days when these strategies feel effortless, and days when they feel like an uphill battle. The key is consistent effort, acknowledging small victories, and adapting your approach as you learn what works best for your unique neurobiology.

The ultimate goal is to move from a reactive state, constantly battling distractions and forgetfulness, to a proactive one, where you are the conscious director of your attention and the master of your mental capacity.

You are equipping yourself not just to cope, but to thrive.

CHAPTER 3

MASTERING PLANNING AND PRIORITIZATION

You have a destination in mind, but how do you get there efficiently, without getting lost or side tracked? This is where planning and prioritization come in. They are the GPS and the strategic map of your executive function command center. Planning is the ability to create a roadmap for achieving a goal, breaking it down into steps and anticipating potential obstacles. Prioritization is the skill of identifying which tasks are most important and urgent, ensuring your efforts are directed where they matter most.

These two skills, when harmonized, provide the crucial framework for converting intentions into tangible accomplishments. For men with ADHD, who often grapple with an internal landscape of competing thoughts and external environments rich with distractions, mastering planning and prioritization is not merely a convenience but a fundamental requirement for reducing overwhelm, enhancing productivity, and fostering a sense of control over one's life. The aim is to move beyond mere reactivity to a state of proactive purpose, where your actions are aligned with your deepest goals and values.

For men with ADHD, these skills can often feel like trying to navigate a dense fog with a faulty compass. The desire to achieve is strong, but the pathway to get there can be murky, leading to:

- **Difficulty initiating large projects**: The sheer scale of a task can be paralyzing without a clear plan. When a task appears as an undifferentiated monolith, the ADHD brain's executive functions, particularly task initiation, struggle to find an entry point. This leads to what's often called "analysis paralysis," where the magnitude of the work prevents any work from beginning at all. The internal dialogue can become a loop of "where do I even start?"
- **Underestimating time**: A tendency to believe tasks will take less time than they actually do, leading to last-minute rushes and missed deadlines. This optimistic bias, sometimes termed "time blindness," is a hallmark of ADHD. It's not intentional deception but a genuine difficulty in accurately perceiving and allocating time, leading to chronic lateness, hurried work, and the stress of always being behind schedule.
- **Getting side tracked by novelties**: The "shiny object" syndrome can derail a carefully laid plan in moments. The ADHD brain's heightened sensitivity to novelty means that new ideas, sudden inspirations, or unexpected stimuli can effortlessly pull attention away from current priorities, no matter how well-planned. This can result in a landscape of half-finished projects and forgotten intentions, as one fascinating tangent leads to another.
- **Struggling to differentiate between urgent and important**: Everything feels urgent, leading to a constant state of reactivity rather than proactive progress. When all incoming stimuli are perceived with similar weight, the capacity to discern true priorities is compromised. This results in a "fire-fighting" mentality, where immediate, often minor, demands consume all available energy, leaving critical long-term goals perpetually neglected.
- **Overwhelm and procrastination**: Without a clear path forward, it's easy to feel inundated and avoid starting altogether. The cumulative effect of these challenges is a deep sense of overwhelm. When the mental map is unclear, the compass is erratic, and every direction seems equally compelling yet daunting, the natural response for many is to simply avoid the journey, leading to significant procrastination and its accompanying guilt.

Mastering these functions isn't about rigid adherence to a perfect schedule, but about developing adaptable systems that work with your ADHD brain, not against it. It's about building external scaffolds that compensate for internal inconsistencies, creating a framework that supports your natural creativity and energy while providing the necessary structure to channel them effectively. These strategies are designed to provide clarity, reduce mental friction, and empower you to move forward with purpose, even when your internal wiring presents unique challenges.

Planning Your Route: Planning Your Route: Creating a Functional Roadmap

Effective planning for the ADHD brain needs to be visual, flexible, and broken down into digestible pieces. The linear, purely mental planning approach that works for some can be a significant barrier for others. By leveraging visual cues and externalizing cognitive load, you create a system that is more forgiving, adaptable, and intuitive for your brain's unique processing style. This approach acknowledges that the challenge isn't a lack of intelligence or capability, but a difference in how information is organized and accessed.

Strategies for Enhanced Planning:

The "Brain Dump" First: Before you can plan, you need to know everything that's occupying your mental space. Dedicate 10-15 minutes to write down everything you need to do, remember, or worry about. Don't filter, just get it all out. This clears your working memory and provides a raw inventory. This initial step is non-negotiable. Your working memory is a finite resource, and constantly juggling a mental list of tasks, worries, and ideas is incredibly draining. The brain dump provides immediate relief from this cognitive burden. Whether it's on a piece of paper, a digital document, or a whiteboard, the act of externalizing these thoughts allows your brain to release them temporarily, freeing up mental space for actual planning and problem-solving. This inventory also brings to light hidden tasks or anxieties that might unconsciously be contributing to your sense of overwhelm. Do this regularly, perhaps at the start or end of each day, or at the beginning of your weekly review.

Visual Planning Tools are Your Friends: Ditch purely mental plans. Utilize whiteboards, large paper calendars, digital mind-mapping tools (e.g., MindMeister, XMind), or project management apps (e.g., Trello,

Asana). Seeing your tasks visually helps you connect the dots and anticipate steps.

For the ADHD brain, which often thinks in webs rather than linear lists, visual tools are invaluable. A large whiteboard where you can map out projects with sticky notes that can be moved around, a digital Kanban board in Trello showing tasks moving from "To Do" to "In Progress" to "Done," or a mind map illustrating the interconnectedness of ideas can make complex plans tangible and less intimidating. These tools leverage your brain's natural affinity for visual information, allowing you to see the entire scope of a project, identify dependencies, and track progress more intuitively. Experiment with different tools to find what resonates best with your personal style.

Reverse Engineering: For larger goals (e.g., "complete project X by end of month"), start at the deadline and work backward. What needs to be done the week before? The day before? This helps break down daunting tasks into smaller, actionable chunks. This strategy combats procrastination by changing your perspective. Instead of looking at a mountain of work, you're looking at the last small step needed to reach the summit, and then identifying the step just before that, and so on. This makes the initial steps less overwhelming and creates a clear sequence. For example, if you have a presentation due on Friday, what must be done by Thursday? What about Wednesday?

This helps identify critical milestones and prevents the last-minute panic that often accompanies time blindness. It also highlights potential bottlenecks early on, allowing you to adjust your plan before it's too late.

Estimate Realistically (and Add a Buffer): Acknowledge your tendency to underestimate time. For each task, estimate how long you think it will take, then add 25-50% more. This built-in buffer accounts for distractions, unexpected issues, or simply needing more time to get into "flow." This is a crucial self-awareness strategy. Time blindness is a real phenomenon in ADHD; you genuinely believe you can do something faster than you can. By consciously adding a buffer, you're building resilience into your schedule. This buffer isn't wasted time; it's an investment in your peace of mind and the quality of your work. It allows for interruptions, unexpected difficulties, and the natural fluctuations in your focus and energy. Over time, as you consistently add buffers and track your actual time, you'll develop a more accurate internal clock.

Identify the "Next Action": For every item on your list, ask yourself: "What's the very next physical action I need to take to move this forward?" Instead of "Plan vacation," the next action might be "Research flights to Bali" or "Ask a partner about preferred dates." This makes starting easier. This concept, popularized by David Allen in "Getting Things Done," is incredibly powerful for task initiation. "Plan vacation" is an overwhelming project, not an actionable step. By breaking it down to the smallest physical action (something you can *do*), you remove the mental barrier to starting. "Research flights to Bali" is a concrete action that can be performed. This micro-commitment lowers the activation energy required to begin, making procrastination less likely. Apply this relentlessly to every large, vague task on your list.

Schedule Transition Time: ADHD brains often struggle with transitions between tasks. Build in small breaks (5-10 minutes) between scheduled activities. This helps reset your focus and prevents the feeling of being constantly rushed. Transitions are points of friction for the ADHD brain.

Shifting from one task to a completely different one without a pause can be jarring and lead to mental "residue" from the previous activity, making it hard to engage with the next. Scheduling short breaks, even just to stand up, stretch, grab water, or look out a window, allows your brain to "reset." This isn't wasted time; it's an intentional re-calibration that primes you for the next period of focus. It reduces the feeling of being perpetually rushed and overwhelmed, which can trigger avoidance behaviors.

The "If-Then" Plan: Anticipate potential obstacles. For example: "IF I get distracted by emails while working on the report, THEN I will close my email client for the next 30 minutes." This pre-planned response reduces decision fatigue in the moment. The ADHD journey is filled with potential sidetracks and unexpected detours. "If-Then" planning (also known as implementation intentions) helps you preemptively navigate these. By deciding *in advance* how you will respond to common challenges, you eliminate the need for real-time decision-making when your executive functions might be compromised by distraction or emotional overwhelm.

This creates automatic, pre-programmed responses to triggers, making it easier to stay on track. Brainstorm your most common pitfalls (e.g., phone notifications, hunger, a sudden urge to clean) and create a corresponding "then" statement.

Prioritizing Your Efforts: Directing Your Focus

Not all tasks are created equal. Prioritization is about deciding what deserves your immediate attention versus what can wait or even be delegated. Without this skill, you risk spending all your energy on urgent but unimportant tasks, leaving the truly significant ones undone. For men with ADHD, the challenge often lies in the brain's tendency to give undue weight to novelty and immediate gratification, making it difficult to defer present desires for future rewards.

This means that an urgent email might feel more compelling than a long-term strategic project, even if the latter holds far greater importance. Developing robust prioritization skills shifts your focus from merely "doing things" to "doing the right things," aligning your efforts with your overarching goals and values. It moves you from a reactive state to one of deliberate, strategic action, significantly impacting your productivity and sense of accomplishment.

Strategies for Smarter Prioritization:

The Eisenhower Matrix: Categorize tasks into four quadrants:

- **Urgent & Important (Do First)**: Crises, deadlines, pressing problems. These tasks demand immediate attention and have significant consequences if neglected. For ADHD, these are often the tasks you feel compelled to address due to immediate pressure, but a healthy system minimizes the number of tasks in this quadrant through proactive planning.
- **Important, Not Urgent (Schedule)**: Planning, relationship building, prevention, long-term goals. This is where you want to spend most of your time. This quadrant is the powerhouse of strategic progress. These tasks are critical for your long-term success and well-being but often lack immediate external pressure, making them easy for the ADHD brain to defer. Deliberately scheduling time for these tasks is paramount.
- **Urgent, Not Important (Delegate/Minimize)**: Interruptions, some emails, minor requests. These tasks create a sense of urgency but contribute little to your core goals. For men with ADHD, these "urgent but unimportant" tasks can be particularly distracting due to their immediate demand for attention. Learn to identify them, delegate if possible, or address them quickly and efficiently without letting them derail your main focus.

- **Not Urgent, Not Important (Eliminate)**: Distractions, time-wasters. This framework provides a clear visual for decision-making. These are the activities that offer little to no value. For the ADHD brain, the allure of easy, low-effort activities in this quadrant can be a major time sink. Ruthlessly identify and eliminate them from your day. The Eisenhower Matrix is powerful because it forces you to think critically about the *value* of each task, not just its immediate pull.

Identify Your "Big Rocks": Before diving into your daily "pebbles" and "sand," identify the 1-3 most important tasks (your "big rocks") that must get done that day or week. Schedule these first. This ensures that even if other things go awry, your most critical priorities are addressed. This metaphor, often attributed to Stephen Covey, highlights the importance of proactive prioritization. If you fill your jar with sand (small, urgent tasks) and pebbles (medium-importance tasks) first, there will be no room for the big rocks (your most important goals). By scheduling and tackling your big rocks early in your most productive periods, you guarantee that what truly matters gets done, even if the rest of your day becomes chaotic. This creates a powerful sense of accomplishment and keeps you aligned with your long-term vision.

The "One Thing" Rule: Each day, pick one single task that, if completed, would make the biggest positive impact. Focus on that one thing, especially during your peak productive hours. This creates a sense of accomplishment and prevents overwhelm. This is a simplification of the "Big Rocks" concept, designed to be even more accessible for days when overwhelm feels imminent. By identifying just *one* crucial task, you reduce decision fatigue and concentrate your limited executive function on a single, high-leverage activity. Completing that one thing provides a significant psychological boost, reducing guilt and building momentum for future days. This is particularly effective for those days where getting started feels impossible; focusing on just one victory makes the day feel purposeful.

Consider Energy Levels: Don't just prioritize by importance; consider when you have the most energy and focus. Schedule your most demanding, "important-not-urgent" tasks during your peak productivity windows (e.g., mornings for many with ADHD), and save the less demanding tasks for times when your energy naturally dips. This is a critical adjustment for the ADHD brain. Your capacity for focused work fluctuates throughout the day. Trying to force intense concentration during a low-energy period is a recipe for frustration and procrastination. Learn to identify your personal "power hours": Times when you are naturally most alert and focused. Reserve these for your most challenging, high-impact tasks (Quadrant 2 of the Eisenhower Matrix). Use your lower-energy periods for administrative tasks, routine emails, or less cognitively demanding work. This leverages your natural rhythms rather than fighting against them.

Review and Adapt Daily/Weekly: Planning and prioritization aren't one-time events. At the end of each day or week, review what worked and what didn't. Did you underestimate time? Did you get side tracked? Adjust your approach for the next planning cycle. This iterative process is crucial for long-term improvement. Your brain is unique, and what works one week might need adjustment the next.

Regular review sessions (e.g., 15 minutes at the end of each day, an hour at the end of the week) allow you to objectively assess your strategies. Ask yourself: "What went well?" "What challenged me?" "What can I learn for tomorrow/next week?" This meta-cognition (in other words, thinking about your thinking) is essential for refining your planning and prioritization systems over time, making them increasingly tailored to your individual needs and patterns.

The 2-Minute Rule: If a task takes less than two minutes to complete, do it immediately. This prevents small, easy tasks from piling up and creating mental clutter that drains your executive function. This simple rule, also from "Getting Things Done," is a powerful antidote to procrastination of small tasks. Minor items such as replying to a quick email, filing a document, or putting away a dish can accumulate quickly, creating a background hum of unfinished business that saps mental energy.

By tackling them immediately, you prevent them from becoming "mental sticky notes" that constantly demand attention and drain your working memory. This frees up your cognitive resources for more significant tasks and provides small, consistent wins throughout your day.

By diligently applying these strategies, you'll transform planning from a source of anxiety into a powerful tool for clarity and direction.

You'll move beyond reacting to daily demands and start proactively shaping your days, ensuring your energy and attention are consistently directed towards what truly matters.

This mastery of planning and prioritization is a cornerstone of taking command of your executive brain, leading to increased productivity, reduced stress, and a greater sense of accomplishment in all areas of your life.

It is the framework upon which a more organized, purposeful, and fulfilling existence can be built, allowing your unique strengths to shine unhindered by the typical challenges of ADHD.

CHAPTER 4

CULTIVATING TASK INITIATION AND FOLLOW-THROUGH

You've meticulously planned your day and prioritized your tasks, a truly commendable feat for any brain, let alone one with ADHD. But then comes the moment of truth: actually starting the thing, and then, perhaps even more challenging, sticking with it until it's done. This is where task initiation and follow-through step onto the stage as critical players in your executive function ensemble. These are the muscles of execution, translating your well-laid plans into tangible progress.

For many men with ADHD, the conceptualization of a task or goal is often effortless, even exciting. The initial burst of inspiration can be exhilarating. However, the chasm between having a brilliant idea or a clear to-do item and actually putting pen to paper (or fingers to keyboard, or body in motion) can feel impossibly wide. This is not a moral failing or a lack of will; it is a neurological hurdle, deeply intertwined with the brain's reward system and its ability to switch between modes of thinking and doing. Understanding this distinction is crucial to developing effective strategies that work *with* your brain's wiring, rather than constantly fighting against it.

Task initiation is the ability to begin a task without excessive delay, to bridge the gap between intention and action. It's the moment you overcome inertia and take that crucial first step. Follow-through, on the other hand, is the persistence to see a task through to completion, even when distractions arise or the initial novelty wears off. It's the sustained effort that transforms a good start into a finished product. For men with ADHD, these two areas are often significant stumbling blocks, manifesting as:

- **The "Just Can't Start" Syndrome**: You know exactly what you need to do, but an invisible wall seems to prevent you from taking that first step. The task feels overwhelming, uninteresting, or just... heavy. This is often described as "activation energy" deficiency. The brain struggles to generate the necessary internal "push" to shift from planning or contemplating to active engagement. The task may be perceived as too complex, too boring, or too effortful, leading to a state of mental paralysis despite a strong desire to begin.
- **Procrastination Spirals**: Delaying tasks until the last possible moment, often leading to rushed, lower-quality work and increased stress. Procrastination is a complex behavior, often serving as a coping mechanism for underlying challenges with task initiation, emotional regulation, or time perception. For men with ADHD, the looming pressure of an imminent deadline can sometimes provide the necessary dopamine rush to finally activate, but this "crisis management" approach is unsustainable, leading to chronic stress, missed opportunities, and a constant feeling of being behind.
- **The "Half-Finished" Project Pile**: A trail of abandoned tasks, half-read books, and partially completed hobbies, victims of dwindling interest or a new, more exciting idea. The initial novelty of a new project provides a dopamine hit, making initiation easier. However, as the task becomes routine or reaches a less stimulating phase, the inherent interest wanes, and the follow-through becomes incredibly challenging. The

"shiny object" syndrome often pulls attention away to the next exciting, novel pursuit, leaving a wake of unfinished endeavors.

- **Difficulty Shifting Gears**: Once you do start, it can be hard to stop or transition to another task, especially if you're hyper focused on something. Paradoxically, while starting is hard, stopping can be just as difficult. When the ADHD brain latches onto something deeply engaging, it can enter a state of "hyperfocus," where attention becomes intensely concentrated, making it challenging to disengage and transition to other necessary tasks, even important ones. This can lead to imbalances, where one area of life receives disproportionate attention while others are neglected.
- **Underestimating the "Small Steps"**: Overlooking the power of tiny actions, leading to the belief that you need a huge burst of motivation to begin. There's a misconception that starting a large task requires an equally large amount of motivation. This leads to waiting for the "perfect" moment or a surge of energy that rarely arrives. The reality for ADHD is that motivation often *follows* action, rather than preceding it. The idea of breaking down tasks into almost trivially small steps is often dismissed as too simple, yet it's profoundly effective in overcoming inertia.

These challenges aren't a sign of laziness; they're a direct consequence of how the ADHD brain processes motivation, reward, and executive signals. The neurological pathways involved in dopamine regulation, which are critical for motivation and reward, function differently. This means that tasks that lack immediate, intrinsic interest or a clear, immediate reward can be extraordinarily difficult to initiate and sustain. The good news is that just like any skill, task initiation and follow-through can be strengthened with the right strategies, creating external structures and mental habits that provide the necessary activation energy and sustained momentum.

Breaking the Inertia: Strategies for Task Initiation

Getting started is often the hardest part. The key is to reduce the perceived effort of beginning. This involves tricking your brain into starting by making the initial step so small or so appealing that the resistance diminishes. The goal is to lower the "activation energy" required for your executive functions to kick in. Once momentum builds, the subsequent steps often become easier, as the brain's reward system begins to engage with the progress being made.

The 5-Minute Rule:

If a task seems daunting, commit to working on it for just five minutes. Tell yourself, "I just need to do this for five minutes." Often, once you start, the inertia breaks, and you'll find yourself continuing far beyond that initial five minutes. If not, you've still made a start, and that's a win. This strategy leverages the psychological principle of momentum. The most difficult part of any task is typically the very beginning. By committing to a ridiculously small amount of time, you bypass the brain's natural resistance to large, overwhelming tasks.

Five minutes feels manageable, even for the most dreaded chore or project. More often than not, once those five minutes are up, the task isn't as bad as you thought, or you've already made enough progress to feel motivated to continue. Even if you stop after five minutes, you've still achieved something, reducing the guilt of full procrastination and building a small but important habit of initiation.

Make the First Step Obvious and Tiny:

Don't think about "writing the report." Think about "opening the document" or "typing the title." For a chore, don't think "clean the kitchen," think "put one dish in the sink." Break the task down until the first action is so small it feels almost ridiculous not to do it. This is about clarifying the *very first physical action* required. Vague tasks such as "study for exam" are overwhelming. "Open textbook to Chapter 3" is a concrete, tiny step. "Exercise" is daunting; "put on running shoes" is a tiny, non-threatening step. The smaller and more explicit the first step, the less mental resistance your brain will encounter. This technique is particularly potent when combined with externalizing your plans.

Writing down that tiny first step can make it feel like a directive you simply have to follow. This bypasses the need for a huge burst of motivation and focuses on the power of micro-actions.

Use an "Action Hook":

Pair a new, difficult task with an established habit. For example, "After I pour my coffee, I will open my planner to review my top three tasks." Or "When I finish lunch, I'll spend 10 minutes on that project." This strategy, often discussed in habit formation, is incredibly effective for task initiation in ADHD. By linking a new, desired behavior (initiating a difficult task) to an existing, automatic habit, you create a "hook" that pulls you into action. Your brain already has a strong neural pathway for the established habit; by attaching a new action to it, you leverage that existing momentum. The key is consistency in the pairing. Over time, the new action will become more automatic, reducing the effort required for initiation. Identify habits you perform daily without thinking (e.g., brushing teeth, checking phone, eating breakfast) and consciously attach a small, desired task to them.

Remove Obstacles:

Clear your workspace. Gather all necessary materials before you start. If you need to make a call, have the number ready. The fewer barriers between you and the task, the easier it is to initiate. Think of this as clearing the runway for takeoff. Any small obstacle, whether physical (a messy desk) or logistical (missing a necessary document or tool), can provide an excuse for the ADHD brain to defer initiation. By proactively setting up your environment for success, you minimize friction. This includes preparing your digital workspace (closing unnecessary tabs, organizing files), ensuring you have all physical supplies, and anticipating any information you might need. The less "setup" a task requires in the moment, the smoother the transition from intention to action. This also reduces decision fatigue, as choices about "what to do next" have already been made.

Gamify It:

Turn tasks into a game. Set a timer, compete with yourself, or use apps that track your progress and reward you for starting. Even small, internal rewards can kick start motivation. The ADHD brain often responds well to novelty, challenge, and immediate feedback. Gamification taps into this. Set a timer for 25 minutes (Pomodoro Technique) and challenge yourself to focus for the entire duration. Use an app that tracks your completed tasks and provides virtual rewards or points. Compete with your past self to beat a certain time limit. The element of play can transform a dreaded chore into a stimulating challenge, leveraging your brain's natural inclination towards engaging activities and providing the intermittent bursts of dopamine that aid in motivation and sustained effort.

"Body Doubling":

Work alongside someone else, even if they're doing something completely different. The mere presence of another person can provide a subtle accountability and energy that helps initiate and sustain focus. This can be in person, via video call, or even in a co-working space.

This is a remarkably effective strategy for many with ADHD. The external presence of another person, even if they are silent and working on their own tasks, provides a gentle, non-judgmental form of accountability. It can create a subtle pressure to stay on task and can reduce feelings of isolation that sometimes accompany solo work. The other person acts as an external executive function, providing a stable, non-distracting presence that helps to anchor your attention and initiate action.

Many online communities now offer virtual body doubling sessions, making this accessible even if you don't have someone physically nearby.

Change Your Environment:

If you're stuck, sometimes simply moving to a different room, a coffee shop, or even just shifting your chair can break the mental block and signal to your brain that it's time to start something new. A change of scenery can provide a powerful cognitive reset. If you're struggling to start a task at your desk, try moving to a different table, a quiet corner, or even a different building. The novelty of the new environment can provide a subtle boost to attention and break the mental association with procrastination in your usual workspace. Even smaller changes, like standing up, stretching, or simply moving your laptop to a different part of the desk, can be enough to signal a fresh start to your brain and help break the inertia.

The Long Haul: Strategies for Follow-Through

Starting is great, but finishing is where the real impact happens. Maintaining momentum is key. The initial excitement of a new project often provides enough dopamine to get you going. However, as the novelty wears off and the grind sets in, maintaining focus and persistence becomes significantly harder for the ADHD brain. This is where strategic reinforcement and intentional motivation come into play, designed to bridge the gap between initial enthusiasm and sustained effort, preventing the dreaded "half-finished" pile.

Visualize the End Goal:

Before and during a task, take a moment to clearly picture the finished product or the positive outcome of completing it. How will it feel? What benefits will it bring? This extrinsic motivation can be powerful for the ADHD brain. When tasks become tedious, the intrinsic reward often diminishes. By consistently visualizing the positive outcome, you provide your brain with a tangible "future reward" that can help bridge the motivational gap. If you're working on a difficult report, imagine the relief and satisfaction of submitting it, or the positive feedback you'll receive. If you're cleaning, picture the calm and order of a tidy space. This mental rehearsal provides a continuous source of positive reinforcement, reminding your brain *why* the sustained effort is worthwhile.

Regular Check-Ins (and Rewards):

Don't wait until the end to acknowledge progress. Break down large tasks into smaller milestones and build in mini-rewards for completing each one. This could be a 5-minute break, a favorite song, or a quick walk. The ADHD brain thrives on immediate feedback and rewards. Large, long-term goals often lack the continuous positive reinforcement needed to sustain attention. By breaking tasks into smaller, more digestible milestones, you create more opportunities for "wins." Each completed milestone can be celebrated with a small, immediate reward. This doesn't have to be anything grand – simply standing up and stretching, listening to one song, or allowing yourself a few minutes of guilt-free Browse. These mini-rewards provide regular dopamine boosts, reinforcing the behavior of following through and making the long haul feel less arduous.

Combat the "Novelty Effect":

The ADHD brain thrives on newness. When a task starts to feel routine or boring, try to inject novelty. Can you do it in a different order? Use a new tool? Listen to different music? Change your environment mid-task? This strategy directly addresses the ADHD brain's hunger for novelty. When a task loses its initial spark, consciously look for ways to make it fresh again. If you're writing, try using a different font or a different writing app. If you're working on data entry, try doing it in a different room or listening to a different genre of music. Even small changes can re-engage your attention and provide a temporary boost of interest, helping you push through the "boring" parts of a long task. This is about creative problem-solving to maintain engagement, rather than waiting for motivation to magically reappear.

Accountability Partners:

Share your goals and progress with a trusted friend, family member, or colleague. Knowing someone else is aware of your commitments can provide a powerful external motivator to follow through. External accountability can be a game-changer for follow-through. When you've publicly stated a goal, there's a natural desire to follow through to maintain your credibility or avoid disappointing someone. This provides an external structure that compensates for internal motivational dips. Choose someone supportive, who understands ADHD, and establish clear expectations for check-ins (e.g., daily text message updates, weekly calls). The simple act of knowing someone will ask about your progress can be enough to push you through moments of resistance.

"Future Self" Letter:

Write a short note to your future self, reminding yourself why this task is important and the positive feelings associated with its completion. Read it when motivation wanes. This technique leverages the power of self-empathy and foresight. When you're in the midst of a tedious task, it's easy to lose sight of the bigger picture. By writing a letter to your "future self" when you're feeling motivated, you create a tangible reminder of the positive outcomes and the "why" behind your efforts. When you hit a wall, reading this letter can re-connect you to your initial intention and provide a much-needed emotional and motivational boost, helping you push through to completion.

Automate and Systemize:

Wherever possible, create systems that reduce the need for conscious effort in follow-through. Set recurring reminders, use templates, or automate routine steps. The less you have to think about it, the more likely you are to do it. The ADHD brain thrives on automation and consistent systems because they reduce decision fatigue and the reliance on inconsistent executive functions. Set up recurring calendar reminders for tasks that need to be done regularly. Use email templates for common responses. Create checklists for multi-step processes. Automate bill payments. The goal is to offload as much routine cognitive load as possible, freeing up your mental energy for tasks that truly require your focused attention and creativity. Systems create predictability and consistency, making follow-through less about willpower and more about habit.

Embrace Imperfection:

The desire for perfection can be a huge blocker to follow-through. Remind yourself that "done is better than perfect." The goal is completion, not flawlessness, especially in the initial stages. Perfectionism is a common, yet often unrecognized, form of procrastination for men with ADHD. The fear of not doing something perfectly can prevent you from starting or, more commonly, from finishing. The ADHD brain can get bogged down in details, endlessly tweaking and refining, leading to unfinished projects. Consciously remind yourself that "perfect is the enemy of good." The goal is to get the task *done* to an acceptable standard, then move on. You can always revisit and refine later if truly necessary. Prioritize completion over unattainable perfection, and watch your pile of half-finished projects shrink.

Cultivating robust task initiation and follow-through means developing a consistent bridge between your intentions and your actions. It's about building momentum and learning to ride that wave, even when it feels like the current is pulling you in another direction. By implementing these strategies, you'll transform your ability to not only start but also complete tasks, moving from a cycle of good intentions to one of consistent accomplishment. This mastery provides a profound sense of control and competence, allowing you to reliably translate your ideas and aspirations into concrete realities, paving the way for sustained success and reduced stress in all areas of your life.

CHAPTER 5

DEVELOPING SELF-REGULATION AND IMPULSE CONTROL

At the very core of your executive function command center lies the critical ability to self-regulate and control impulses. Think of these as your brain's internal brakes and steering wheel, allowing you to pause, think, and choose a deliberate response rather than simply reacting to every urge, emotion, or distraction. While planning and initiation help you start and guide your journey, self-regulation and impulse control ensure you stay on course, avoid collisions, and reach your destination safely and efficiently. These are not merely optional skills but fundamental capacities that dictate your ability to navigate complex social situations, manage personal finances, maintain professional decorum, and pursue long-term goals without being constantly derailed by immediate gratification or emotional surges. For men with ADHD, the development of these capacities is not about eliminating the unique energetic and responsive nature of your brain, but rather about channelling it with greater intentionality and purpose. It's about empowering you to direct your inner force, rather than being swept away by it.

For men with ADHD, the internal brakes can sometimes feel a bit spongy, and the steering wheel might occasionally get a mind of its own. This isn't a moral failing; it's a neurological difference that often manifests as a disjunction between intention and action, particularly when faced with a strong immediate stimulus or emotion. The underlying neurobiology of ADHD, involving variations in the function of the prefrontal cortex and the regulation of neurotransmitters like dopamine and norepinephrine, means that the brain's "stop" signals and its ability to delay gratification are less robust. This translates into a heightened sensitivity to immediate rewards and a reduced capacity to inhibit automatic responses, even when those responses are counterproductive to long-term goals or positive relationships. This foundational difference contributes to common challenges such as:

- **Difficulty managing emotions**: Intense frustration, anger, or excitement can lead to outbursts or withdrawal, without a pause for thoughtful response. For men with ADHD, emotions can often feel amplified and rapidly shifting. A minor inconvenience might trigger a disproportionate burst of anger, or perceived criticism could send you into a spiral of intense shame or despair (often linked to Rejection Sensitive Dysphoria, as discussed in Book 4). The "lag time" between feeling an intense emotion and acting on it is significantly shorter, leading to regrettable words or actions that can strain personal and professional relationships. The challenge isn't the emotion itself, but the lack of an effective internal buffer to process it before reacting.
- **Impulsive spending**: Acting on a sudden desire to buy something, leading to financial strain or regret. The allure of immediate gratification, coupled with a reduced ability to foresee long-term consequences, can make impulsive purchases a significant challenge. Whether it's a new gadget, an expensive meal, or an online shopping spree, these decisions are often made in the moment, driven by a desire for a quick dopamine hit, only to be followed by financial stress and regret.
- **Interrupting conversations**: The thought feels so urgent, it bursts out before you can process politeness or turn-taking. This often stems from a rapid flow of ideas and a difficulty inhibiting the urge to express them immediately. While not intended as rude, frequent interruptions can make others feel unheard, devalued, or frustrated, impacting social connections and professional interactions. The internal experience is one of a thought feeling so critical that if not expressed immediately, it will be lost forever.

- **Jumping to conclusions**: Reacting to incomplete information without taking time to gather all the facts. The ADHD brain's tendency to process information quickly and sometimes superficially, combined with a difficulty inhibiting initial interpretations, can lead to hasty judgments. This can result in misunderstandings, miscommunications, and reactive behaviors based on partial or inaccurate information, particularly in emotionally charged situations.
- **Struggling with gratification delay**: Choosing immediate, smaller rewards over larger, long-term benefits (e.g., scrolling social media instead of working on a crucial project). The "now" bias is strong in ADHD. The brain is wired to prioritize immediate pleasure or relief from discomfort, making it exceptionally difficult to defer satisfaction for a more significant, but distant, reward. This directly impacts long-term goal achievement, health habits, and financial planning.
- **Addictive behaviors**: A heightened susceptibility to developing habits around things that provide immediate dopamine hits, from gaming to unhealthy food. The brain's search for stimulation and reward, combined with challenges in self-control, can make individuals with ADHD more vulnerable to developing habits that provide quick dopamine boosts, whether through excessive screen time, substance use, or other compulsive behaviors. These behaviors can become self-perpetuating, offering temporary relief from internal discomfort but ultimately undermining overall well-being.

These challenges can impact every facet of life, from professional reputation to personal relationships and overall well-being. The good news is that just like strengthening a muscle, you can train your brain to improve its capacity for self-regulation and impulse control. This training involves a combination of environmental adjustments, cognitive restructuring, and behavioral practices that create a more robust internal regulatory system. It's about building a conscious buffer between stimulus and response, allowing you to make intentional choices that align with your long-term values and goals, rather than being driven by fleeting urges or intense emotions.

Hitting the Brakes: Strategies for Impulse Control

The first step in controlling impulses is creating a pause – a small window between stimulus and response. This pause is where the power of choice resides. Without it, your actions are automatic reactions. For the ADHD brain, this pause is often short or non-existent, making intentional intervention crucial. By consciously inserting this moment, you gain the opportunity to engage your executive functions – to think, plan, and then act deliberately.

The "Stop, Think, Act" Method:

This is a foundational strategy. When you feel an impulse arising (to interrupt, to buy something, to lash out), physically **STOP** what you're doing. Take a deep breath. **THINK**: What is the consequence of this action? What is my goal right now? What are alternative responses? Then, **ACT** deliberately. This simple, three-step process is a powerful circuit breaker for impulsivity. The "STOP" doesn't just mean a mental pause; it often benefits from a *physical* stop. Put down what you're holding, take a step back, or even clench your fist and release it. This physical interruption helps to disengage the automatic, reactive pathways in your brain. The "THINK" phase is where you engage your prefrontal cortex, asking questions that force a consideration of consequences and alternatives.

For example, if you feel an urge to angrily reply to an email, the "THINK" step involves considering: "If I send this now, how will it impact my professional relationship? Is there a more constructive way to communicate my point?" Only after this deliberate thought process do you "ACT" with intention, choosing a response that aligns with your desired outcome. Consistent practice with this method gradually extends the pause, making deliberate action more accessible.

Delay Gratification with a Timer:

If you have an impulse to do something distracting or less productive (e.g., check social media, eat a snack), set a timer for 10-15 minutes. Tell yourself, "I can do this, but not right now." Often, the urge will pass or diminish in that time. This strategy directly targets the "now" bias inherent in ADHD. The brain desires immediate reward or relief from discomfort. By setting a timer, you acknowledge the urge ("Yes, I want to check social media"), but you defer the gratification. This simple act trains your brain to tolerate discomfort and delay reward. You're teaching it that the reward *will* come, just not instantly. In many cases, by the time the timer goes off, the intensity of the urge has significantly decreased, or you've become re-engaged in your productive task. Start with short delays and gradually increase them as your capacity for gratification delay improves.

Physical Barriers:

Make impulsive actions harder to do. If you impulsively buy online, delete saved credit card details or unsubscribe from tempting retail emails. If you interrupt, try putting a hand over your mouth or biting your tongue gently (without hurting yourself!) to create a physical reminder to pause. This is about creating "friction" between the impulse and the action. By making impulsive behaviors more difficult or inconvenient, you give your executive functions a chance to intervene. For online shopping, moving credit cards to a harder-to-reach location, unsubscribing from marketing emails, or even using a browser extension that forces a "cooling-off" period before purchase can be effective. In conversations, a subtle physical cue like gently pressing your tongue to the roof of your mouth, or lightly gripping your hands under the table, can serve as a non-verbal "stop" signal, allowing you to pause before an interruption slips out. The goal is to build an external or physical "speed bump" for your impulses.

"Think It Through" Questions:

Before making a quick decision, especially a significant one, ask yourself:

- "Is this truly necessary right now?"
- "What are the immediate and long-term consequences?"
- "Is there a better way to address this?"
- "Am I feeling a strong emotion that's influencing this decision?" These questions serve as a mental checklist, forcing a more comprehensive and rational evaluation of an impulse before acting. The ADHD brain often operates on "fast-thinking" (System 1 thinking), relying on intuition and immediate emotional responses. These questions encourage "slow-thinking" (System 2 thinking), which is more analytical and deliberate. By consciously asking about necessity, consequences, alternatives, and emotional influence, you engage the prefrontal cortex, providing an opportunity for wiser decision-making. This is particularly helpful for major financial decisions, significant relationship discussions, or high-stakes professional interactions where impulsive actions can have lasting negative repercussions.

Identify Triggers:

Become aware of what situations, emotions, or thoughts tend to precede your impulsive behaviors. Is it stress? Boredom? Certain people? Once you identify your triggers, you can develop proactive strategies to avoid or navigate them. Impulse control is often about proactive prevention rather than reactive suppression. By diligently observing and logging your impulsive behaviors, you can start to discern patterns. Do you tend to interrupt more when you're tired, or when a specific topic comes up? Do you overspend when you're feeling stressed or bored? Once identified, triggers become points of intervention. You can then create an "If-Then" plan for each: "IF I feel bored during a meeting, THEN I will doodle notes instead of checking my phone." Or "IF I feel stressed, THEN I will take a 5-minute walk before opening any online shopping sites." This moves you from a reactive stance to a proactive one.

Scheduled "Impulse Releases":

Sometimes the urge to do something (like check your phone) is overwhelming. Instead of constantly fighting it, schedule specific short "release" times throughout your day where you allow yourself to indulge in those impulses for a brief period. This can reduce the constant mental battle. This strategy acknowledges the ADHD brain's powerful need for novelty and stimulation. Trying to suppress all impulses for an extended period can lead to intense mental fatigue and eventual relapse. Instead, create controlled "release valves." For example, if you know you have an urge to check social media every 30 minutes, schedule a 5-minute social media break every hour. This gives your brain permission to look forward to the "reward" and reduces the need to constantly fight against the urge. It turns an unconscious, disruptive behavior into a conscious, managed one, allowing for greater focus during your designated work periods.

Guiding the Wheel: Strategies for Self-Regulation

Self-regulation extends beyond impulse control; it's about consciously managing your states – your energy, your focus, and your emotions – to align with your goals. It's the overarching ability to monitor and adjust your thoughts, feelings, and behaviors to achieve desired outcomes, particularly in the face of challenging situations or tempting distractions. For men with ADHD, cultivating robust self-regulation means building a flexible internal steering mechanism that can navigate the unpredictable terrain of daily life, keeping you aligned with your values and long-term aspirations. It's about developing an internal compass that guides you back on track when you drift, not just slamming on the brakes when you're about to crash.

Mindfulness and Body Scans:

Regularly check in with your body and mind. What are you feeling? Where is tension? Is your mind racing? Simple mindfulness exercises (e.g., focusing on your breath for one minute) can create a mental space to observe your internal state without immediately reacting to it. This awareness is the foundation of self-regulation. Mindfulness trains your attention to the present moment, which is a key skill for self-regulation. For the ADHD brain, which often operates at high speed or drifts into past regrets/future worries, mindfulness provides an anchor. A quick body scan – mentally checking in with sensations in different parts of your body – can ground you and reveal underlying tension or emotional states you weren't consciously aware of. This increased interoception (awareness of internal bodily states) helps you recognize emotional arousal *before* it escalates, providing a crucial window for intervention. Regular short mindfulness practices (2-5 minutes daily) build this foundational awareness, making you more attuned to your internal landscape.

Emotional Labeling:

When strong emotions arise, try to identify and name them: "I'm feeling intense frustration right now." "This is anger." Labeling emotions helps to distance yourself from them slightly, giving you a chance to respond thoughtfully rather than being swept away. Research in affect labeling shows that simply putting a name to an emotion can reduce its intensity by activating the prefrontal cortex and dampening the amygdala's response. For men with ADHD, who may experience emotions with greater intensity and less processing time, this is incredibly powerful. Instead of just feeling "bad" or "overwhelmed," explicitly identifying "This is sadness," or "This is anxiety," creates a small but significant cognitive distance from the emotion. This distance allows for a more rational assessment and prevents being completely consumed by the feeling, opening the door for a more measured response.

The "Zone of Regulation" Check-in:

Learn to recognize your emotional zones (e.g., Green Zone: calm, focused; Yellow Zone: anxious, agitated; Red Zone: angry, out of control). Develop a toolkit of strategies for each zone to help you return to the Green. For Yellow, it might be taking a walk; for Red, it might be deep breathing or stepping away. This framework, often used in emotional education, helps you categorize and proactively manage your emotional state. Instead of waiting for an emotional crisis, you learn to identify early warning signs (Yellow Zone) and apply preventative strategies. This might involve a personalized list of "calming tools" for the Yellow Zone (e.g., listening to music, talking to a trusted friend, doing a quick chore) and "crisis tools" for the Red Zone (e.g., intense exercise, splashing cold water on your face). Regularly checking in with your "zone" allows for continuous, proactive emotional steering.

Strategic Breaks and Movement:

Your brain needs regular resets. Short, intentional breaks (5-10 minutes) can prevent emotional build-up and mental fatigue. Physical movement, even just stretching or walking around, can significantly aid in self-regulation by discharging excess energy and helping you reset your focus. The ADHD brain is not built for sustained, static effort. Movement is a natural regulator of dopamine and norepinephrine, helping to manage restlessness and improve cognitive function.

Strategic breaks, beyond just Pomodoro-style work breaks, are essential for emotional well-being. This might involve stepping outside for a few minutes, doing some push-ups or jumping jacks, or even just dancing to a favorite song. These "brain breaks" prevent cognitive and emotional overload, allowing you to return to your tasks with renewed focus and emotional equilibrium.

Prepare for High-Stimulus Environments:

If you know you're going into a situation that triggers impulsivity or overstimulation (e.g., a noisy meeting, a crowded store), have a plan. This might involve setting a time limit, wearing noise-canceling headphones, or having an exit strategy. Anticipation is a powerful self-regulation tool. For men with ADHD, certain environments can be highly dysregulating, leading to overwhelm, irritability, or impulsive actions. By pre-planning how to navigate these situations, you reduce the in-the-moment cognitive load. This might mean deciding in advance to only stay at a crowded event for a set amount of time, bringing noise-canceling headphones to a busy office, or having pre-scripted phrases to politely exit a conversation if you feel overwhelmed. This proactive approach reduces the likelihood of an emotional or behavioral derailment.

Practice Self-Compassion:

Developing self-regulation is a journey, not a destination. You will make mistakes. Instead of dwelling on them, practice self-compassion. Acknowledge the misstep, learn from it, and recommit to your strategies. Harsh self-criticism only depletes the emotional resources needed for regulation. For men with ADHD, who often carry a lifetime of perceived failures or criticisms, the inner critic can be particularly damaging. Self-compassion is not self-indulgence; it's a powerful motivator.

When you inevitably stumble, treating yourself with kindness and understanding (as you would a good friend) helps you recover faster, learn from the experience, and re-engage with your strategies. Harsh self-criticism triggers shame and anxiety, which further undermine self-regulation. By fostering an inner ally, you build emotional resilience and create a supportive internal environment for growth.

By diligently practicing these strategies, you'll find yourself increasingly capable of pausing before reacting, making more intentional choices, and navigating your emotional landscape with greater control. Developing self-regulation and impulse control is not about suppressing who you are, but about empowering you to direct your energy and attention towards the life you genuinely want to build. It's the ultimate command over your own brain's operations, transforming inherent challenges into cultivated strengths, allowing you to live with greater purpose, peace, and sustained effectiveness.

CONCLUSION

YOUR SHARPENED MIND

You've reached the end of Book 1, and in doing so, you've taken a significant step toward understanding and strengthening the very core of your cognitive abilities: your **executive functions**. These functions are largely managed by the prefrontal cortex, which, as we touched on in Chapter 1, shows different activity patterns and neurotransmitter regulation in individuals with ADHD. For example, challenges in **response inhibition** (the ability to stop or hold back impulses) are directly linked to these neurobiological differences, often contributing to impulsivity in thought, speech, and action.

We've journeyed through the intricacies of your brain's command center, acknowledging the unique ways ADHD impacts these crucial skills, not as deficits, but as areas ripe for strategic cultivation.

From enhancing your **working memory** and focusing your **attention**, to mastering the art of **planning and prioritization**, and finally, cultivating resilient **task initiation and follow-through** alongside powerful **self-regulation and impulse control**, you've gained invaluable insights and practical strategies.

This book isn't just about theory; it's about equipping you with actionable tools to reclaim control over your daily life. You've learned to:

- **Externalize and visualize** information to bolster your memory.
- **Create "attention zones"** and use techniques like Pomodoro to sharpen your focus.
- **Break down daunting tasks** and prioritize effectively with frameworks like the Eisenhower Matrix.
- **Overcome inertia** with the 5-Minute Rule and build consistent follow-through.
- **Pause and choose** your responses more deliberately, managing impulses and emotions.

Remember, the journey of strengthening your executive functions is an ongoing process. There will be days when the strategies click into place effortlessly, and days when the old patterns re-emerge. This is normal. The key is **consistency**, **self-compassion**, and a willingness to **adapt** what you've learned to suit your unique neurobiology.

The foundation you've built in this book is crucial. You now have a deeper understanding of *how* your brain works and *what* you can do to support its optimal performance. This sharpened mind isn't about eradicating ADHD; it's about empowering you to leverage your strengths, navigate challenges with greater ease, and ultimately, live a more intentional and fulfilling life.

As you move forward, carry these tools with you. Practice them daily. Observe what works best for *you*. With each conscious effort, you're not just managing ADHD; you're actively shaping a more responsive, resilient, and effective version of yourself.

Let's pause for a moment and reflect on what you've just read. What resonates with you? What are the strategies you feel you can apply to work and life now versus those that seem more challenging or daunting?

BOOK TWO

MASTERING FOCUS: SUSTAINED ATTENTION IN A DISTRACTING WORLD

CHAPTER 1

UNDERSTANDING THE ADHD FOCUS CHALLENGE

In Book 1, we explored your brain's command center and its executive functions, laying the groundwork for better self-management. We established that executive functions are the sophisticated managers of your mind, guiding you through planning, task initiation, and self-regulation. Now, we're going to dive deeper into one of the most persistent and often misunderstood aspects of ADHD: focus. It's not just about paying attention; it's about sustained attention: the ability to maintain your mental spotlight on a task or thought for an extended period, especially when there are countless other things vying for that light. This capacity for sustained, directed attention is the bedrock upon which productivity, deep learning, and meaningful engagement are built.

For individuals with ADHD, this bedrock often feels less like solid ground and more like shifting sand, presenting a unique and often frustrating challenge that impacts every facet of daily life. The distinction between merely "paying attention" and "sustaining attention" is critical; the former is a fleeting moment, while the latter is an enduring state, a continuous act of conscious mental direction.

For many men with ADHD, the concept of "focus" can feel like a cruel paradox. On one hand, you might experience intense periods of hyperfocus, where you become completely engrossed in a task or interest, often to the exclusion of everything else—food, sleep, or urgent responsibilities. This state, while sometimes incredibly productive for specific, engaging tasks, is often uncontrolled and can lead to imbalances, such as neglecting critical deadlines for a captivating new hobby. On the other hand, for tasks that lack immediate novelty, stimulation, or personal interest, maintaining focus can feel like trying to catch smoke with your bare hands. Your attention flits, jumps, and scatters, leaving you feeling frustrated and unproductive. This isn't a deliberate choice or a sign of laziness; it is an inherent characteristic of how your brain processes and prioritizes stimuli.

The mental effort required to maintain attention on a mundane task can be immense, leading to rapid cognitive fatigue and the constant allure of more stimulating alternatives. This constant battle for sustained attention creates a pervasive sense of internal struggle, leading to feelings of inadequacy and a cyclical pattern of starting and abandoning tasks.

This isn't a lack of desire or willpower; it's a fundamental difference in how your brain regulates attention. While a neurotypical brain might act like a sophisticated filter, effortlessly tuning out irrelevant stimuli, the ADHD brain often struggles with this inhibition. This challenge stems from differences in neurochemistry, particularly in the pathways involving dopamine and norepinephrine, which are vital for motivation, reward, and attention.

Dopamine, often called the "feel-good" neurotransmitter, is crucial for regulating the brain's reward system, motivation, and the ability to find tasks interesting enough to sustain focus. In ADHD, there's often a dysregulation in how dopamine is transported and utilized, leading to a diminished baseline level of stimulation. This means that tasks that are inherently boring or effortful provide less intrinsic reward, making it harder to initiate and sustain engagement. Norepinephrine plays a key role in alertness and arousal; its dysregulation can impact the brain's ability to maintain an optimal state of readiness for focused work.

Also, variations in the activity of specific brain networks, such as the Default Mode Network (DMN), which is associated with mind-wandering and introspection, and the Task Positive Network (TPN), which is involved in focused, goal-directed attention, contribute to the difficulty in sustaining attention and inhibiting distractions. In the neurotypical brain, these networks operate in a kind of "seesaw" fashion: when one is active, the other is suppressed. In the ADHD brain, the DMN can remain overly active even when the TPN is supposed to be engaged, leading to intrusive thoughts and a struggle to stay "on task." This under-filtering of both internal and external stimuli means the ADHD brain is constantly bombarded, making it difficult to select and maintain focus on any single input.

The 'ADHD focus challenge' isn't a single issue, but a multifaceted one:

- **Distractibility:** Both external (a phone notification, a colleague walking by, a siren outside) and internal (a sudden memory, a new idea, a nagging worry about an upcoming task, a self-critical thought) stimuli can pull your attention off course with remarkable ease. For the ADHD brain, every piece of information, whether relevant or not, seems to register with almost equal weight. It's as if the brain's sensory gates are perpetually open, allowing a flood of data to enter, making it incredibly difficult to prioritize and filter. This leads to a constant internal "pinging" effect, where your attention is fragmented, leading to a pervasive sense of mental exhaustion. A quick glance at a notification can turn into 20 minutes lost down an internet rabbit hole, or a fleeting thought about what to cook for dinner can derail an hour of productive work. The challenge is not a lack of *ability* to focus, but a profound difficulty in *choosing* what to focus on and then *ignoring* everything else. This constant battle against stimuli is a significant drain on executive function.
- **Difficulty Shifting Focus:** While easy to distract, it can also be difficult to intentionally shift focus back to a less stimulating but important task once diverted, or even to transition from

one task to another. This is often referred to as "attentional inertia" or "stickiness." Once the ADHD brain latches onto a new, stimulating input (a distraction or an engaging new project), it can be incredibly difficult to disengage from it. It's like a train that's hard to get started, but once it's moving, it's also hard to stop or switch tracks. This means that a brief distraction can lead to extended periods of being off-task. Similarly, transitioning between different types of tasks, even planned ones (e.g., from creative writing to administrative work), can be a significant hurdle, requiring a substantial amount of mental energy to "unstick" from one cognitive mode and initiate another. This contributes to the feeling of being "stuck" or paralyzed when attempting to move between items on a to-do list.

- **Inconsistent Focus (The "On/Off" Switch):** Your ability to focus might fluctuate wildly throughout the day, or even within an hour, often leaving you at the mercy of your brain's unpredictable shifts. Unlike a neurotypical individual who might experience a gradual dip in focus, the ADHD brain's focus can feel like an erratic light switch – either intensely on (hyperfocus) or completely off (scattered and unfocused), with little in-between. This inconsistency makes it incredibly difficult to plan reliable work blocks or predict your productivity. One day you might power through a complex task, and the next, the same task feels insurmountable. This unpredictability can lead to significant frustration, as you're constantly battling an internal state that seems outside your control. This also contributes to the "ADHD tax": the extra time, effort, and often financial cost incurred due to inconsistent performance, missed deadlines, or redoing work.
- **Under-stimulation vs. Overstimulation:** You might struggle to focus because a task is too boring (under-stimulating), leading to mind-wandering and a desperate search for internal or external novelty, or because your environment is too chaotic (overstimulating), leading to overwhelm and scattered attention. The ADHD brain is constantly seeking an optimal level of stimulation. If a task is not engaging enough (e.g., repetitive data entry, reading a dense policy document), the brain will actively seek out alternative, more stimulating internal or external stimuli, leading to boredom, restlessness,

and mind-wandering. Conversely, if the environment is too rich with sensory input (e.g., open-plan office noise, multiple conversations, bright lights, cluttered space), the brain becomes overstimulated, leading to sensory overload, irritability, and an inability to filter out irrelevant information. Finding the "just right" level of stimulation is a constant balancing act for optimal focus, requiring careful environmental design and self-awareness.

- **"Time Blindness":** A poor internal sense of time can exacerbate focus issues, making it hard to accurately perceive the passage of time, estimate how long tasks will take, or understand the immediacy of future events. While not a formal diagnostic term, "time blindness" is a widely recognized and impactful experience for many with ADHD. This means that "soon" or "later" can feel like an abstract concept, and even short intervals can be misjudged. This contributes to chronic lateness, difficulty allocating appropriate attention to tasks (either underestimating or overestimating time needed), and a struggle to prioritize based on future deadlines. The future often feels less "real" than the immediate present, making it challenging to invest in long-term goals when immediate gratification or a pressing, last-minute demand beckons. This makes sustained, future-oriented focus particularly challenging, as the reward seems too distant to motivate consistent effort.

The impact of these challenges ripples through every aspect of life. Professionally, it can mean missed deadlines, incomplete projects, difficulty staying engaged in meetings (leading to perceptions of disinterest), or struggling with complex, multi-stage assignments. Your career progression might feel stalled, or you might find yourself consistently underperforming despite possessing high intelligence and capability. Personally, it can lead to miscommunications in relationships (e.g., forgetting details of conversations, not being present), forgotten chores, an inability to relax and be present with loved ones (as your mind races), or neglecting personal health goals.

The cumulative effect of these daily struggles is significant: it contributes to pervasive feelings of overwhelm, anxiety, and a deep-seated sense that you're constantly fighting your own brain. This internal battle often leads to self-criticism, shame, and a belief that you are simply not "good enough" or "disciplined enough," further eroding self-esteem and hindering your ability to engage effectively with strategies that could help. The mental load of managing these challenges is exhausting, leading to burnout and a cycle of underachievement relative to potential.

But here's the empowering truth: while your brain is wired differently, you can absolutely learn to exert greater influence over your attention. Mastering focus for the ADHD brain isn't about forcing yourself to conform to neurotypical norms; it's about understanding your unique cognitive landscape and implementing strategies that work *with* your brain's natural tendencies. It's about recognizing that your brain's unique wiring, while presenting challenges, also often comes with strengths like creativity, divergent thinking, high energy for novel tasks, and the capacity for intense hyperfocus when engaged. The goal is to harness these strengths and build compensatory systems and habits that mitigate the challenges. This involves strategic environmental design, internal cognitive shifts, and the consistent practice of new behaviors that gradually re-wire your brain's attentional pathways. It's a journey of self-discovery and tailored optimization, recognizing that a "one-size-fits-all" approach to focus will likely fail.

In the chapters to come, we'll delve into practical, actionable strategies specifically designed for the ADHD brain's unique attentional patterns. We'll explore how to design your environment for optimal concentration by minimizing distractions and curating sensory input. We'll learn to harness the power of mindfulness to anchor your attention in the present moment, building greater self-awareness and control over your internal landscape. You'll discover how to master single-tasking and cultivate periods of deep work, leveraging techniques that reduce context switching and honor your brain's preference for focused engagement. Furthermore, we'll address strategies to build resilience to sustain focus without burning out, incorporating self-compassion and realistic expectations into your approach. This isn't about becoming a robot, devoid of your unique spontaneity and creativity; it's about empowering you to direct your mental energy where you want it to go, when you need it to go there. Get ready to transform your relationship with focus and unlock a powerful new edge in navigating a distracting world, allowing your inherent strengths to shine through with greater clarity and purpose.

CHAPTER 2

ENVIRONMENTAL DESIGN FOR FOCUS

You now have a clearer understanding of how your ADHD brain approaches focus. We've seen that focus isn't a singular, monolithic skill, but a complex interplay of attention regulation, impulse control, and the brain's unique wiring regarding stimulation and reward. The good news is that while your internal landscape might be unique, you have significant control over your external environment. Just as a pilot checks their instruments and clears the runway before take-off, designing your surroundings can dramatically reduce distractions and prime your brain for sustained attention. This isn't about imposing rigid, uncomfortable rules, but rather about creating a supportive ecosystem for your brain, a space that minimizes friction and maximizes your capacity for deep, meaningful work. Think of it as creating a personalized, high-performance cockpit for your mind, tailored to its specific needs.

For men with ADHD, the environment isn't just a backdrop; it's an active participant in your ability to focus. A cluttered desk, a noisy office, a constantly vibrating phone, or even a strong visual stimulus from a window can be insurmountable barriers to deep work. Your brain is highly sensitive to external stimuli, and every unexpected sound, fleeting movement, or visual distraction acts like a siren call, pulling your mental spotlight away from your intended target. This isn't a sign of weakness, but a characteristic of the ADHD brain's reduced ability to filter out irrelevant information. While a neurotypical brain might effortlessly tune out the hum of the refrigerator or the distant chatter of colleagues, the ADHD brain registers these inputs with near-equal importance, demanding cognitive resources that could otherwise be directed towards your task. This constant barrage of competing stimuli leads to mental fatigue, frustration, and a diminished capacity for sustained attention.

The goal of environmental design isn't to create a sterile, silent chamber (unless that works for you!), but to consciously curate a space that supports your specific needs for concentration. It's about reducing friction, minimizing tempting distractions, and creating cues that signal "this is where I focus." This personalized approach recognizes that what's distracting for one person might be a helpful background for another. The aim is to proactively sculpt your surroundings to work *with* your brain's unique tendencies, rather than constantly fighting against them. This involves an iterative process of observation, experimentation, and adjustment, identifying what truly helps you achieve and maintain your desired state of focus. It's about taking command of your external world to empower your internal one.

Crafting Your "Attention Zone": Physical Space Strategies

Your physical workspace plays a monumental role in your ability to concentrate. Small, intentional changes can yield significant returns, transforming a chaotic environment into a sanctuary for focus. This isn't necessarily about having a dedicated home office, but rather about optimizing whatever space you have to create a distinct "attention zone" that cues your brain for productive work.

Declutter Ruthlessly:

A cluttered environment leads to a cluttered mind. Clear your desk or workspace of everything not directly related to your current task. For paperwork, use simple filing systems; for objects, give them a designated "home." The less visual noise, the easier it is for your brain to zero in on what matters. Visual clutter is a significant source of distraction for the ADHD brain. Each item on your desk or in your line of sight is a potential mental "ping," demanding a fraction of your attention. By ruthlessly decluttering, you reduce the number of competing stimuli, making it easier for your visual attention to settle on your work. This isn't about achieving a minimalist aesthetic, but about creating functional order. Implement a "one-touch" rule: if you pick something up, either put it away immediately, or take the next action on it. Regularly schedule 5-minute "micro-decluttering" sessions to prevent accumulation. Consider having only the essential tools for your *current* task on your desk, with everything else stored away in drawers or dedicated organizers. This practice frees up cognitive bandwidth by reducing the constant visual scanning and mental processing required to filter out irrelevant items.

Optimize for Your Senses:

Your sensory environment profoundly impacts your ability to focus. Tailoring it to your unique needs is critical.

- **Sound:** Experiment with sound. Some thrive in complete silence, others benefit from noise-cancelling headphones or ambient noise (e.g., white noise, nature sounds, classical music without lyrics). Find what helps you concentrate and consistently use it. For some, silence can be too under-stimulating, leading to internal distractions. For others, even minimal background noise is a significant interruption. Experiment: try a white noise generator, binaural beats, or instrumental music. Avoid music with lyrics if you find yourself getting distracted by them. Noise-cancelling headphones can create a powerful personal sound bubble in an otherwise noisy environment, signaling to your brain that it's time to focus. Consistently using your chosen sound environment helps build a habit, acting as an auditory cue for focus.
- **Sight:** Position your desk facing a wall, or in a way that minimizes foot traffic or windows with busy views. If you have a highly visual brain, even a picture frame on your desk can be a distraction. Use desk partitions or visual barriers if needed. Visual distractions are potent attention hijackers for the ADHD brain. A busy hallway, a window overlooking an active street, or even a lively office environment can constantly pull your gaze and mind away from your work. If possible, arrange your workspace to minimize these visual inputs. If you can't reorient your desk, consider a small, portable partition or even strategically placed plants to block distracting lines of sight. For highly sensitive individuals, even personal decor items can be distracting; opt for a clean, visually calm workspace during focused periods.

- **Lighting:** Ensure adequate, natural light if possible. Poor lighting can cause eye strain and fatigue, making focus harder. Avoid harsh overhead lights that can be distracting. Natural light is generally beneficial for mood and alertness, supporting sustained focus. Position your workspace near a window, if possible, but be mindful of glare. If natural light isn't available, use warm, diffused lighting that mimics natural light and minimizes shadows or harsh glares. Task lighting (e.g., a desk lamp) can help illuminate your immediate work area without overstimulating the entire space. Avoid fluorescent lights, which can cause eye strain and be audibly distracting to some.
- **Comfort:** An uncomfortable chair, a too-hot or too-cold room, or even restrictive clothing can be constant, low-level distractions. Optimize your physical comfort. Persistent physical discomfort creates a constant, subtle pull on your attention. If your chair is uncomfortable, your body will constantly fidget or shift, diverting mental resources. If the room is too cold, you'll be preoccupied with warmth; too hot, and you'll be battling lethargy. Address these fundamental needs first. Invest in an ergonomic chair if possible. Keep a sweater or small fan nearby. Wear comfortable, non-restrictive clothing. The less your body has to complain, the more your mind can focus.

Dedicated Work Zones:

If possible, designate a specific area only for deep work or specific tasks. This cues your brain that when you're in that spot, it's time to focus. Avoid working in bed or on the couch if those spaces are associated with relaxation. Even a specific chair or side of a table can serve this purpose. The principle here is strong environmental association. Your brain learns to associate certain places with certain activities. If you work, relax, eat, and sleep in the same spot, your brain receives mixed signals. By dedicating a "work zone," you train your brain to enter a focused state merely by being in that area. This doesn't mean you need a separate room; it could be a specific desk in a corner, a particular chair, or even just the dining table used *only* for work during certain hours. The consistency of this spatial cue helps trigger your "focus mode."

"Tools In, Distractions Out":

Before starting a task, gather all the tools you'll need (pens, paper, specific documents, water bottle, etc.). Simultaneously, remove all potential distractions (phone in another room, social media tabs closed, irrelevant books put away). This minimizes reasons to break focus. This is a crucial pre-work ritual. The goal is to eliminate any reason to interrupt your flow once you've started. Running to grab a forgotten pen, looking for a file, or realizing you need a drink can all become opportunities for distraction and derailment. Conversely, proactively removing potential distractions *before* you start creates a clear path for your attention. This "preparation phase" helps you transition into focused work smoothly and reduces the cognitive load of decision-making during your work session.

Digital Discipline: Taming the Online World

The digital realm is often the biggest culprit for attention fragmentation for men with ADHD. The internet, with its infinite novelty and instant gratification, is uniquely designed to hijack the ADHD brain's attention. Mastering digital discipline is therefore non-negotiable for sustained focus in the modern world. This requires a proactive and often aggressive approach to managing notifications, browser habits, and smartphone usage.

Notification Annihilation:

This is paramount. Turn off all non-essential notifications on your phone, tablet, and computer. Email, social media, news alerts—they are designed to hijack your attention. Schedule specific times to check them, rather than being at their mercy. Each notification is a micro-interruption that pulls your attention away, even if just for a second. For the ADHD brain, that micro-interruption often leads to a lengthy derailment, as the brain "sticks" to the new stimulus. Be ruthless. Turn off banners, sounds, and badges for anything that isn't absolutely critical. For emails, close your email client unless you are specifically in an "email processing" block. For social media, consider deleting the apps from your phone and only accessing them via a desktop browser during scheduled breaks. The less your devices are constantly vying for your attention, the more mental energy you'll have for your actual work.

Strategic App & Tab Management:

The digital workspace, much like a physical one, can become cluttered and distracting.

- **Browser Extensions:** Use extensions like "StayFocusd" or "Freedom" to block distracting websites during work periods. These tools act as external accountability partners, preventing you from impulsively drifting to time-wasting sites. Set them up to block social media, news sites, or entertainment platforms during your designated work hours. This creates a powerful barrier that bypasses the need for constant willpower.

- **Tab Limiting:** Commit to having only 1-3 tabs open at any given time. Each additional tab is an invitation for distraction. Open tabs are like open loops in your brain, each demanding a piece of your working memory. The more tabs you have, the more visual and mental clutter you create, making it harder to focus on the active task. Cultivate the habit of closing tabs immediately once you're done with them.
- **Dedicated Browsers/Profiles:** Consider having a separate browser (e.g., Firefox for work, Chrome for personal) or different user profiles to keep work and personal browsing separate. This creates a clear boundary between your professional and personal digital life. When you open your "work browser," your brain receives a strong cue that it's time to focus, as all personal distractions (bookmarks, saved passwords, open tabs) are not immediately available.

Phone Hygiene:

Your smartphone is a powerful tool and a potent distraction. It is arguably the single greatest threat to sustained focus in the modern era.

- **Physical Distance:** Put your phone in another room or a drawer while working. Out of sight, out of mind. This is the most effective strategy. If your phone is within arm's reach or line of sight, the temptation to check it will be constant. By physically separating yourself from it, you remove the immediate cue and significantly reduce the likelihood of impulsive checking.
- **Do Not Disturb Mode:** Use this feature liberally. Customize it to allow calls from emergencies only. This allows you to control who can reach you, preventing unnecessary interruptions while still ensuring you're available for critical contacts.
- **App Organization:** Group distracting apps into folders on your phone's last screen, making them less accessible. Make the process of getting to these apps slightly more cumbersome. The extra taps or swipes can provide just enough friction to engage your executive functions and allow you to reconsider the impulse.

Scheduled Digital Breaks:

Instead of letting digital distractions pull you away randomly, schedule short, intentional breaks (e.g., 5 minutes every hour) to check emails, messages, or social media. This gives your brain permission to look forward to these "release" times. Fighting every urge to check your phone or email is exhausting. By scheduling designated "digital breaks," you legitimize the desire for stimulation but contain it to specific periods. This reduces the constant mental battle and allows you to fully engage with your work during your focused blocks, knowing that a controlled "release" is coming.

Offline First:

Whenever possible, download documents, read articles, or do work that doesn't require an internet connection. Then, disconnect your Wi-Fi. This creates an immediate, strong barrier against online distractions. If your work doesn't absolutely require an internet connection, removing the possibility of online distractions altogether is the ultimate environmental design hack. This forces you to focus only on the materials at hand and eliminates the temptation of endless browsing.

By consciously designing both your physical and digital environments, you are not just reacting to distractions, but proactively building a fortress for your focus. This isn't about perfection, but about creating systems that support your brain's natural tendencies. Take the time to observe your current habits, identify your biggest environmental culprits, and then implement these strategies to clear the runway for sustained, productive attention. This proactive approach transforms your workspace from a source of struggle into a powerful ally, empowering you to achieve deeper concentration and more consistent productivity.

CHAPTER 3

MINDFULNESS AND PRESENCE FOR ATTENTION

We've explored how to shape your external world for better focus, recognizing that a thoughtfully designed environment can significantly reduce the pull of distractions. Now, we turn inward to cultivate your internal landscape. This is where mindfulness and presence become incredibly powerful tools for the ADHD brain. Often, the greatest distractions aren't external pings and notifications, but the relentless chatter of our own minds—the planning for tomorrow, the regrets of yesterday, the rehashing of past conversations, or the sudden, exciting new idea that pulls you off track with compelling urgency. This internal world, while a source of creativity and spontaneity, can also become a chaotic torrent of thoughts and emotions, making sustained attention a formidable challenge. For men with ADHD, who frequently experience a mind that races ahead, gets stuck in loops, or drifts effortlessly into imaginative realms, mastering this internal terrain is not just beneficial, but transformative.

Mindfulness is simply the practice of paying attention, on purpose, to the present moment, without judgment. It's about observing your thoughts, feelings, and sensations as they arise, rather than getting entangled in them or being carried away by their current. Presence is the natural outcome of mindfulness—a state of being fully engaged with what's happening right now, whether it's a conversation, a task, or a quiet moment of reflection. For men with ADHD, who often experience a mind that races ahead or drifts behind, cultivating mindfulness can feel like learning to gently lasso your runaway thoughts and bring them back to the here and now. It's a process of becoming the observer of your internal experience, rather than being solely subject to its whims. This allows for a crucial pause, a moment of intentionality, before your automatic reactions take over.

This isn't about emptying your mind or achieving some zen-like state of perfect stillness (which is often unrealistic for anyone, let alone someone with ADHD). The ADHD brain is inherently active, a vibrant engine of thought and energy. Trying to force it into absolute stillness is often counterproductive and frustrating. Instead, mindfulness for ADHD is about building your attentional muscle by repeatedly guiding your focus back to the present. Each time your mind wanders and you gently, without self-reproach, bring it back to your chosen anchor or current task, you're doing a "rep" for your attention. This consistent, compassionate redirection strengthens your capacity for sustained focus, making it easier over time to choose where your mental spotlight shines, even amidst internal noise. It's a pragmatic, iterative approach that acknowledges the brain's natural tendencies while gently nudging it towards greater control.

Anchoring Your Attention: Mindfulness Practices

The core of mindfulness for attention is having an "anchor"—something to consistently bring your focus back to when your mind inevitably drifts. For the ADHD brain, which can struggle with internal filtering and sustained mental effort, an accessible and consistent anchor provides a point of return, a home base for your attention amidst the chaos. These practices are not meant to be rigid rituals, but flexible tools to build awareness and control.

The Breath Anchor:

Your breath is always with you and is a constant, subtle sensation. It is perhaps the most fundamental and universally accessible anchor because it is always present, it is neutral, and its rhythm can be both observed and subtly influenced.

- **Simple Breath Focus:** Sit comfortably. Close your eyes or soften your gaze to minimize visual distraction. Bring your attention to the sensation of your breath entering and leaving your body. Notice the rise and fall of your chest or abdomen, the feeling of air at your nostrils, or the gentle expansion and contraction of your diaphragm. When your mind wanders (and it will, relentlessly at first!), gently acknowledge the thought without judgment. Don't criticize yourself for drifting; simply note, "There's a thought about my to-do list," or "My mind has wandered to that conversation." Then, gently, as if guiding a small child, guide your attention back to your breath. Start with 2-5 minutes of this practice daily, perhaps at the beginning of your day or before a challenging task, and gradually increase the duration as your capacity grows. The key is the *gentle return*, not the absence of wandering. Each return is a strengthening of your attentional muscle.
- **Counting Breaths:** As you exhale, count "one." On the next exhale, "two," up to "ten," then start over from "one." If your mind wanders and you lose count, simply start again from "one" without judgment. This adds a gentle, rhythmic structure that can be particularly helpful for a busy or restless mind. The act of counting provides just enough mental engagement to keep the ADHD brain from getting bored, while still directing attention to the breath. It creates a clearer focal point than just "noticing" the breath, offering a tangible metric for your practice.

Sensory Check-Ins (5-4-3-2-1 Method):

When your mind is racing, you feel overwhelmed by internal chatter, or you're stuck in a thought loop, this exercise can quickly ground you in the present by bringing your awareness to external reality.

- **5 things you can see:** Look around and name five distinct things you can see. Focus on details—colors, textures, shapes. (e.g., "the blue of the wall," "the grain of the wooden table," "the dust motes dancing in the sunlight").
- **4 things you can feel:** Notice four things you can feel (e.g., your feet on the floor, the texture of your clothes against your skin, the air temperature, the pressure of your chair). Really lean into the sensation.

- **3 things you can hear:** Listen for three distinct sounds (e.g., distant traffic, your own breathing, the hum of a computer, the chirping of a bird). Don't judge them, just notice their presence.
- **2 things you can smell:** Notice two distinct smells (even if faint, e.g., lingering coffee, fresh air from an open window, the scent of your shirt).
- **1 thing you can taste:** Notice one taste in your mouth (e.g., the lingering taste of your last meal, the freshness from toothpaste, or just your own saliva). This exercise is a rapid, powerful circuit-breaker for an overactive mind. It quickly pulls your attention away from internal distractions, such as worries, regrets, or future planning, and redirects it into your immediate, external reality, providing a quick reset for your attention. It's an excellent tool to use before starting a task, during a moment of overwhelm, or when you notice your mind spiraling.

Mindful Movement:

Integrate mindfulness into physical activity. This is particularly beneficial for the ADHD brain, as movement can help discharge excess energy and provide a tangible anchor for attention.

- **Walking Meditation:** As you walk, shift your attention from your thoughts to the physical sensations of walking. Pay attention to the sensation of your feet touching the ground, the heel-to-toe roll, the swing of your arms, the movement of your legs, and the rhythm of your breath. Notice the sights and sounds around you without labeling or judging them; simply observe. This is an excellent way to combine the benefits of physical activity (which helps regulate dopamine) with attentional training.
- **Mindful Stretching/Yoga:** Focus intensely on the sensations in your body as you stretch or hold a pose. Notice the stretch, the release, the tension, and the relaxation. This can be a great way to combine physical activity with mental anchoring, promoting both body awareness and mental focus. Even simple stretches at your desk can become mindful moments.
- **Mindful Eating/Drinking:** Instead of mindlessly consuming food or drink, choose one meal or beverage a day to practice mindful eating. Before you even take a bite or sip, notice the colors, textures, smells. As you chew, pay attention to the taste, the temperature, how the food feels in your mouth, and the act of

swallowing. Chew slowly, savoring each bite. This engages multiple senses and trains your attention by slowing down a common, often rushed activity, fostering a deeper connection to the present moment.

Integrating Presence into Daily Life: Beyond Formal Practice

Mindfulness isn't just for meditation cushions or structured exercises; it's a way of approaching everyday moments, transforming routine activities into opportunities for attentional training and greater presence. The goal is to weave moments of conscious awareness throughout your day, making presence a habit rather than an occasional event.

The "One-Minute Mindfulness Break":

Set an alarm for once or twice an hour, or at natural transition points in your day (e.g., when a meeting ends, before starting a new task). When it goes off, pause whatever you're doing. Take three deep breaths, focusing on the sensation of each breath. Look around you and notice one thing you haven't seen before, or one detail you often overlook. Then return to your task.

This acts as a micro-reset for your attention, preventing mental fatigue, reducing accumulation of internal distractions, and bringing you back to the present moment before you get completely derailed. It's a powerful way to integrate consistent "attentional reps" without needing long, dedicated meditation sessions.

Active Listening:

In conversations, make a conscious effort to truly listen to the other person, rather than planning your response, letting your mind drift, or formulating counter-arguments. When you notice your mind wandering, gently bring it back to their words. Try to silently paraphrase what they've said in your head to ensure comprehension and active engagement.

For men with ADHD, rapid-fire thinking often means your brain is already three steps ahead, anticipating the conversation's direction or formulating your next brilliant point. This can lead to interrupting, missing crucial details, or others feeling unheard. Practicing engaged listening not only improves your relationships but also trains your sustained attention in a real-world, dynamic context. Ask open-ended questions to encourage the other person to elaborate, which further anchors your attention.

Single-Task Awareness:

As you work on a task, bring your full, conscious attention to it. When you notice your mind drifting (and it *will*), acknowledge the distraction without judgment ("There's a thought about what to eat for lunch"). Then, gently but firmly redirect your attention back to the task. This is the "attentional rep" in action – each time you bring your attention back, you strengthen the neural pathways for focus. Avoid multitasking, as it fragments attention and reduces efficiency for the ADHD brain. Commit to one task at a time, and every time your mind pulls away, practice the gentle return. Over time, the periods of sustained single-task focus will naturally lengthen.

The "Curiosity Mindset":

Approach tasks, even mundane or boring ones, with a sense of genuine curiosity. What can you learn from this? What details can you observe? What is the underlying mechanism? Engaging your natural curiosity can make mundane tasks more palatable and easier to focus on by providing an internal source of stimulation. For example, if you're doing paperwork, instead of just seeing "forms," observe the design of the form, the font, the sequence of information. If you're washing dishes, notice the temperature of the water, the feel of the soap, the shine of the clean plate. This approach injects novelty and engagement into tasks that might otherwise feel under-stimulating, leveraging your brain's natural inclination towards new information.

Acknowledge and Let Go:

When distracting thoughts or emotions arise, instead of fighting them or getting lost in them, simply acknowledge their presence ("There's a thought about X," "I'm feeling impatient," "There's an urge to check my phone"). Then, consciously choose to let them go and return your attention to your anchor or your task. Trying to suppress thoughts often makes them stronger, like trying not to think about a pink elephant. Instead, practice non-judgmental observation: observe the thought or emotion as if it's a cloud passing by in the sky. You notice it, but you don't jump on it and ride it away. By acknowledging without engagement, you weaken its power to hijack your attention and reinforce your capacity to choose where your focus lies. This is a subtle but profoundly effective self-regulation skill.

Cultivating mindfulness and presence is a lifelong practice, not a quick fix or a destination. For men with ADHD, it offers a powerful pathway to greater control over your attention, reduced reactivity, and a richer, more engaged experience of the present moment. By regularly training your internal spotlight, you'll find it easier to direct your focus where you intend, even in a world clamoring for your attention and a mind prone to wandering. This internal mastery is a vital complement to designing your external environment for sustained focus, creating a holistic approach that empowers you to truly take command of your attention and, by extension, your life. The journey is ongoing, but the rewards of greater presence and control are immeasurable.

CHAPTER 4

SINGLE-TASKING AND DEEP WORK STRATEGIES

We've explored how to shape your external world for better focus by designing an environment conducive to concentration, and we've begun to cultivate your internal landscape through mindfulness and presence, anchoring your attention to the present moment. Now, it's time to put those principles into practice with some of the most potent strategies for sustained focus: single-tasking and deep work. In a world that constantly pushes for multitasking, these approaches are revolutionary, especially for the ADHD brain. The pervasive myth that juggling multiple tasks simultaneously enhances productivity is deeply ingrained in modern work culture. However, for an ADHD brain, constantly switching between tasks is not just inefficient; it's actively detrimental. Each switch depletes valuable mental energy, fragments attention, and leads to more errors, superficial work, and less actual completed output. This "context switching cost" is astronomically higher for an ADHD brain, as the effort required to disengage from one task and re-engage with another is immense, often involving a significant "reboot" of mental resources and a hunt for the necessary dopamine to kickstart the new activity.

Single-tasking is simply the practice of focusing on one task at a time, giving it your undivided attention until it's complete or a designated time period ends. It's a deliberate act of choosing singularity over fragmentation. Deep work, a term coined by author Cal Newport in his seminal book, takes this a step further: it's the ability to focus without distraction on a cognitively demanding task. It's the kind of work that creates new value, improves your skills, and is difficult to replicate, requiring sustained intellectual effort at the highest level. For the ADHD brain, achieving this state of deep work is not always easy, given its natural inclination towards novelty and immediate stimulation, but it is profoundly rewarding. The moments of true deep work are where innovation happens, where complex problems are solved, and where significant personal and professional growth occurs. It's the antithesis of the shallow, fragmented work that often characterizes modern productivity.

The challenge lies in your brain's natural inclination for novelty and stimulation. A single, demanding task, especially if it involves sustained effort and lacks immediate gratification, can quickly feel boring or difficult, prompting your mind to seek out more immediate dopamine hits from distractions. The prefrontal cortex, responsible for executive functions like sustained attention, relies on dopamine for optimal functioning. When a task isn't providing enough novel stimulation, the brain's dopamine levels may dip, leading to a search for external stimulation (distractions) to get that quick hit. This makes single-tasking and deep work feel like pushing against a strong current. However, by deliberately engaging in single-tasking and structuring your environment and time for deep work, you can train your brain to embrace sustained effort and achieve higher levels of productivity and satisfaction. You are not fighting your brain but *teaching* it to find reward in sustained, focused effort through structured practice and strategic reinforcement.

The Power of One: Embracing Single-Tasking

The core principle here is simplicity and dedication. It's about stripping away unnecessary complexity and committing fully to the task at hand. This approach counteracts the ADHD brain's tendency to scatter attention and provides a clear, unwavering target for your mental energy.

- **Identify Your One Task:** Before you begin a work session, clearly decide on the single task you will focus on. Write it down. Make it specific and tangible. For example, instead of "work on report," choose "write introduction for report" or "outline Chapter 2 of the proposal." The specificity reduces ambiguity and decision fatigue, which are significant energy drains for the ADHD brain. Having only one designated task on your mental radar provides immense relief, as your brain doesn't have to constantly juggle competing priorities or wonder what to do next. This clear focus point makes initiation easier and reduces the likelihood of immediate distraction.

- **Eliminate All Other Options:** This is where environmental design and digital discipline from Chapter 2 come into play with full force. Close all irrelevant tabs, put your phone on silent and out of reach (ideally in another room or a drawer), close your email client and messaging apps, and clear your physical workspace of anything not pertaining to that one task. Make it physically and digitally difficult to switch. Use browser extensions that block distracting websites during your focus sessions. Turn your chair to face a blank wall if necessary. The fewer opportunities your brain has to wander to an easier, more stimulating alternative, the more likely it is to engage with the designated task. This external barrier reduces the reliance on willpower, which is a finite resource.
- **Use a Timer (The Pomodoro Technique Refined):** This is perhaps the most effective single-tasking tool for ADHD because it works *with* the brain's need for novelty and breaks, rather than fighting against it.
    - **Set a timer for 25 minutes (your "Pomodoro").** This short, manageable burst of time feels less daunting than an open-ended work session, making initiation easier.
    - **Commit to working *only* on your chosen task for that entire duration.** This is the core of single-tasking. If a distracting thought arises (and it will!), quickly jot it down on a "Distraction List" (a simple piece of paper next to you) and immediately return to your task. Do *not* act on the distraction; simply externalize it for later. This honors the thought without allowing it to derail your current focus.
    - **When the timer rings, take a mandatory 5-minute break.** Get up, stretch, grab water, look out a window, or do a quick mindful body scan. Critically, do *not* check email, social media, or get involved in another task during this

short break. This break is designed for mental reset, not for new stimulation.

    - **After four Pomodoros, take a longer break (20-30 minutes).** Use this time for more substantial recovery, checking messages, or engaging in a short, preferred activity. The power of this technique for ADHD lies in its structured breaks, which provide regular dopamine hits, and its defined work periods, which manage the feeling of overwhelm. It trains your brain to focus intensely for short, manageable bursts, gradually extending your capacity for sustained attention.

- **Batch Similar Tasks:** While the goal is single-tasking *within* a work session, you can still improve efficiency by batching similar tasks together across your day or week. For example, dedicate a specific block of time solely to answering emails, another block for making phone calls, and yet another for administrative paperwork. This minimizes the "context switching" cost: the mental energy wasted when your brain has to constantly reorient itself to different types of tasks and different cognitive demands. By grouping similar activities, you allow your brain to stay in a particular "mode," reducing the friction and cognitive load associated with frequent transitions.
- **Focus on "Inputs" Not Just "Outputs":** For highly challenging or overwhelming tasks, sometimes the "output" (e.g., finishing the whole report, completing a complex coding project) feels too daunting, leading to procrastination or task paralysis. Instead, shift your focus to the "input" you need to provide: "I will work on this report for 45 minutes," or "I will read 2 chapters of this book," or "I will write 200 words." This shifts your brain's focus from a potentially overwhelming, distant goal to a manageable, immediate action. This approach reduces the pressure for perfectionism, makes initiation easier, and allows your brain to find satisfaction in the act of *doing* rather than solely in the completed product. The momentum generated by consistent input often naturally leads to the desired output.

Creating Your Deep Work Sanctuary: Strategic Implementation

Deep work requires more than just willpower; it requires strategic planning and protection. It's about proactively carving out and defending periods of uninterrupted, focused effort, creating a "sanctuary" where your most demanding cognitive work can flourish.

- **Schedule Deep Work Blocks:** Don't wait for inspiration or a sudden burst of motivation; schedule your deep work time just like you would a critical meeting. Identify your peak focus times (often mornings for many with ADHD, before the day's distractions fully set in) and block out 1-2 hour segments for your most demanding, cognitively intensive tasks. Treat these blocks as sacred, non-negotiable appointments in your calendar. Use a different color in your digital calendar or physically block out the time. This intentional scheduling reduces decision fatigue and signals to your brain that this period is dedicated to focused effort.
- **Communicate Your Intent:** If you work in an open office, share a workspace, or live with others, communicate your deep work periods clearly. Put up a "Do Not Disturb" sign, use headphones (a universal signal for focus), or let family members know you need uninterrupted time for specific blocks. Be explicit about your need for quiet and lack of interruption. Setting clear boundaries with colleagues, family, and friends protects your focus blocks from external encroachment. Consider using a tool like Slack's "Do Not Disturb" feature or setting an auto-responder on your email to manage expectations.
- **The "Pre-Flight Checklist":** Before starting a deep work session, develop a brief, consistent ritual or "pre-flight checklist." This ritual cues your brain that it's time to engage in sustained focus and helps you smoothly transition into deep work. This could include:
  - Reviewing your single, specific task for the session.
  - Gathering all necessary materials (documents, specific software, water, a light snack).
  - Getting a fresh drink of water or coffee.
  - Closing all unnecessary programs, tabs, and silencing *all* notifications.

    - Doing a quick 60-second mindfulness check-in (as discussed in Chapter 3) to ground yourself. This consistent ritual acts as a psychological trigger, preparing your mind and body for intense concentration.

- **Limit "Shallow Work" Time:** Shallow work, such as checking email, administrative tasks, casual meetings, or responding to messages, is necessary but often less demanding and more prone to distraction. For the ADHD brain, shallow work can be a dopamine trap, providing frequent, small hits of gratification that deter you from tackling more challenging, less immediately rewarding deep work. Consciously limit the time you spend on these activities, perhaps grouping them into specific "shallow work blocks" outside of your prime deep work hours. Process email only 2-3 times a day, for example, rather than having it open constantly. This protects your most valuable mental energy for the tasks that truly move the needle.
- **Build in Recovery Time:** Deep work is mentally taxing. Just as you wouldn't expect to run a marathon every day, don't expect to do intense deep work for eight hours straight. Schedule regular, meaningful breaks between sessions and allow for ample recovery time between deep work blocks, and certainly at the end of the day. This prevents cognitive burnout, replenishes mental energy, and maintains your ability to engage in focused work over the long term. Recovery could involve physical movement, spending time in nature, engaging in a non-stimulating hobby, or simply resting. For the ADHD brain, understanding the need for rest and actively building it into your schedule is crucial for sustainable productivity.
- **Review and Reflect:** After a deep work session (or at the end of the day), briefly reflect on how it went. What helped you stay focused? What were the biggest distractions or challenges? What can you adjust for the next session? Did you manage your Pomodoro breaks effectively? Did you honor your single-task commitment? This iterative learning is key to refining your deep work habits. By consistently analyzing your performance, you gain valuable insights into your personal focus triggers and distractions, allowing you to continuously optimize your environment and strategies. This self-awareness accelerates your mastery of deep work.

Embracing single-tasking and deep work is a powerful counter-cultural act in our hyper-connected world, and it's especially transformative for men with ADHD. By deliberately creating mental and environmental space for sustained focus on one thing at a time, you'll not only complete more meaningful work but also experience a profound sense of accomplishment and clarity, moving beyond the chaos of constant distraction. This intentional approach allows you to harness your considerable potential, achieving a level of productivity and satisfaction that might have previously seemed out of reach.

CHAPTER 5

SUSTAINING FOCUS AND PREVENTING BURNOUT

You've learned to understand the ADHD focus challenge, designed your environment for optimal concentration, cultivated mindfulness to anchor your internal attention, and implemented powerful single-tasking and deep work strategies. These are foundational tools for getting into a state of sustained focus. But what happens after that intense period of concentration? How do you maintain that newfound ability without hitting a wall of exhaustion, or worse, burning out completely? This final chapter in Book 2 addresses the crucial, often overlooked, aspect of the focus equation: sustaining your attention over the long haul and building resilience against mental fatigue. It's not enough to be able to access deep focus; the true mastery lies in managing your energy and protecting your well-being so that these periods of intense concentration are sustainable, consistent, and ultimately contribute to a flourishing life, rather than leading to a crash.

For men with ADHD, the pursuit of focus can sometimes feel like a high-stakes sprint. The effort required to overcome internal and external distractions, initiate challenging tasks, and maintain cognitive grip can be immense, leading to disproportionate mental exhaustion, irritability, and even a feeling of being "fried." This is particularly true if you rely heavily on stimulating activities (like hyper-focusing, external novelty, or last-minute adrenaline rushes) to get things done, rather than building sustainable attentional habits rooted in consistent energy management. The ADHD brain often operates on a feast-or-famine cycle regarding stimulation and dopamine. Periods of intense, unmanaged focus, especially hyperfocus, can neglect fundamental needs like eating, sleeping, or taking breaks, leading to a significant energy debt. Without proper recovery and self-care, this cycle can quickly lead to reduced productivity, increased stress and anxiety, heightened symptom severity (e.g., more distractibility, greater impulsivity), and an inevitable return to old patterns of scattered attention and avoidance. The consequence is not just lost productivity, but a significant toll on mental and physical health.

Sustaining focus isn't just about the moments you're "on" and working intensely; it's about optimizing your entire daily rhythm to support your attention. It's about recognizing the subtle signs of fatigue, proactively managing your energy levels throughout the day, and building a lifestyle that allows your brain to perform at its best without succumbing to the relentless demands of modern life. This holistic approach acknowledges that focus is deeply intertwined with overall well-being, and that neglecting one will inevitably compromise the other. It's about proactive maintenance, not just reactive repair.

Fueling Your Focus: Energy Management Strategies

Think of your focus as a finite resource, much like a battery. You need to consistently charge it, use it wisely, and prevent it from running completely flat. Ignoring these fundamental inputs is akin to trying to drive a car with an empty fuel tank or a failing engine—no amount of driving skill will make it perform.

Strategic Breaks (Beyond Pomodoro):

While Pomodoro breaks (as discussed in Chapter 4) are excellent for short, focused bursts, you need longer, more restorative breaks tailored to the unique needs of the ADHD brain. These breaks are not a luxury but a necessity for cognitive replenishment.

- **Micro-Breaks:** Every 15-20 minutes, take a 30-second to 1-minute "brain break." Look away from your screen, stretch, take a few deep breaths, or simply close your eyes. This prevents cognitive overload and the build-up of mental fatigue by allowing for brief moments of cognitive disengagement. For the ADHD brain, which processes so much stimuli, these micro-pauses prevent overstimulation and allow your prefrontal cortex a brief moment of rest.
- **Movement Breaks:** Stand up, walk around, do some push-ups or squats every hour. Physical movement boosts circulation, increases blood flow to the brain, and helps regulate neurotransmitters like dopamine and norepinephrine, effectively re-energizing your brain and combating the mental stagnation of prolonged sitting. Movement can also help discharge restless energy that often accompanies ADHD, making it easier to return to a focused state.
- **Nature Breaks:** If possible, step outside for 5-10 minutes. Even looking at a tree, feeling the sun on your face, or hearing the sounds of birds can be incredibly restorative for your attention. "Green space" exposure has been shown to reduce mental fatigue and improve cognitive function, offering a powerful antidote to screen-induced brain drain.

Optimize Sleep:

This is foundational, not optional. Chronic sleep deprivation is a major enemy of focus, emotional regulation, and impulse control for everyone, but especially for those with ADHD, whose brains are already working harder to self-regulate. Prioritize consistent, quality sleep (7-9 hours for most adults). Create a relaxing bedtime routine (e.g., dimming lights, reading a physical book, taking a warm bath) that signals to your body it's time to wind down. Ensure your bedroom is dark, quiet, and cool, and avoid screens (phones, tablets, computers, TV) for at least 60-90 minutes before bed, as their blue light interferes with melatonin production. Sleep is when your brain cleanses itself and consolidates learning; sacrificing it directly impairs your next day's cognitive function.

Nutrition and Hydration:

Your brain needs consistent, high-quality fuel to function optimally. Dehydration and erratic blood sugar levels can wreak havoc on your attention and mood, mimicking or exacerbating ADHD symptoms. Drink plenty of water throughout the day, aiming for consistent hydration rather than large infrequent intakes. Opt for balanced meals with lean protein (for sustained amino acid supply), healthy fats (crucial for brain cell membranes), and complex carbohydrates (for steady glucose release) to maintain stable energy levels and prevent energy crashes. Avoid excessive simple sugars and highly processed foods, which lead to rapid blood sugar spikes and subsequent crashes, leaving you feeling sluggish and unfocused.

Mindful Consumption of Stimulants:

Caffeine, nicotine, and even some ADHD medications are stimulants. While they can be powerful tools for focus, their effects can be a double-edged sword for ADHD. Pay close attention to how caffeine specifically affects your focus, anxiety levels, and sleep. Some individuals with ADHD find it helpful in moderate doses, while others experience increased anxiety or a significant "crash" later in the day that severely impairs focus. Consider when and how much you consume, avoiding caffeine late in the day. Be aware of the "post-caffeine crash," which can lead to increased irritability and difficulty concentrating. Experiment with different types and amounts, and observe your personal response to find your optimal balance.

Regular Physical Activity:

Exercise is a natural mood and focus enhancer, often likened to "medication for ADHD" due to its profound neurochemical benefits. It increases dopamine and norepinephrine, helps regulate energy levels, reduces restlessness, and improves sleep quality. Find an activity you genuinely enjoy and make it a consistent part of your routine. This could be lifting weights, running, cycling, team sports, hiking, or even brisk walking. Even 20-30 minutes of moderate activity most days can make a significant difference in your ability to initiate tasks, sustain attention, and manage emotional regulation throughout the day. Exercise helps to both release pent-up energy and provide a calming, regulating effect on the brain.

Building Resilience: Protecting Against Burnout

Burnout is not just about being tired; it's a state of chronic physical, emotional, and mental exhaustion caused by prolonged or excessive stress. For men with ADHD, the constant effort to manage symptoms, fight distractions, regulate emotions, and navigate a demanding world can make you particularly susceptible to this debilitating state. Building resilience is about creating buffers and practices that protect your vital energy reserves.

Recognize Your Burnout Signals:

Learn your personal warning signs. Early detection is key to intervention. Are you more irritable than usual, snapping at loved ones? Having significantly more trouble initiating tasks, even simple ones? Feeling cynical or detached from your work or hobbies? Experiencing increased forgetfulness or "brain fog"? Are you withdrawing socially? Are you experiencing physical symptoms like persistent headaches, stomach issues, frequent colds, or muscle tension? Catching these subtle cues early allows you to intervene before full burnout sets in, enabling you to step back and recharge proactively. Keep a simple journal to track your mood and energy levels if you find it hard to identify patterns.

Schedule True Downtime:

This isn't just "not working" or collapsing on the couch to scroll aimlessly. True downtime is intentionally unplugging and engaging in activities that genuinely recharge you, providing restorative rest for your mind and body. This might include engaging in hobbies (without turning them into another "task"), spending time in nature, pursuing creative outlets, connecting meaningfully with loved ones without distraction, or simply doing nothing active. Treat downtime as important as work time; schedule it in your calendar and defend it vigorously. For the ADHD brain, which is prone to overstimulation, true downtime means disengaging from screens and mentally demanding activities to allow for quiet processing and restoration.

Practice Realistic Self-Expectations:

Avoid the trap of perfectionism or constantly comparing yourself to neurotypical productivity standards. Acknowledge and accept your brain's unique wiring and its inherent challenges. It's okay to have "off" days where focus is elusive, or when you don't achieve everything on your to-do list. Be kind to yourself when things don't go as planned;

harsh self-criticism only depletes the emotional and cognitive resources needed for regulation and resilience. Focus on consistent, sustainable effort and progress, rather than unrealistic bursts of productivity or unattainable ideals. Celebrate small wins and acknowledge the effort involved in managing ADHD symptoms. Self-compassion is a powerful antidote to the shame and frustration that can fuel burnout.

Delegate and Say No:

Learn to identify tasks that can be delegated or opportunities that you need to politely decline. Men with ADHD can sometimes overcommit due to enthusiasm, difficulty estimating time requirements, or a desire to please. Overcommitment is a fast track to overwhelm and burnout, especially when you have ADHD, as it stretches your limited executive function resources too thin. Protect your energy and time for your true priorities. Practice saying "No" to new commitments by having polite scripts ready (e.g., "I appreciate you thinking of me, but I'm fully committed right now," or "I need to check my schedule before I can commit, I'll get back to you"). This empowers you to manage your boundaries effectively.

Cultivate a Support System:

You don't have to navigate this alone. Connect with friends, family, a partner, or support groups who understand ADHD. Having people you can talk to openly, share challenges with, and receive encouragement and practical advice from can be a powerful buffer against stress, isolation, and burnout. Consider joining an online or in-person ADHD support group, or seek out a coach or therapist specializing in ADHD. Sharing your experiences and learning from others can validate your struggles and provide fresh perspectives and strategies, reinforcing that you are not alone in your journey.

Review and Reflect on Your Focus Habits:

At the end of each day or week, briefly reflect on how your focus strategies worked. What enabled you to sustain focus? What led to fatigue or distraction? Were your breaks restorative? Did you honor your boundaries? This continuous learning process allows you to refine your approach, making your focus efforts more efficient and less draining over time. This meta-awareness, a core component of executive function, allows you to become an active, informed manager of your own attention and energy. Use a simple journal or a mental check-in to periodically assess and adapt your strategies.

Sustaining focus isn't a relentless grind; it's a mindful dance between intense effort and intelligent recovery. By implementing these strategies for energy management and burnout prevention, you'll not only extend your capacity for attention and productivity but also foster a deeper sense of well-being, resilience, and personal control. This integrated approach ensures that your sharpened focus becomes a consistent, reliable asset, helping you thrive in a world that constantly vies for your attention, rather than merely survive it. It's about building a life where focus is a tool for flourishing, not a pathway to exhaustion.

CONCLUSION
YOUR FOCUSED EDGE

You've now completed Book 2, "Mastering Focus: Sustained Attention in a Distracting World," and in doing so, you've equipped yourself with a profound understanding of how to harness your attention in a world designed for distraction. We've journeyed from dissecting the unique ways the ADHD brain approaches focus to implementing tangible strategies that empower you to direct and sustain your mental spotlight.

You've learned to:

- **Deconstruct the ADHD focus challenge**, recognizing it not as a personal failing, but as a neurological difference that can be strategically managed.
- **Design your environment** for optimal concentration, transforming both your physical and digital spaces into powerful allies for deep work.
- **Cultivate mindfulness and presence**, anchoring your attention to the present moment and gently guiding your mind back when it wanders.
- **Master single-tasking and deep work**, embracing the power of focused effort on one thing at a time, rather than falling prey to the myth of multitasking.
- **Sustain your focus and prevent burnout**, understanding that consistent attention is built on smart energy management, strategic breaks, and genuine self-care.

This focused edge isn't about eradicating your ADHD; it's about learning to work *with* your brain's unique rhythms. It's about empowering you to choose where your attention goes, rather than being pulled by every fleeting impulse or external demand. You're building resilience, enhancing your capacity for deep work, and ultimately, gaining a significant advantage in achieving your goals and living a more intentional life.

The strategies covered in this book are not one-time fixes; they are practices to be integrated into your daily routine. Experiment with them, adapt them to your personal style, and observe their impact. There will be days of effortless flow and days of struggle, but with each mindful effort, you're strengthening your attentional muscles and creating a more reliable, consistent ability to focus.

As you move forward, carry these principles with you. Your ability to direct your attention is one of your most valuable assets. Continue to protect it, nourish it, and deploy it with purpose. You now have the blueprint to navigate a distracting world with a sharper, more sustained focus, giving you a distinct advantage in all your endeavors.

Let's pause for a moment and reflect on what you've just read. What resonates with you? What are the strategies you feel you can apply to work and life now versus those that seem more challenging or daunting?

BOOK THREE

UNLEASHING PRODUCTIVITY

TURNING INTENTIONS INTO ACCOMPLISHMENTS

CHAPTER 1

REDEFINING PRODUCTIVITY FOR ADHD MEN

You've honed your executive functions, transforming your brain's command center from a chaotic control room into a more organized and effective hub. You've sharpened your focus, gaining greater influence over your attention and learning to direct your mental spotlight with intentionality. Now, it's time to channel that cultivated power into tangible results. This book, "Unleashing Productivity," isn't about simply doing more; it's about redefining productivity for the ADHD brain: moving beyond the conventional, often frustrating, metrics to a personalized system that truly works for you, aligning your unique cognitive landscape with meaningful output. It's about working smarter, with less friction, and achieving a sustainable sense of accomplishment.

For many men, particularly in a culture that glorifies endless grind and quantifiable output, productivity is often measured by a relentless pursuit of a never-ending to-do list, hours meticulously clocked, or the sheer volume of tasks completed. Success is frequently equated with being perpetually busy, with visible output being the ultimate arbiter of worth. For someone with ADHD, this traditional definition can be a source of immense frustration, self-criticism, and even profound shame. You might recognize yourself in the pattern of having bursts of incredible output: Moments of hyperfocus where you achieve in hours what might take others days, only to be followed by periods of overwhelm, crippling procrastination, or the maddening inability to translate brilliant ideas and urgent intentions into concrete, consistent actions. It's a common experience to feel like you're working harder, expending immense mental effort just to initiate or stay on track, but not necessarily smarter, leaving a trail of unfinished projects, missed opportunities, and unmet goals. This often leads to a crushing sense of inadequacy, a feeling that despite your intelligence and effort, you are perpetually "behind" or "not enough."

The challenge isn't a lack of desire, intelligence, or even capability. It stems directly from the inherent difficulties with executive functions we discussed in Book 1 (like planning, initiation, working memory, and emotional regulation) and the unique focus patterns explored in Book 2. Your brain might thrive on novelty, urgency, and high-intensity stimulation, making sustained, methodical, and often repetitive progress a significant hurdle. The very tasks that require consistent, unglamorous effort often feel under-stimulating for the ADHD brain, prompting it to seek out more immediate dopamine hits from distractions or more exciting, albeit less critical, new endeavors. The conventional wisdom often prescribed by productivity gurus, "just push through" or "use more willpower," frequently backfires for someone with ADHD, leading not to breakthrough, but to rapid mental exhaustion, increased anxiety, and ultimately, burnout. This is because it asks the ADHD brain to function against its natural wiring, without providing the necessary support structures or understanding of its unique needs.

So, how do we redefine productivity in a way that truly serves the ADHD brain? It's about shifting from a sole emphasis on raw quantity to a focus on quality, consistency, and, most critically, alignment with your unique strengths and energetic fluctuations. It's a more compassionate, effective, and sustainable approach that respects your neurobiology. This redefinition involves several key paradigm shifts:

- **Understanding your personal energy cycles and attention patterns, including the common experience of time perception challenges (often referred to as 'time blindness'):** This means recognizing that your brain's internal clock might operate differently from a neurotypical one, often struggling to accurately perceive the passage of time, estimate how long tasks will take, or grasp the immediacy of future deadlines. This can lead to chronic lateness, underestimation of task duration, and a feeling that deadlines suddenly appear out of nowhere. Simultaneously, your attentional capacity isn't a constant. You likely have periods of peak alertness and focus (your "prime time") and periods of lower energy and increased distractibility. Redefining productivity means learning to identify these unique fluctuations—when your brain is naturally more engaged, when it needs a break, and when it's better suited for administrative or less demanding tasks, and then working *with* these unique fluctuations, not against them. This involves employing external aids and strategies (like visual timers, breaking tasks into smaller chunks, and scheduling accordingly) to compensate for internal time perception challenges and leverage your natural energy ebbs and flows.
- **Celebrating momentum over perfection:** For many with ADHD, the pursuit of perfection can be a significant barrier to initiation and completion. The "all-or-nothing" thinking pattern can lead to paralysis: if it can't be done perfectly, it might not be started at all, or an almost-finished project remains incomplete because of the perceived need for a flawless final touch. Redefining productivity means recognizing that progress, however small, however imperfect, is infinitely more valuable than paralysis caused by aiming for flawless execution. The goal is to build consistent momentum. Acknowledge that "done is better than perfect," especially in initial stages. The act of simply starting, or completing a rough draft, builds crucial momentum and provides a sense of accomplishment that fuels further action. This shifts the focus from an intimidating, distant ideal to a series of manageable, achievable steps.
- **Creating sustainable systems:** For the ADHD brain, which often struggles with working memory, organization, and consistent follow-through, relying solely on willpower is a recipe for exhaustion and frustration. Redefining productivity

means developing habits, routines, and external structures, such as consistent schedules, organizational frameworks, and automated reminders, that reduce decision fatigue and friction. These systems act as external scaffolding, compensating for internal challenges and making it easier to start tasks, follow through, and manage information without constant conscious effort. When a process is systematized, your brain doesn't have to expend energy reinventing the wheel each time, freeing up mental energy for the actual work that truly matters. This creates a predictable and reliable environment that supports consistent output.

- **Prioritizing impact over activity:** A common ADHD productivity trap is getting caught in "busywork": tasks that feel productive because they keep you occupied, but don't genuinely move you towards your most important goals. This can stem from a desire for immediate gratification from checking off easy tasks, or from getting lost in the details rather than focusing on the bigger picture. Redefining productivity means consciously shifting your focus to tasks that genuinely create the most impact, that align with your highest priorities, and that move you significantly closer to your long-term aspirations. It's about becoming a strategic filter, learning to differentiate between high-leverage activities and those that merely keep you spinning your wheels. This requires clear goal setting and regular evaluation of where your efforts are truly making a difference.
- **Acknowledging and leveraging your ADHD strengths:** This is perhaps the most empowering aspect of redefining productivity. Instead of viewing ADHD solely as a deficit, recognize that your neurodiversity comes with inherent strengths that can be harnessed for extraordinary output when managed strategically. Your rapid thinking, ability to make novel connections, natural curiosity, boundless creativity, entrepreneurial spirit, and capacity to hyperfocus when engaged are not weaknesses; they are powerful assets. Redefining productivity involves understanding how to integrate these strengths into your workflow. For instance, leveraging hyperfocus for deep dives into engaging projects, using rapid idea generation for brainstorming sessions, or channeling your novelty-seeking into exploring new, innovative

solutions. This shifts the narrative from "what's wrong with me?" to "how can I maximize my unique potential?"

This isn't about becoming a productivity robot or forcing yourself into a rigid, soul-crushing routine that extinguishes your spontaneity and creativity. Instead, it's about building a compassionate, effective framework that helps you turn intentions into accomplishments consistently, with less stress and more satisfaction. It's about recognizing that your optimal productivity system will be uniquely yours, a reflection of your individual brain and preferences. We will explore how to break down overwhelming tasks into manageable steps, conquer the inertia of procrastination, optimize your workflow to minimize friction, and build robust systems that support your unique way of working, rather than trying to fit you into a conventional mold.

Get ready to shed the guilt of "not enough" and the frustration of "should be doing more." Embrace a powerful, personalized approach to productivity that truly works for your ADHD brain. By the end of this book, you'll have a clear roadmap to unleash your potential, transform your aspirations into tangible achievements, and cultivate a sustainable sense of accomplishment that honors your unique neurodiversity. You will learn to move beyond merely coping, to truly thriving in your work and life.

CHAPTER 2

TASK BREAKDOWN AND ACTIONABLE STEPS

You've redefined productivity, understanding that it's about smart, consistent action tailored to your ADHD brain, rather than a relentless pursuit of endless tasks. You've acknowledged your unique strengths and the challenges posed by executive function differences and fluctuating focus. Now, let's get practical. One of the biggest and most persistent roadblocks to turning intentions into tangible accomplishments is the sheer overwhelming nature of a large, complex task. When your brain sees something like "Write Book," "Launch New Product," or "Complete Annual Report" on a to-do list, it often translates that formidable entry into an "Impossible Mountain to Climb." This perception triggers an immediate shutdown response, leading to intense feelings of overwhelm, paralyzing anxiety, or the familiar spiral of procrastination. The solution? Task breakdown – a systematic and powerful process of transforming that intimidating mountain into a series of manageable, actionable, and psychologically approachable steps.

For men with ADHD, the ability to break down tasks is not just a useful skill; it's an essential survival strategy for navigating work and life effectively. Your working memory, which is often a significant challenge in ADHD, can struggle with holding too many complex parts of a project simultaneously. When a task is too big and vague, your brain is forced to juggle an immense amount of information and potential steps, leading to mental clutter and a sense of being lost before you even begin. Furthermore, your task initiation often falters when faced with an abstract, enormous goal that lacks clear, immediate entry points. The "start button" for the ADHD brain requires a spark of clarity and achievable steps. By systematically dissecting a large task into its constituent components, you create clear, distinct entry points that reduce cognitive load, increase motivation by providing frequent small wins, and offer a tangible, visual sense of progress that fuels continued effort. This process bypasses the overwhelm and provides the necessary structure that your brain craves to move forward.

Think of it like dismantling a complex machine. You wouldn't try to move the whole thing at once, or even figure out how to operate it without understanding its parts. Instead, you'd logically identify the smaller components, understand how they fit together, and then work on one piece at a time. This process not only makes the task less daunting but also clarifies the exact, concrete actions needed to move forward. Each step becomes a small, self-contained mission, rather than an overwhelming segment of an endless journey. This methodical approach is precisely what helps the ADHD brain gain traction and maintain momentum.

The Art of Dissection: How to Break Down Any Task

The goal here is to get from a vague idea or an amorphous project to a series of concrete, "doable" actions that are easy to initiate and complete. This process externalizes the cognitive burden, leveraging your visual and kinesthetic senses to support your planning.

- **The "Mind Map" or "Brain Dump" Start:** Begin by writing down the main task or project at the center of a large space. Then, brainstorm *everything* and anything associated with it, letting your thoughts flow freely without censorship. Don't worry about order, logic, or completeness at this stage. Just get all the sub-ideas, related concepts, questions that arise, known steps, potential obstacles, resources needed, and even anxieties out of your head and onto a visual medium. Use a large whiteboard, a big piece of paper, sticky notes, or a digital mind-mapping tool (like MindMeister, XMind, or even a simple bullet-point list in a note app). This "brain dump" serves a crucial purpose: it externalizes the cognitive burden from your working memory, freeing up mental space and allowing you to see the entire landscape of the project, no matter how chaotic it initially appears. It's the first step in taming the mental storm.
- **Identify the Major Phases/Categories:** Look at your brainstormed, often messy, list. Can you group related items into logical phases or overarching categories? For example, for "Plan a Trip to Europe," categories might naturally emerge: "Research Destinations," "Book Flights," "Book Accommodation," "Create Itinerary," "Pack," "Budgeting," "Visa & Documentation." For "Write a Business Proposal," categories could be: "Research Market," "Outline Proposal Sections," "Write Content," "Design Visuals," "Review & Edit." This step helps to bring order to the initial chaos, creating a higher-level structure that makes the project feel less overwhelming and more modular. It's like sorting a pile of laundry into darks, lights, and delicates before washing.
- **Break Each Phase into Smaller Sub-Tasks:** Now, take each major phase you've identified and break it down further into smaller, more manageable sub-tasks. The critical rule here is to make each sub-task small enough that it feels achievable in a single focused session, typically ranging from 30 to 90 minutes for an ADHD brain. If a sub-task still feels too large or abstract, break it down again. For "Book Flights," sub-tasks could be: "Research flight comparison sites," "Set budget for flights," "Check dates for best prices for specific routes," "Select airline based on criteria," "Input passenger information," "Complete payment." The psychological benefit of this step is immense: by creating these "bite-sized" chunks, you reduce the intimidation

factor and create clear, approachable starting points that are less likely to trigger procrastination.

- **Define the "Next Action" (The Smallest Unit):** For every sub-task, identify the absolute smallest, most immediate *physical* action required to start it. This is your "next action." This step is paramount for task initiation, especially for the ADHD brain which can get stuck in "analysis paralysis." If you can't identify a physical action (something you can *do*), the task is still too big. It should be so simple that you can perform it almost without thinking, requiring minimal decision-making or mental energy to begin.
    - **Bad:** "Do taxes." (Too vague, overwhelming)
    - **Better:** "Gather tax documents." (Still a bit vague, what *exactly* do I do first?)
    - **Best:** "Find last year's tax return in filing cabinet." (Clear, specific, physical action) The "next action" is your clear starting pistol, removing the ambiguity that often traps the ADHD brain in a cycle of hesitation.
- **Estimate Time (and Add Your ADHD Buffer):** For each "next action" and small sub-task, estimate how long it will realistically take. Be generous with your estimates. As discussed in previous chapters, the ADHD brain often struggles with "time blindness"—underestimating how long tasks will take and how quickly time passes. To account for potential distractions, unexpected complications, or the need for a quick mental break, add a "buffer" of 25-50% extra time to your initial estimate. If you think it will take 20 minutes, block out 30. If it's an hour, give yourself 90 minutes. This helps in realistic scheduling, reduces frustration when things take longer than expected, and builds a more accurate internal clock over time. Consistent overestimation is far less damaging than consistent underestimation.
- **Sequence Your Steps:** Once you have a detailed list of actionable steps and their estimated times, put them in a logical order. What absolutely needs to happen first? What steps are dependent on another step being completed? Use arrows, numbers, a simple outline format, or even drag-and-drop features in a digital tool to visualize the flow of the project. This creates a clear, sequential pathway from beginning to end,

reducing ambiguity and showing you the logical progression. This structured view is incredibly supportive for the ADHD brain, providing a clear roadmap rather than a confusing tangle of possibilities.

Making It Actionable: Beyond the List

A beautifully broken-down list is useless if it just sits there, an elegant blueprint for inaction. The next critical phase is to ensure these steps lead directly to *action* and ultimately, accomplishment.

- **Use Visual Checklists:** Once broken down, transfer your actionable steps into a visual checklist. This could be a simple pen-and-paper list, a physical whiteboard, a digital task manager like Trello, Asana, Todoist, or a dedicated to-do app. The visual satisfaction of physically or digitally checking off small items provides valuable, immediate dopamine hits. These mini-rewards reinforce the positive behavior of task completion and build crucial momentum, which is particularly motivating for the ADHD brain. Seeing visible progress counteracts feelings of stagnation and overwhelm.
- **Schedule the "Next Action":** Don't just list the steps; integrate them into your calendar or daily plan. Block out specific time slots for those "next actions." This transforms an intention into a concrete commitment, creating external accountability and reducing the cognitive load of deciding what to work on next. For example, instead of just "Research flight comparison sites," your schedule should read: "10:00 AM - 10:30 AM: Research flight comparison sites (Project Europe Trip)." This scheduled commitment provides a clear start time, minimizing procrastination.
- **Start with the Easiest or Most Appealing:** While logical sequencing is important, sometimes the best way to build initial momentum for the ADHD brain is to tackle the easiest, most appealing, or most novel "next action" first, even if it's not the absolute highest priority. This "easy win" provides an immediate burst of dopamine and a sense of accomplishment, propelling you forward into the more challenging tasks. It's a strategic form of "dopamine farming" that leverages your brain's natural tendencies to get started. Once you're in motion, staying in motion often becomes easier.

- **Focus on One Step at a Time:** Once you're working on a specific step, actively resist the urge to jump ahead, think about other parts of the project, or get distracted by unrelated tasks. Your current mission is *only* that one small, actionable step you've identified. Employ the single-tasking principles from Chapter 4. When your mind tries to wander to the next step or a different distraction, gently bring it back to the current, manageable action. When it's done, then (and only then) move to the next item on your sequenced list. This hyper-focus on the micro-task prevents the overwhelming feeling of the entire project from derailing your progress.
- **Acknowledge and Reward Progress:** Every time you complete a small step, take a moment to acknowledge it. Check it off with satisfaction. This small win provides a mini-burst of dopamine that reinforces the behavior and encourages you to keep going. Don't underestimate the power of these micro-rewards. They are the fuel for consistent motivation for the ADHD brain. This could be a mental high-five, a stretch break, a quick look out the window, or a small, pre-planned non-distracting reward. Over time, your brain will associate the feeling of completing a small step with positive reinforcement, making the entire process less of a struggle.

By consistently employing task breakdown, you transform overwhelming, nebulous projects into a series of manageable, psychologically less intimidating actions. You shift from being stuck at the base of a seemingly impossible mountain to confidently taking one well-defined step after another, seeing visible progress with each completed item. This clarity, systematic approach, and built-in reinforcement are fundamental to unleashing your productivity and consistently turning your ambitious intentions into concrete, satisfying accomplishments, paving the way for a more organized and effective way of working with your ADHD brain.

CHAPTER 3

OVERCOMING PROCRASTINATION AND RESISTANCE

You've learned to break down tasks into actionable steps, a crucial strategy for managing the overwhelm that often paralyzes the ADHD brain. You've discovered how to transform intimidating "mountains" into manageable "hills," making projects less daunting and more approachable. Yet, even with a perfectly detailed plan, the invisible wall of procrastination and resistance can loom large, casting a long shadow over your intentions. This isn't a sign of laziness, a character flaw, or a deficiency in your work ethic; it's a common, often frustrating, symptom for men with ADHD, deeply rooted in how your brain processes motivation, reward, and the perceived difficulty or stimulation level of a task. It's a neurobiological hurdle, not a moral failing.

Procrastination, for the ADHD brain, often isn't about avoiding work altogether. Instead, it's a sophisticated, often unconscious, mechanism for avoiding the *discomfort* associated with initiating or engaging with a task. This discomfort can manifest in various ways, each signaling a specific challenge for your unique brain wiring:

- **Low Stimulation:** The task is perceived as boring, repetitive, abstract, or uninteresting, leading your dopamine-seeking brain to wander in search of more immediate novelty or engagement. The brain struggles to generate the necessary intrinsic motivation when the task itself doesn't provide enough external stimulation or an immediate reward.
- **Overwhelm:** Even a broken-down task can feel daunting if the sum of its parts still appears too large, too complex, or requires a sustained mental effort that feels beyond your current capacity. The sheer cognitive load of holding the task in mind, even in its smaller pieces, can trigger a shutdown response.
- **Fear of Failure/Perfectionism:** The desire to do something perfectly, coupled with an awareness of past struggles or perceived imperfections, can lead to paralysis. The perceived effort required to achieve an ideal outcome is too high, leading to an avoidance of starting altogether rather than risking imperfection. This is often an unconscious self-protection mechanism.
- **Difficulty with Future Self-Talk:** The "future you" seems capable of handling anything with ease, so the "present you" can comfortably defer the unpleasantness of the task. There's a disconnect where the consequences of inaction feel abstract and distant, making it easy to rationalize delay, believing that "future me" will have more energy, more time, or more motivation.
- **Time Blindness:** Without a strong, accurate internal sense of urgency, a deadline can feel distant and abstract until it's critically, overwhelmingly close. This makes it challenging to prioritize tasks based on their true time sensitivity, often leading to a reliance on last-minute adrenaline to kickstart action, a highly unsustainable and stressful approach.

Overcoming these internal barriers is fundamental to unleashing your productivity and transforming your intentions into consistent accomplishments. It requires a blend of psychological understanding, clever practical tricks, and consistent, compassionate practice that acknowledges and works *with* your ADHD brain, not against it.

Busting the Block: Strategies for Overcoming Procrastination

The key to beating procrastination is to lower the activation energy required to start and to make the initial steps so small, so appealing, or so supported that your brain's resistance is minimized.

The "2-Minute Rule" (with an ADHD Lens):

This popular productivity guideline suggests that if a task takes less than two minutes to complete, you should do it immediately. For the ADHD brain, this can be a powerful starting strategy for low-friction tasks that don't trigger significant internal resistance. Quickly tackling tasks like replying to a quick email, putting away a single dish, or throwing out a piece of trash can indeed prevent a multitude of tiny tasks from building up into an overwhelming mental burden. The immediate completion provides a small, satisfying dopamine hit. **However**, it's crucial to acknowledge that even a two-minute task can feel insurmountable if it's boring, highly resistant, or lacks immediate novelty for your particular brain in that moment. If you find yourself consistently unable to apply this rule to certain "two-minute" tasks, don't view it as a personal failing or a sign you're "broken." Instead, it's a signal to apply deeper strategies: perhaps that specific two-minute task needs to be paired with something enjoyable, you need the presence of a body double, or it needs to be broken down even further into a *one-minute* or *30-second* step. The rule is a guideline, not a rigid law, and its effectiveness depends on the individual task and your current internal state.

The "Just Start" or "Tiny Task" Strategy:

Forget about finishing the whole project or even completing a large section. Just commit to starting the tiniest possible first step. "Open the document." "Read the first paragraph." "Type the title." "Write one sentence." "Send one email." "Put on my running shoes." This micro-commitment bypasses the brain's overwhelm response. The momentum generated by even this minuscule action is often enough to propel you forward, as the brain's reward system begins to engage with the act of doing. This strategy works because the "cost" of starting feels so low, it becomes easier to overcome the initial inertia.

Harness the Power of Urgency (Strategically):

Your ADHD brain often responds well to urgency, as the pressure can provide a much-needed dopamine boost. While relying solely on last-minute panic isn't sustainable or healthy, you can create artificial, controlled urgency to your advantage:

- **Set Micro-Deadlines:** For a sub-task or even a tiny action, give yourself aggressive, internal deadlines, even if the actual project deadline is far off. Use a timer (e.g., "I will complete this section in the next 30 minutes"). This creates a mini-pressure cooker that can help activate your focus and bypass procrastination.
- **Public Accountability:** Tell someone (a trusted friend, a colleague, a mentor, or an online support group) what specific task you plan to accomplish by a specific time. Knowing someone else is aware of your commitment can provide a powerful external motivator, leveraging social pressure to push through resistance. This can be as simple as a quick text: "I'm going to finish the first draft of that report by 3 PM."

"Pairing" or "Temptation Bundling":

Combine a dreaded or boring task with something you genuinely enjoy or find highly stimulating. This strategy leverages the ADHD brain's natural inclination towards novelty and reward.

- "I will only listen to my favorite podcast or a specific genre of music while I'm doing the laundry."
- "I will only eat this specific, slightly indulgent snack while I'm working on that tedious report."
- "I will only watch this new show while I'm on the treadmill." This associates a positive, immediate reward or enjoyable stimulus with the undesirable task, making the dreaded activity more palatable and easier to initiate. The brain learns to anticipate the reward, reducing the friction of starting the less appealing task.

Change Your Environment/Context:

If you're stuck in a procrastination loop, a simple change of scenery can be enough to break the mental block and signal to your brain that it's time for a fresh start. Move to a different room, go to a coffee shop, or even just shift your chair, stand up, or walk to a different part of your desk. This physical shift can create a mental reset, breaking the negative association with your current environment that might be contributing to the procrastination. It's a way to introduce novelty and signal a new beginning, which can be highly effective for the ADHD brain.

"Body Doubling":

Work alongside someone else, even if you're working on completely different things. Their mere presence, either in person or virtually, can provide a subtle sense of accountability, structure, and shared focus, making it easier to start and stay on task. The other person acts as an external executive function, providing a stable, non-judgmental anchor that helps to activate and sustain your own focus. Many online communities and apps offer virtual body doubling sessions, making this a highly accessible strategy. The knowledge that someone else is working nearby can significantly reduce the feeling of isolation and inertia.

Address the Underlying Discomfort:

When you find yourself procrastinating, take a moment to pause and honestly identify *why* you're resisting. Is the task genuinely boring? Does it feel overwhelmingly large? Are you afraid of making a mistake, or of the outcome? Are you feeling tired or overwhelmed? Acknowledging the specific discomfort allows you to apply a targeted strategy. For example, if it's overwhelming, break it down further. If it's boring, try temptation bundling or gamification. If it's fear of failure, remind yourself of "done is better than perfect." This metacognitive step empowers you to be a detective of your own procrastination, leading to more effective interventions.

Navigating Resistance: The Deeper Mental Blocks

Resistance goes beyond mere procrastination; it's a deeper, often subconscious, mental or emotional barrier that keeps you from engaging with important work, even when you logically know you should. It's the insidious internal voice that whispers, "You can't do this," "This isn't important enough," or "You'll fail anyway." These blocks often stem from past negative experiences, perfectionism, or internalized shame.

"Done is Better Than Perfect":

For men with ADHD who struggle with perfectionism, the pursuit of an ideal, flawless outcome can be incredibly paralyzing. The effort required to reach "perfect" feels insurmountable, leading to indefinite delay. Remind yourself constantly that a completed, even imperfect, task creates momentum, provides tangible progress, and allows for iteration and refinement later. Good enough, released, and in motion, is always better than perfect, perpetually stuck in your head or on your to-do list. This mantra combats the "all-or-nothing" thinking pattern that often traps the ADHD brain.

Externalize the Resistance:

Sometimes, just acknowledging and naming the resistance can lessen its power. When you feel that invisible wall, that deep reluctance, don't suppress it. Instead, externalize it: "Okay, I'm feeling a lot of resistance to starting this proposal right now. My brain is telling me it's too hard." Write it down. Speak it aloud to yourself. Acknowledging it without judgment helps you separate yourself from the feeling, allowing you to observe it rather than be consumed by it. This creates a small but significant cognitive distance, opening a space for choice.

The "Swiss Cheese" Method:

For tasks you truly dread or those that feel like an insurmountable block, don't try to tackle them head-on. Instead, "poke holes" in them. Spend just 10-15 minutes doing the easiest part, or a completely random small part, even if it's out of logical order. This breaks the intimidating solid block of the task, making it feel less formidable and more approachable. For a research paper, you might just find three sources. For a messy room, you might just clear one small surface. Each "hole" you poke reduces the perceived size and density of the "cheese," making the rest of it seem less daunting. This tactic capitalizes on your brain's need for small wins.

Embrace the "Messy Middle":

All projects, especially large ones, have a point where the initial excitement and novelty wear off, and the end isn't yet in sight. This "messy middle" is where many with ADHD abandon projects, as the dopamine hit from novelty fades. Recognize this phase as a normal, predictable part of the creative or productive process. Remind yourself that it's normal to feel less engaged, bored, or frustrated here. Instead of seeking a new, exciting project, double down on your tiny, actionable steps and leverage your accountability and reward systems to push through this phase. Knowing it's coming can help you prepare for it and not be derailed by it.

Self-Compassion and Reframing:

When you find yourself procrastinating or hitting a wall of resistance, avoid harsh self-criticism. Instead of thinking "I'm so lazy and undisciplined," try reframing it: "My brain is finding this task hard right now. What small step can I take to make it easier or more interesting?"

Or "This resistance is a signal that I need a different strategy." Reframe procrastination and resistance as signals to adjust your approach or to apply a specific strategy, not as personal failings. Harsh self-criticism only triggers shame, anxiety, and a feeling of inadequacy, which further deplete the emotional resources needed for motivation and self-regulation. Cultivate an inner voice that is supportive, curious, and problem-solving, rather than judgmental.

Celebrate Small Wins:

The ADHD brain thrives on positive feedback and immediate reward. Don't wait until the entire project is finished to celebrate. Acknowledge and celebrate each small task completed, each tiny step taken, each moment of resistance overcome. This consistent, positive reinforcement provides crucial dopamine rewards that reinforce productive behavior and make future initiation and follow-through easier. Make it a deliberate practice: physically check off items, tell your accountability partner, or give yourself a pre-planned mini-reward. These small, frequent celebrations are the fuel that keeps your motivation tank from running empty during the long haul of productivity.

Overcoming procrastination and resistance is an ongoing battle, but one you can absolutely win by equipping yourself with these practical, neurobiologically informed strategies. By understanding *why* you procrastinate and by actively breaking down those barriers with targeted interventions, you'll unleash a powerful new level of consistent action, transforming your intentions into tangible accomplishments with greater ease, less internal struggle, and a profound sense of self-efficacy. This is about working smarter, not just harder, with your unique ADHD brain.

CHAPTER 4

WORKFLOW OPTIMIZATION AND SYSTEM BUILDING

You've mastered breaking down tasks into manageable steps, a fundamental skill for bypassing the overwhelm that often paralyzes the ADHD brain. You've also confronted the insidious nature of procrastination and armed yourself with strategies to break through those invisible walls of resistance. Now, to truly unleash consistent, sustainable productivity, we need to move beyond individual tasks and focus on the bigger picture: workflow optimization and system building. This isn't just about doing more; it's about creating a streamlined, predictable path for your work, minimizing friction, and reducing the constant mental effort required to decide "what's next?" It's about creating an operating system for your life that supports your unique neurobiology, allowing your brilliant ideas and energy to flow effortlessly into concrete action.

For men with ADHD, a chaotic or unpredictable workflow is an enormous drain on executive function, almost like trying to run a race while constantly tripping over loose obstacles. Your brain thrives on novelty and excitement, but paradoxically, it also benefits immensely from underlying structure and predictability. Without clear, intuitive systems, every task becomes a fresh act of initiation, a new decision point, and an open invitation for distraction. This constant need to re-evaluate, re-prioritize, and re-locate information leads to:

- **Constant decision fatigue:** Spending valuable mental energy on *how* to do something, *where* to find information, or *what* to do next, rather than just doing the actual work. Each micro-decision drains your limited willpower and cognitive bandwidth, leading to exhaustion before you've even begun the core task.
- **Lost information:** Brilliant ideas, crucial notes, important documents, or pending tasks disappearing into the ether of a disorganized physical or digital system. This leads to wasted time searching, re-doing work, and the frustration of missed opportunities.
- **Inefficient transitions:** Wasting significant time and mental energy switching between different types of work, trying to locate necessary tools, or recalling where you left off on a project. Each transition becomes a potential derailment point for the ADHD brain.
- **A feeling of being overwhelmed by the sheer volume of "stuff":** Emails, physical documents, digital files, tasks, and fleeting ideas piling up without a clear home or a defined process for handling them. This creates a constant background hum of anxiety and the sensation of perpetually being behind, feeding the cycle of procrastination and avoidance.

Optimizing your workflow and building reliable systems isn't about becoming rigid or stifling your natural creativity; it's about creating freedom. It frees up your working memory by offloading information to trusted external systems, reduces the need for constant willpower by automating decisions, and provides a clear, well-worn path for your brilliant ideas and bursts of energy to flow into concrete action. It's about setting up the track so your ADHD brain can run on it with minimal friction, rather than constantly trying to build the track while simultaneously running the race. This intentional design empowers you to leverage your strengths, transforming potential chaos into structured efficiency.

Streamlining Your Flow: Optimizing Your Workflow

Workflow optimization focuses on the minute-to-minute, task-to-task movements of your work, actively reducing points of friction, eliminating unnecessary steps, and minimizing decision-making at every turn. It's about designing a smoother, more intuitive cognitive pathway for your daily tasks.

- **Define Your "Default State":** What happens when you finish a task? Without a conscious plan, the ADHD brain might default to checking email, scrolling social media, or getting a snack – activities that provide immediate dopamine hits but derail productivity. Instead, define a *productive* default for yourself: "When I finish task X, I will immediately check my 'Next Actions' list for task Y," or "I will review my schedule for the next pre-blocked task," or "I will do a 5-minute brain dump." This proactive definition reduces decision fatigue and creates a consistent, positive loop. By replacing a reactive default with a proactive one, you maintain momentum and direct your attention towards your true priorities.
- **Batch Similar Tasks:** Group similar activities together into dedicated time blocks. For example, process all emails at specific, pre-determined times (e.g., 9 AM, 1 PM, 4 PM) rather than reacting to each one as it arrives. Make all your phone calls in a dedicated block. Do all your "shallow work" (administrative tasks, quick replies, filing) at one time, and reserve your "deep work" (cognitively demanding tasks) for another, often earlier, block in your day. This strategy is incredibly powerful because it minimizes the mental "context switching" cost that is so draining for the ADHD brain. Each time you switch tasks, your brain has to reorient itself, load new information into working memory, and discard the old. Batching reduces this overhead significantly, allowing you to build momentum within a single cognitive mode.
- **Create Checklists and Templates:** For repetitive tasks, recurring projects, or even complex one-off endeavors, create detailed checklists or templates. Whether it's for launching a new project, preparing for a weekly meeting, handling client onboarding, or even your morning routine, a checklist reduces the mental load of remembering every step and ensures consistency. Templates for emails, reports, or common

documents prevent you from having to "start from scratch" each time. This is especially useful for preventing steps from being missed due to working memory challenges and provides external structure for reliable execution. Checklists effectively outsource the "remembering" function from your brain to a reliable system.

- **"One Touch" Rule for Information:** When you handle a piece of information (an email, a physical document, a note, a voicemail), try to process it, file it, or take an action on it immediately, rather than letting it sit and become "clutter." If it can't be dealt with in two minutes (as per the 2-minute rule), don't leave it in your immediate workspace. Instead, put it directly into your designated capture system (e.g., your inbox for later processing, a "to file" folder) to be reviewed and acted upon later. The goal is to minimize the number of times you touch or mentally process the same piece of information, reducing cognitive fatigue and preventing mental and physical clutter from accumulating.
- **Simplify Your Tools:** Resist the urge to use too many different apps, software, or analog systems. While the novelty of a new tool can be appealing for the ADHD brain, constantly switching between or managing multiple systems adds unnecessary complexity and cognitive load. Find one or two core tools for tasks, notes, and scheduling that you genuinely use consistently and that integrate well. The fewer systems you have to manage, the less mental energy is required to maintain them, ensuring reliability and reducing the chance of information falling through the cracks. Master your chosen tools rather than endlessly searching for the "perfect" one.
- **Review Your Workflow Regularly:** Your workflow isn't set in stone; it's a living system that needs periodic adjustment. At the end of each week (or even monthly), spend 15-20 minutes reviewing what worked well in your workflow, what caused bottlenecks or friction points, and what could be improved. Are there steps you can automate further? Can you eliminate unnecessary steps? Did you consistently follow your default states and batching strategies? This iterative process of review and adjustment is key to continuous improvement and ensuring your workflow remains optimized for your evolving needs and projects.

Building Your Foundation: Creating Reliable Systems

Systems are the underlying, often invisible, structures that support your optimized workflow. They reduce chaos, build predictability, and provide a trusted scaffolding for your executive functions. These are the habits and tools that prevent cognitive overload and ensure consistency, even on "off" days.

- **The Master Capture System:** You need one, and only one, reliable place to capture *all* your ideas, tasks, notes, commitments, and stray thoughts as they arise. This could be a single physical notebook that's always with you, a specific digital note-taking app (Evernote, Notion, Obsidian, Google Keep), or even a simple voice recorder. The key is that it's always available, easy to use, and you implicitly *trust* that anything captured there will be reviewed and processed later. This prevents valuable thoughts from being lost (which is a huge source of anxiety for ADHD) and immediately reduces mental clutter, freeing up your working memory. The capture system is the funnel for all incoming mental data.
- **A Consistent Review Schedule:** Having a capture system is useless without a rigorous, consistent review system. This is the crucial step where you process the captured information, organize it, and integrate it into your actionable plans.
    - **Daily Review:** At the start or end of each day, spend 10-15 minutes reviewing your capture system, processing new inputs, planning the next day's top 1-3 priorities ("Big Rocks"), and cleaning up any lingering tasks from the previous day. This ritual provides a clear start or end to your workday, helping with transitions and ensuring you wake up or go to bed with clarity.
    - **Weekly Review:** This is perhaps the most important system for long-term productivity and stress reduction. Dedicate 30-60 minutes each week (e.g., Friday afternoon or Sunday evening) to conduct a comprehensive review of all your projects, commitments, and goals. Clear out old notes, process your email and physical inboxes, review your calendar, and plan the week ahead in detail. This holistic review is crucial for staying on top of everything, preventing overwhelm from accumulating, identifying potential bottlenecks, and

ensuring your efforts are aligned with your overarching objectives. It's your personal strategic planning session.

- **Filing System (Digital & Physical):** A simple, intuitive, and *consistently used* filing system saves immense time, reduces stress, and prevents the feeling of being disorganized.
    - **Digital:** Implement a consistent, logical folder structure on your computer and cloud storage (e.g., by project, by year, by client). Crucially, favor search functions over overly complex, nested folder hierarchies. Learn to use the search bar effectively to find files quickly.
    - **Physical:** Implement a basic "Action" (for things needing immediate attention), "Archive" (for completed or reference items), and "Reference" (for frequently accessed information) system for physical papers. Don't let papers pile up on surfaces; process them into these categories immediately. Label clearly and consistently.
- **Scheduled Maintenance/Tidying:** ADHD brains often struggle with ongoing, spontaneous organization. Instead of aiming for constant, unattainable tidiness, schedule dedicated "reset" times. This acknowledges that things will get messy and builds in time to address it. This could be 15 minutes at the end of each workday to clear your desk and digital desktop, 30 minutes every Friday to clear out email, or an hour on Saturday morning to reset your entire workspace and main living areas. By scheduling these resets, you prevent small messes from becoming overwhelming mountains, providing regular opportunities to refresh your environment.
- **Project-Specific Systems:** For larger, ongoing projects, create dedicated, centralized "homes" for all related information, notes, tasks, and communications. This could be a dedicated folder on your computer, a specific section or page in your note-taking app (like Notion or OneNote), or a simple physical binder. This prevents information from being scattered across multiple platforms and allows you to quickly dive into a project when needed, without wasting time searching for relevant materials or recalling context. All project-related items should live here.

- **Automate Wherever Possible:** Explore tools, apps, and software features that can automate repetitive tasks or reminders. This could include setting up email filters to sort messages, using scheduling tools for appointments, setting recurring reminders for bills or habits, or linking different apps with services like Zapier or IFTTT to create automatic workflows (e.g., a new email with a specific subject creates a task in your to-do list). Automation reduces the need for manual initiation and frees up valuable mental bandwidth, allowing your executive functions to focus on more complex, non-automatable tasks.

By investing time and effort in optimizing your workflow and building robust, reliable systems, you are essentially outsourcing decision-making and organization from your conscious mind to a trusted, external framework. This proactive approach significantly reduces the mental overhead associated with getting things done, allowing your focused attention and cultivated executive functions to be directed towards meaningful, high-impact work rather than fighting against inefficiency, disorganization, or constant cognitive friction.

This is how you create sustainable, powerful productivity for the ADHD brain, turning aspirations into consistent, tangible achievements.

CHAPTER 5

REVIEW, ADAPT, AND ITERATE

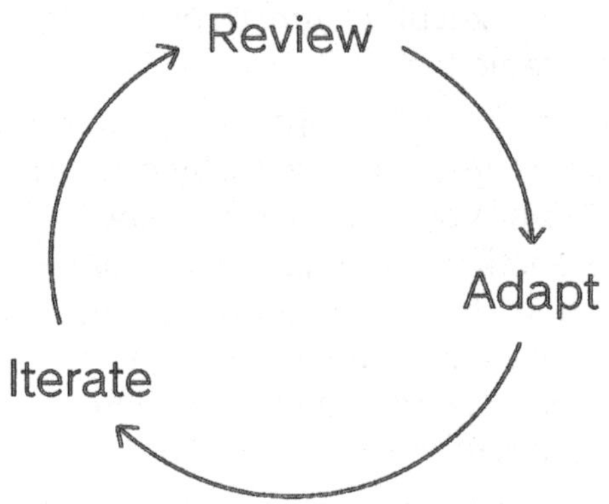

You've learned to break down daunting tasks into approachable steps, effectively dismantling the "impossible mountains" into navigable paths. You've also confronted the pervasive grip of procrastination and resistance, arming yourself with practical strategies to lower activation energy and initiate action. Furthermore, you've begun to build robust workflow optimizations and reliable systems, laying down the tracks for your productivity train to run smoothly. These are undeniably powerful steps toward unleashing your full productive potential. Yet, the journey to optimized productivity for the ADHD brain isn't a one-time setup, a static blueprint you follow indefinitely; it's a dynamic, continuous cycle of **review, adapt, and iterate**. Your brain isn't static, your life circumstances are constantly evolving, and neither should your productivity systems be.

For men with ADHD, rigid, inflexible systems often fail precisely because they don't account for the natural, often pronounced, fluctuations in energy, focus, interest, and the inherent novelty-seeking tendencies of your brain. What works perfectly one week – perhaps a specific time-blocking method or a particular environment – might feel impossible, boring, or utterly ineffective the very next. The novelty of a new system can wear off, the challenges of a new project might demand a different approach, or simply a shift in your internal rhythm can throw everything off balance. This is why a consistent, built-in practice of review, critical assessment, and strategic adaptation is not just helpful, but absolutely essential. Without this iterative loop, even the best-laid plans and most promising initial strategies can gather dust, lose their effectiveness, and the initial enthusiasm for new approaches can wane into familiar frustration and a return to old, less productive habits.

Think of it like a seasoned scientist in a lab, or an elite athlete training for a competition. They don't simply read a manual once and then execute blindly. They constantly experiment, observe the results of their efforts, collect data (whether informal or formal), tweak their methods based on what they learn, and try again with refined approaches. They learn as much, if not more, from what *doesn't* work as they do from what *does*. This iterative process of hypothesis, experiment, observation, and adjustment is how true mastery is achieved in any complex domain. For your productivity, it translates to:

- **Learning from experience:** Actively identifying what truly helps your unique ADHD brain thrive and what consistently creates friction, distraction, or overwhelm. It's about becoming an expert on *your own* operating system.
- **Catching issues early:** Preventing small problems – a forgotten task, a neglected inbox, a subtly draining habit – from snowballing into overwhelming chaos, missed deadlines, or a complete system collapse.
- **Refining your strategies:** Continuously making your systems more efficient, more intuitive, and more deeply personalized to your evolving needs, challenges, and strengths over time.
- **Building self-awareness:** Deepening your understanding of your own unique rhythms, triggers, energy cycles, and executive function fluctuations. This awareness is the foundation for genuine self-mastery.

This chapter will guide you through establishing a sustainable rhythm of self-reflection and proactive adjustment, ensuring your productivity strategies remain dynamic, effective, and perfectly tailored to your evolving needs, allowing you to consistently build on your progress.

The Power of Reflection: Why Review Matters

Regular, structured review periods are your brain's designated opportunity to pause, step back from the daily grind, assess what has happened, and recalibrate for what's next. They are the intentional moments that transform raw past experiences into invaluable future wisdom, providing the critical feedback loop that the ADHD brain often struggles to create organically.

- **The Daily Huddle (5-10 minutes):** This brief, powerful check-in can be done either at the very end of your workday (to close things out with clarity) or at the beginning of the next (to prime your focus). The key is consistency and brevity. During this time, take a few minutes to:
    - **Review yesterday:** What did you accomplish? Be specific. What did you *not* accomplish? Why? This is a moment for non-judgmental observation. Avoid self-criticism or dwelling on shortcomings. Simply notice the facts. Did a task take longer than expected? Was there a specific distraction?
    - **Identify wins:** Even small ones! What went well? Did you initiate a dreaded task? Did you stay focused for a solid 30 minutes? Did you remember to take your break? Acknowledging these micro-wins provides a vital dopamine hit, reinforcing positive behaviors and building self-efficacy.
    - **Note challenges:** Where did you get stuck? What was particularly distracting? Was a tool cumbersome? Was the task itself too vague? Pinpointing these moments helps you identify patterns for future adaptation.
    - **Plan your "Big Rocks" for tomorrow:** Based on your review, identify the 1-3 critical tasks that absolutely *must* get done tomorrow. This laser focus provides a clear target for initiation and ensures you prioritize impact over mere activity.
    - **Clear your mental desktop:** Quickly process any lingering thoughts, unexpected tasks, or ideas into your master capture system. This prevents mental clutter from bleeding into your personal time or the next day, ensuring you start fresh.

- **The Weekly Recharge (30-60 minutes):** This is your strategic planning and clearing session, a non-negotiable appointment with yourself. Choose a consistent time that works best for you – perhaps Friday afternoon to close out the week, or Sunday evening to prepare for the next. This dedicated time is crucial for preventing overwhelm from accumulating and for aligning your actions with your larger goals.
    - **Clear the decks:** Process your email inbox to zero (or close to it), clear your physical desk, and tidy up your digital desktop (downloads folder, open tabs). This physical and digital decluttering clears the mental space for strategic thinking.
    - **Review all projects:** What's the current status of each project you're involved in? Are there any looming deadlines you overlooked? Are there dependencies you need to act on? This prevents "out of sight, out of mind" syndrome common with ADHD.
    - **Review your task management system:** Go through your master capture system, organize newly added tasks, delete irrelevant notes, update due dates, and add any new tasks that emerged from your project review. This ensures your trusted system is up-to-date and reliable.
    - **Assess the past week:** Beyond the daily huddle, take a broader look: What worked effectively this week in your productivity? What challenges did you consistently encounter? What strategies did you try, and what strategies fell flat? This is a deeper dive into patterns.
    - **Plan the upcoming week:** Map out your "Big Rocks" and top priorities for the next 7 days. Schedule specific deep work blocks, allocate time for your "friction points," and deliberately plan for personal time, exercise, and rest to ensure balance.
    - **Reflect on energy and mood:** How was your overall energy this week? Where did you feel most productive and engaged? Where did you feel drained, stressed, or prone to procrastination? This insight helps you refine your schedule to leverage your natural energy cycles.

- **The Quarterly Recalibration (1-2 hours):** Every three months, step back further for a broader, higher-level strategic look at your life and work. This prevents you from getting caught in the weeds and ensures your daily actions are still serving your long-term vision.
    - **Review your larger goals:** Are your annual goals, career aspirations, or personal development objectives still relevant? Are you making consistent progress toward them? Do they need adjustment based on new information or shifting priorities?
    - **Assess your systems:** Are your core tools (task manager, calendar, note-taking app, filing system) still serving you optimally? Do you need to try a new app, a different calendar view, or a fundamentally new approach to a recurring problem (e.g., managing specific types of distractions)? This is where you consider more significant changes.
    - **Identify recurring issues:** Are there patterns of procrastination, disorganization, or overwhelm that persist despite your daily and weekly efforts? What underlying causes can you identify and address at a systemic level? This might point to needing professional support or a more radical change in habit.
    - **Plan for the next quarter:** Set new, inspiring goals for the upcoming three months, refine existing ones, and consider new habits, strategies, or experiments you want to implement to further optimize your productivity and well-being. This creates a fresh horizon to aim for.

Adapting and Iterating: Making Your Systems Agile

The purpose of these systematic review periods is not just reflection for its own sake, but purposeful, informed change. This is where you transform insights into action, making your productivity systems truly agile and responsive.

- **Embrace Experimentation:** Think of yourself as a kind of personal productivity scientist running micro-experiments. If a specific strategy isn't working for you (e.g., the Pomodoro Technique feels too rigid, or a particular app is too distracting), don't abandon the *idea* of systems altogether; adapt it. Try a different timer, a shorter or longer focus block, a different environment, or a new way of breaking down tasks. Frame it as: "This didn't work *for me* right now. What's one small thing I can change for next time to see if that helps?" This mindset removes the judgment and replaces it with curiosity and problem-solving, which is far more empowering for the ADHD brain.

- **Identify "Friction Points":** During your daily, weekly, and quarterly reviews, pay close attention to where you consistently get stuck, overwhelmed, distracted, or feel undue resistance. These are your "friction points" – the places where your intended workflow grinds to a halt. Examples include: constantly getting derailed by emails, struggling to start a particular type of task, or repeatedly losing track of certain documents. Once identified, brainstorm specific, targeted strategies to reduce that friction (e.g., if emails are a constant distraction, commit to closing the email client completely during deep work blocks, or uninstall it from your phone). The more precisely you can identify the friction, the more effectively you can address it.
- **"Just One Tweak" Mentality:** Resist the powerful ADHD tendency to try and overhaul your entire system at once when you identify a problem. Drastic overhauls are rarely sustainable and often lead to burnout and abandonment. Instead, identify just one or two small, actionable changes you can implement based on your review. Small, consistent improvements are far more sustainable and effective for the ADHD brain than large, disruptive revolutions. Think of it as chipping away at a statue: small, deliberate actions eventually reveal the masterpiece. A single new reminder, a minor change to your morning routine, or a different way to label a file can have a ripple effect.
- **Listen to Your Brain:** Your ADHD brain sends you constant signals – you just need to learn how to interpret them. If a task feels overwhelmingly boring, it might be too large and needs further breakdown, or you might need to pair it with a strong external reward or novel stimulus. If you're constantly forgetting appointments, you might need a more robust visual or auditory reminder system. If you're constantly losing focus, perhaps your environment needs more "noise" or less, or you need to experiment with different types of background sound.

Pay attention to these signals of discomfort, frustration, or lack of engagement, and adapt your strategies accordingly. Your brain is trying to tell you what it needs to thrive.

- **Be Kind to Yourself:** This is arguably the most crucial element of the entire iterative process. There will be times when you fall off the wagon. Procrastination will reappear, systems will feel clunky, and you'll have "bad" productivity days or weeks. When this happens, avoid harsh self-criticism, shame, or guilt. These emotions are counterproductive; they deplete your mental resources and push you further into avoidance. Acknowledge what happened, observe it without judgment, learn from it, and gently guide yourself back to the process of reviewing and adapting. Remember that every successful man with ADHD has these moments. Self-compassion is not laziness; it is the essential fuel that keeps the iterative cycle going. It allows you to learn from mistakes without being crippled by them.
- **Celebrate Adaptation:** When you successfully identify a problem, brainstorm a solution, implement a tweak, and see it make a positive difference, take a moment to consciously acknowledge that win. This could be a mental high-five, a note in your journal, or sharing it with an accountability partner. This specific celebration reinforces your ability to learn, adjust, and solve problems, building profound confidence in your ongoing capacity for productivity. It provides the positive feedback loop that solidifies new habits and empowers you to continue the cycle.

By building in these consistent review, adaptation, and iteration practices, you transform your productivity journey from a rigid, potentially frustrating path into a dynamic, responsive, and deeply personalized process. You'll ensure your systems remain effective, perfectly tailored to your unique needs as a man with ADHD, and truly supportive of your overarching goals and aspirations. This continuous improvement is the ultimate key to unleashing consistent, powerful productivity, moving you from intention to accomplishment with increasing ease, effectiveness, and a profound sense of self-mastery.

CONCLUSION

YOUR PRODUCTIVE POWER

You've journeyed through Book 3, "Unleashing Productivity: Turning Intentions into Accomplishments," and in doing so, you've gained a truly transformative understanding of how to harness your energy and focus to create tangible results. This book wasn't about conforming to generic productivity hacks, but about **redefining productivity for *your* ADHD brain**, building systems that genuinely support your unique way of working.

We've covered essential ground, from the foundational principles of:

- **Redefining productivity** to align with your strengths and natural rhythms, moving beyond conventional, often frustrating, metrics.
- Mastering **task breakdown** and identifying actionable steps, transforming daunting projects into manageable sequences that invite initiation.
- Developing powerful strategies to **overcome procrastination and resistance**, understanding the underlying mechanisms of these common ADHD challenges and providing practical solutions to break free.
- Implementing **workflow optimization and system building**, creating streamlined, predictable paths for your work that reduce mental effort and minimize friction.
- And finally, establishing a crucial cycle of **review, adapt, and iterate**, ensuring your productivity strategies remain dynamic, effective, and perfectly tuned to your evolving needs.

The true power of this book lies in its practical application. You now possess the knowledge and tools to consistently bridge the gap between your brilliant ideas and their real-world manifestation. You're learning to work *with* your ADHD, not against it, converting its unique aspects into an advantage. This isn't about becoming a robot; it's about reclaiming your agency, reducing overwhelm, and experiencing the profound satisfaction of consistent accomplishment.

Remember, productivity for the ADHD brain is a journey of continuous learning and refinement. Embrace the process of experimentation, celebrate every small win, and approach challenges with curiosity rather than criticism. Your ability to get things done, to move from intention to accomplishment, is no longer a roll of the dice; it's a skill you are actively honing, a powerful command you are exerting over your own productive potential.

As you continue forward, apply these strategies diligently. Watch how they transform your days, your projects, and your overall sense of self-efficacy. You now have the blueprint to unleash your authentic, productive power and consistently turn your aspirations into reality.

Let's pause for a moment and reflect on what you've just read. What resonates with you? What are the strategies you feel you can apply to work and life now versus those that seem more challenging or daunting?

BOOK FOUR

MASTERING YOUR EMOTIONS WITH CBT TOOLS
NAVIGATING THE INNER LANDSCAPE

INTRODUCTION

THE EMOTIONAL ROLLERCOASTER AND YOUR GUIDING HAND

You've worked diligently through strengthening your executive functions, sharpening your focus, and unleashing your productivity. These are critical external skills, but they often rest upon a foundational, yet frequently turbulent, internal landscape: your emotions. For many men with ADHD, emotional regulation can feel like an entirely separate and often more challenging frontier. While you might be able to plan a complex project, the sudden surge of frustration, the sting of rejection, or the overwhelming rush of excitement can derail your best intentions in moments.

Imagine your brain as a finely tuned sports car. Executive functions are the steering, brakes, and accelerator. But if the engine is running on highly volatile fuel, prone to sudden surges and stalls, even the most skilled driver will struggle to maintain control. For men with ADHD, that volatile fuel often comes in the form of intense, rapidly shifting, and sometimes dysregulated emotions.

This isn't a character flaw or a sign of weakness. Research consistently shows that **emotional dysregulation** is a core, often overlooked, aspect of ADHD. It manifests not just as difficulty managing "big" emotions like anger or sadness, but also as:

- **Emotional Intensity:** Feeling emotions more deeply and intensely than neurotypical peers.
- **Rapid Mood Shifts:** Moving quickly from one emotional state to another, often without a clear trigger.
- **Difficulty Soothing Yourself:** Struggling to calm down or recover from emotional upset.
- **Impaired Impulse Control Related to Emotions:** Reacting emotionally without a pause for thought, leading to regrettable words or actions.
- **Low Frustration Tolerance:** Giving up easily on tasks or goals when faced with even minor obstacles.

The impact of this emotional rollercoaster can be profound. It can strain relationships, undermine professional progress, lead to self-medication (e.g., overeating, excessive gaming), and erode self-esteem. You might find yourself saying or doing things you later regret, struggling with perceived criticism, or feeling overwhelmed by everyday stressors.

This book will provide you with a powerful guiding hand to navigate this inner landscape: **Cognitive Behavioral Therapy (CBT) tools**. CBT is a widely recognized and **extensively researched evidence-based therapeutic approach** that has demonstrated significant effectiveness in helping individuals identify and change unhelpful thinking patterns and behaviors. While CBT is not a direct treatment for the core symptoms of ADHD, its components are highly effective for managing the emotional dysregulation, anxiety, depression, and stress that frequently co-occur with ADHD. It offers a structured way to develop skills for navigating emotional difficulties and building resilience.

It's not about suppressing your emotions or pretending they don't exist. Instead, it's about developing a keen awareness of your emotional triggers, understanding the connection between your thoughts, feelings, and actions, and building a robust toolkit to respond to emotions more effectively and constructively.

We'll start by exploring the specific emotional landscape of adult ADHD, then dive into practical CBT techniques for challenging distorted thoughts, implementing behavioral strategies for regulation, building emotional resilience, and fostering compassionate self-talk. This isn't a quick fix, but a journey towards greater emotional mastery, allowing you to move from reactivity to thoughtful response. Get ready to develop your guiding hand, transform your relationship with your emotions, and unlock a deeper sense of inner strength and peace.

CHAPTER 1

THE EMOTIONAL LANDSCAPE OF ADULT ADHD

In the introduction, we touched upon the idea that emotions for men with ADHD can often feel like a dizzying, unpredictable rollercoaster, a turbulent ride through peaks of intense excitement and valleys of deep despair, often with sharp, sudden drops in between. Now, let's explore this "emotional landscape" in more detail, shining a light on the intricate ways your unique brain wiring processes and responds to the full spectrum of human feelings. Understanding how ADHD profoundly impacts your emotional experience is not about pathologizing your feelings or labeling them as "wrong"; rather, it's the first crucial step toward validating your lived experience, building self-compassion, and ultimately navigating your inner world more effectively and strategically. It's about recognizing the unique neurobiological underpinnings that shape your emotional life.

The traditional view of Attention-Deficit/Hyperactivity Disorder (ADHD) has historically focused predominantly on its "core" diagnostic symptoms: inattention (difficulty sustaining focus, being easily distracted), hyperactivity (fidgeting, restlessness, excessive talking), and impulsivity (acting without thinking, interrupting). While these are undeniably central to the diagnosis, a rapidly growing body of contemporary research, coupled with the consistent, often heart-wrenching, lived experience of countless men with ADHD, increasingly highlights that **emotional dysregulation** is a pervasive, profoundly impactful, and often debilitating aspect of adult ADHD. This means a significant difficulty in managing, modulating, and appropriately expressing emotions. It is so central to the daily struggles that many researchers and clinicians now argue it should be formally recognized as a core symptom of the disorder, or at least an intrinsic and highly significant feature. For many, it's the emotional turbulence, rather than the inattention, that causes the most significant distress and impairment in relationships, work, and overall well-being.

So, what does this nuanced and often challenging emotional landscape actually look like for men with ADHD? Let's unpack the key features:

- **Intense and Rapid Emotional Shifts:** Imagine your emotional thermostat is not just highly sensitive, but also lacks a robust internal "buffer" or dampening mechanism. While neurotypical individuals might experience a gradual build-up or fading of emotions, your emotional responses can flare up with startling speed and intensity. You might go from a state of calm to intensely frustrated or enraged by a minor inconvenience, then abruptly shift to profound boredom, followed by a surge of unbridled excitement, all within a remarkably short span of time – sometimes mere minutes. These dramatic and rapid shifts can be bewildering not only to you, leaving you feeling out of control of your own internal experience, but also to those around you who struggle to keep pace with your fluctuating moods. A small irritation, like a misplaced key or a delayed email response, can quickly escalate into disproportionate anger or a volcanic outburst. Similarly, a minor disappointment or perceived slight can trigger a deep, overwhelming wave of sadness or despair that feels all-consuming. This isn't simply about being "moody" or "overly emotional"; it's a genuine, neurobiologically-based difficulty in modulating the intensity, duration, and even the type of emotional response. The prefrontal cortex, often implicated in ADHD, plays a crucial role in emotional regulation, and its dysregulation can lead to a less filtered, more raw emotional experience.

- **Emotional Sensitivity to Rejection (often described as Rejection Sensitive Dysphoria - RSD):** This is a particularly painful, frequently misunderstood, and incredibly common characteristic experienced by a significant number of individuals with ADHD. You might find that even mild criticism, a perceived social snub, a hint of disapproval, or a sense of failure (even a minor one) can trigger an intense, disproportionate emotional storm within you. This isn't just feeling hurt; it's an immediate, overwhelming emotional pain that can feel physically agonizing, sometimes described as akin to being punched in the gut or stabbed in the heart. It's important to note that while Rejection Sensitive Dysphoria (RSD) is a widely recognized descriptive term and a profoundly impactful experience for many with ADHD, enabling them to articulate a previously nameless pain, it is not currently a formal, standalone diagnosis in official diagnostic manuals like the DSM-5. However, its profound impact on daily life is undeniable. RSD vividly describes the intense emotional pain and heightened sensitivity that stems from the *perception* (which is often more powerful than the reality) of being rejected, criticized, teased, or failing to meet expectations. This hypersensitivity can make navigating interpersonal relationships, professional feedback, and social interactions incredibly challenging, often driving compensatory behaviors such as intense people-pleasing, perfectionism (to avoid any perceived flaw), or social withdrawal and isolation (to avoid the potential for judgment or rejection altogether). The fear of this intense emotional pain can be paralyzing, leading to avoidance of situations that might trigger it, even if those situations are opportunities for growth or connection.
- **Difficulty with Impulse Control in Emotional Contexts:** Just as ADHD can manifest as impulsive actions (e.g., interrupting conversations, making spontaneous purchases, blurting out thoughts without filtering), it can also lead to impulsive emotional reactions. This means there's a shorter fuse between feeling a strong emotion and acting on it, with less time for the internal "stop and think" mechanism to engage. In the heat of an argument, you might blurt out hurtful words that you immediately regret. When frustrated, you might make rash decisions that have negative long-term consequences. When feeling overwhelmed or angry, you might lash out at loved ones

or engage in behaviors that sabotage your own goals, simply because the emotional surge bypasses your internal brakes. The reduced inhibitory control associated with ADHD directly impacts your ability to pause, reflect, and choose a considered emotional response rather than a reactive one. This can lead to a frustrating cycle of impulsive emotional outbursts followed by profound regret and self-recrimination, further damaging self-esteem and relationships.

- **Chronic Feelings of Overwhelm:** The ADHD brain is often likened to a highly sensitive antenna, constantly bombarded by a multitude of internal thoughts and external sensory stimuli. This relentless input, coupled with inherent difficulties in executive functions such as prioritization, organization, working memory, and task management, can lead to a pervasive, enduring sense of being overwhelmed. This isn't just about having too much on your plate; it's a profound, emotional state where you feel flooded, mentally paralyzed, and genuinely unable to cope with the demands of daily life. Even minor stressors or seemingly simple tasks can trigger this feeling. When in this state, the brain often goes into a shutdown mode, leading to complete paralysis, avoidance of tasks, or emotional meltdowns when faced with situations that feel even slightly beyond your perceived capacity. This chronic overwhelm often contributes to procrastination, as the brain seeks to avoid the feeling of being flooded, even if it means delaying important responsibilities.
- **Struggles with Motivation and Emotional Energy:** While often discussed in terms of focus and task initiation, motivation has a profound emotional and neurochemical component, particularly for the ADHD brain. Your brain's dopamine reward system is crucial for motivation, and when tasks are perceived as boring, repetitive, abstract, or uninteresting, they struggle to generate sufficient dopamine for initiation or sustained engagement. This isn't laziness; it's a neurobiological reality. This can manifest as apathy, lethargy, a profound lack of emotional "oomph" for important but unstimulating activities (like paperwork, chores, or long-term planning), leading to chronic underachievement despite high intelligence and capability. Conversely, activities that are novel, highly stimulating, or intensely interesting can lead to "hyperfocus," an almost obsessive absorption. While

hyperfocus can be incredibly productive, it often comes at the expense of other responsibilities, self-care, or other emotional needs, leading to an imbalance in emotional energy allocation. The inability to direct emotional energy efficiently where it's needed is a significant barrier.

- **Challenges with Self-Soothing and Emotional Regulation:** When intense emotions hit – whether it's anger, anxiety, sadness, or frustration – many neurotypical individuals have developed an unconscious repertoire of automatic coping mechanisms to calm themselves down, process the emotion, and return to a baseline state. For men with ADHD, these internal self-soothing skills can be underdeveloped, less effective, or simply not readily accessible in the heat of the moment. You might struggle to calm down after an argument, find yourself stuck in a prolonged loop of anxiety or resentment, or be unable to shift your emotional state even when you rationally know you should. This difficulty in internal regulation can lead to prolonged emotional distress, impacting sleep, relationships, and physical health. Without effective internal strategies, individuals may resort to less healthy external coping mechanisms such as excessive screen time, substance use, overeating, or other impulsive behaviors to temporarily escape or numb uncomfortable emotions.

Understanding these profound aspects of the emotional landscape isn't about making excuses for behavior, but rather about building a solid foundation for empathy, self-compassion, and most importantly, effective intervention. Recognizing that your intense emotional reactions, rapid shifts, or chronic overwhelm are often a direct result of neurobiological differences in your brain, rather than a personal failing, a character flaw, or a lack of willpower, can be incredibly liberating. It shifts the focus from "What's wrong with me? Why can't I just control my feelings like everyone else?" to a more empowering and actionable question: "How does my unique brain work, and what specific tools and strategies can I learn and consistently apply to manage it effectively?"

This crucial shift in perspective is the gateway to real change. In the following chapters, we will move from understanding to application, diving into specific Cognitive Behavioral Therapy (CBT) tools and techniques that directly address these emotional challenges. These tools will provide you with a structured, practical framework to observe your emotional patterns without judgment, challenge the unhelpful thought processes that often fuel emotional dysregulation, and develop tangible, actionable strategies to regulate your emotional responses. This will give you a guiding hand through your inner emotional landscape, transforming it from an unpredictable rollercoaster into a navigable terrain where you are increasingly in the driver's seat.

CHAPTER 2

IDENTIFYING AND CHALLENGING DISTORTED THOUGHTS (CBT)

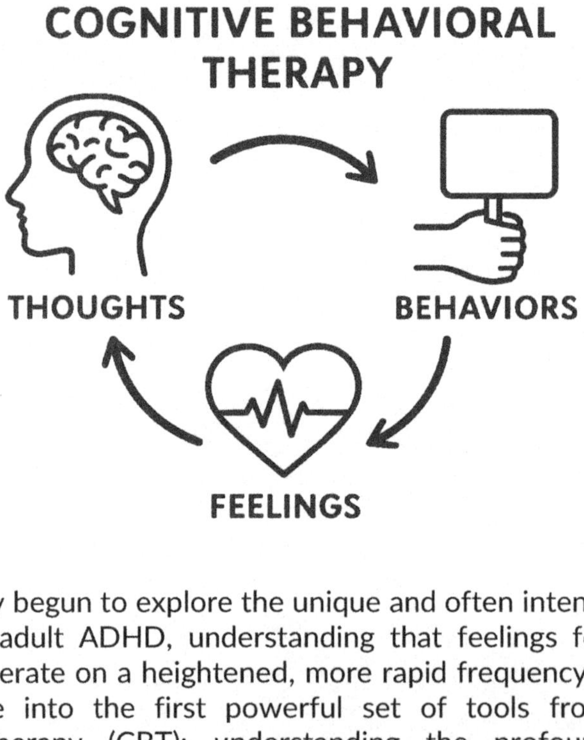

You've bravely begun to explore the unique and often intense emotional landscape of adult ADHD, understanding that feelings for men with ADHD can operate on a heightened, more rapid frequency. Now, we're going to dive into the first powerful set of tools from Cognitive Behavioral Therapy (CBT): understanding the profound, intricate connection between your thoughts, feelings, and behaviors, and learning to identify and challenge the distorted, unhelpful thoughts that often fuel emotional distress and dysregulation. This direct intervention on your internal monologue is a cornerstone of gaining greater control over your emotional responses.

The fundamental premise of Cognitive Behavioral Therapy (CBT), a well-established, extensively researched, and highly effective approach for addressing a wide range of emotional and behavioral challenges, is elegantly simple yet profoundly impactful: **your thoughts are not facts.** They are interpretations of reality, often automatic and unexamined, and these interpretations directly and powerfully influence how you feel and how you act. Decades of rigorous research have demonstrated CBT's efficacy in helping individuals learn to identify, evaluate, and ultimately change unhelpful thinking patterns, leading to significant and lasting improvements in mood, anxiety, stress levels, and overall well-being. The tools presented in this chapter are core components of CBT, widely used to build cognitive flexibility (the ability to consider multiple perspectives) and enhance emotional regulation by breaking the automatic link between a distorted thought and an intense emotional reaction.

For example, imagine a common scenario: you receive a critical email from your boss. The event itself is neutral; it's the *interpretation* of the event that dictates your subsequent emotional and behavioral response.

Scenario: Critical email from your boss.

Thought A (Distorted/Unhelpful): "I'm a complete failure. I can never do anything right. This proves I'm incompetent, and they're definitely going to fire me for this small mistake."

Feeling A: Intense shame, crippling anxiety, deep despair, a sense of hopelessness, perhaps even anger at yourself.

Behavior A: Procrastinate further on the task, avoid interacting with the boss, withdraw from colleagues, ruminate endlessly on the negative thought, leading to reduced productivity and increased stress.

Thought B (Balanced/Helpful): "Okay, this feedback is tough to hear. It points out an area where I can improve. What specifically can I learn from this? How can I implement this feedback and improve next time? Everyone makes mistakes."

Feeling B: Concern, determination, mild disappointment, a healthy sense of responsibility, but without the crushing weight of shame.

Behavior B: Review the email objectively, ask for clarification if needed, plan specific corrective actions, and perhaps schedule a follow-up conversation with the boss to discuss improvement.

The same external event (the critical email) can lead to vastly different emotional and behavioral outcomes based solely on your initial, often automatic, thought. For men with ADHD, who often experience rapid shifts in mood and intense emotional responses due to neurochemical differences (e.g., in dopamine regulation affecting motivation and emotional processing), these quick, often automatic, and unhelpful thought patterns are particularly impactful. Your brain's speed, its tendency to jump to conclusions, and its difficulty with emotional regulation can make you especially susceptible to these pervasive "thinking traps" or cognitive distortions, which then amplify your emotional rollercoaster.

Common Cognitive Distortions for Men with ADHD

Cognitive distortions are irrational or exaggerated thought patterns that reinforce negative thinking, undermine self-esteem, and exacerbate emotional distress. They are like mental shortcuts that, while sometimes quick, often lead you down a wrong path. Recognizing them is the first crucial step toward challenging them and reclaiming control over your emotional responses. Here are some common ones often experienced by men with ADHD, often amplified by the unique challenges of the condition:

- **All-or-Nothing Thinking (Black-and-White Thinking):** Seeing things in extremes, with no middle ground, no shades of gray. Everything is either perfect or a total disaster, a complete success or an utter failure.
    - **Example:** "I missed that deadline, so I'm a total failure and completely incompetent at my job." (Discounts all past successes and efforts). Or "If I can't do it perfectly, there's no point in starting it at all." (Feeds procrastination and perfectionism). This distortion often stems from the ADHD brain's tendency to struggle with nuance and moderation.
- **Catastrophizing:** Exaggerating the negative consequences of an event, jumping to the worst possible conclusion, even when it's highly unlikely.
    - **Example:** "If I forget to pay this bill today, my credit will be ruined, I'll go bankrupt, and I'll lose everything I own." (Turns a minor oversight into an apocalyptic scenario). Or "My partner looked annoyed when I spoke, so they must be furious with me, our relationship is irreparable, and they're on the verge of leaving me." (Often heavily linked to RSD, where perceived disapproval escalates to relationship termination). This is a common pattern when the ADHD brain's anxiety response is triggered, blowing a small issue out of proportion.

- **Mind Reading:** Assuming you know what others are thinking or feeling, usually negatively, without any actual evidence. This often involves inferring negative judgments about yourself.
    - **Example:** "My boss didn't say hello to me this morning and walked past without a smile, so he must think I'm doing a terrible job and is disappointed in my performance." (No evidence; boss might be distracted, stressed, or tired). This is extremely common and painful for individuals with RSD, as their sensitivity to perceived rejection makes them prone to jumping to negative conclusions about others' intentions and feelings towards them.
- **"Should" Statements:** Holding rigid, often unrealistic, expectations for yourself or others, often expressed with words like "should," "must," or "ought." When these expectations aren't met, it leads to intense guilt, shame, frustration, or resentment.
    - **Example:** "I *should* be able to focus for hours without any distractions, just like everyone else." (Ignores the neurobiological reality of ADHD). Or "I *shouldn't* feel so overwhelmed by simple household tasks; I'm a grown man." (Leads to self-criticism and invalidates your own experience). These "shoulds" are often internalized from societal expectations that don't account for neurodiversity.
- **Emotional Reasoning:** Believing something is true solely because you feel it strongly, treating your feelings as definitive evidence of reality.
    - **Example:** "I feel like a lazy, unproductive person today, so I must *be* inherently lazy and incapable." (Discounts effort and past accomplishments). Or "I feel incredibly anxious about this presentation, so it *must* be disastrous and I'm going to humiliate myself." (Ignores the possibility of performance anxiety and leads to avoidance). The intensity of ADHD emotions can make this distortion particularly compelling and difficult to challenge.
- **Overgeneralization:** Drawing a sweeping negative conclusion based on a single event or piece of evidence, assuming that if something happened once, it will always happen, or that it applies to all situations.

- **Example:** "I messed up that presentation last week, so I'm terrible at public speaking and will never succeed in any leadership role." (One event defines entire capability). Or "My partner got frustrated with me for forgetting one thing, so I'm always going to disappoint everyone." (Exacerbates feelings of inadequacy).

- **Personalization:** Blaming yourself for external events or taking things personally that aren't actually your fault, or over-attributing events to your own actions.
  - **Example:** "Our team project failed because I didn't push hard enough on my part, even though multiple factors were involved." (Taking disproportionate responsibility). Or "My friend didn't invite me out last night; it must be because I'm boring." (Assumes personal blame without checking facts). This can tie into RSD, where any negative outcome is quickly internalized as a personal failing.
- **Disqualifying the Positive:** Ignoring, discounting, or dismissing positive experiences, compliments, or achievements, often by saying they "don't count" or were due to luck.
  - **Example:** "I finished that tough project ahead of schedule, but anyone could have done it; it was just easy." (Minimizes your effort and skill). Or "My boss praised my work, but he was probably just trying to be nice." (Prevents genuine self-esteem from building). This distortion sabotages efforts to build self-worth and recognize progress, a key motivator for the ADHD brain.

How to Identify and Challenge Distorted Thoughts

The key to breaking free from the grip of distorted thoughts is to become a detective of your own mind. This is an active process of observation, questioning, and re-framing. When you notice a strong negative emotion, pause and investigate the thoughts that immediately preceded it.

1. **Catch the Thought (The "Pause and Observe"):**
   - When you feel a sudden surge of a strong negative emotion (anger, shame, intense anxiety, crushing frustration, deep sadness, acute self-criticism), use this emotion as a trigger. Ask yourself: "What thought just went through my mind right before I felt this way?" or

"What am I telling myself right now about this situation or about myself?"

- Write it down immediately, even if it feels silly or fragmented. The act of externalizing the thought (even briefly, on a sticky note or in a simple journal) helps you gain some crucial distance from it, allowing you to view it as an object of analysis rather than an undeniable truth. This is the first, most vital step in breaking the automatic emotional reaction.

2. **Question the Thought (The "Courtroom Test"):**
   - Once you've identified the thought, put it on trial. Imagine you are a neutral judge or a rigorous lawyer, meticulously examining the evidence for and against this thought. Ask yourself:
     - "Is this thought 100% true? Is there *any* evidence to the contrary, no matter how small?"
     - "What's the concrete evidence *for* this thought?" (Be specific and factual, not just general feelings or past assumptions).
     - "What's the concrete evidence *against* this thought?" Are there other ways to interpret the situation? What might someone else, a neutral observer, see?
     - "Am I falling into one of the thinking traps or cognitive distortions I just learned about?" (Refer back to the list above and identify the specific distortion: Is it all-or-nothing thinking? Catastrophizing? Mind reading?). Naming the distortion helps to depersonalize it.
     - "What would I tell a friend in this exact situation if they came to me with this thought?" (We are often far kinder, more rational, and more compassionate to others than to ourselves).
     - "Is this thought helpful? Does it move me towards my goals or away from them? Does it help me feel better or worse?" (A thought can be partially true but still unhelpful).

        - "What's the absolute worst that could happen if this thought were true, and could I cope with it? What's the *most likely* outcome?" (Particularly for catastrophizing).
3. **Reframe and Replace (The "Constructive Alternative"):**
    - Based on your rigorous questioning, formulate a more balanced, realistic, and ultimately more helpful thought. This isn't about forced positive affirmations that feel untrue or saccharine; it's about finding a more accurate, nuanced, and empowering perspective that reflects reality more fully.
    - **Original Distorted Thought (All-or-Nothing):** "I didn't finish everything on my to-do list today, so today was a complete waste and I'm a failure."
    - **Challenging Questions:** "Is it 100% true it was a complete waste? What *did* I get done? Did I accomplish anything helpful at all? What would I tell a friend who felt this way?"
    - **Reframed Thought:** "I didn't finish everything, but I did complete [X, Y, and Z important tasks], and that's solid progress. It wasn't perfect, but it wasn't a total waste. I'll re-prioritize for tomorrow and continue my momentum."
    - **Original Distorted Thought (Catastrophizing/RSD):** "My partner looked annoyed when I brought up the chore list, they must be mad at me, and our relationship is in trouble; they'll probably leave me."
    - **Challenging Questions:** "Did they *say* they were mad at *me*? Is there another reason they might look annoyed (tired, stressed from work, thinking about something else)? Have they been annoyed before and it resolved? Am I mind-reading? What's the evidence that our entire relationship is in trouble from this one moment?"
    - **Reframed Thought:** "My partner looked annoyed. I'm going to take a breath and assume they might be tired or thinking about something else, or I can gently ask them later if everything is okay without immediately assuming it's about me or a catastrophe."

The practice of identifying and challenging distorted thoughts takes consistent, compassionate effort. These unhelpful patterns are often deeply ingrained, automatic shortcuts developed over a lifetime. But with persistent practice, you'll find yourself catching these thoughts earlier, questioning them more effectively, and ultimately choosing more balanced, realistic, and empowering interpretations of your experiences. This direct intervention on your thought patterns is a cornerstone of emotional regulation, giving you profound greater control over your inner landscape, transforming it from a turbulent, reactive space to one of greater clarity and intentional response.

CHAPTER 3

BEHAVIORAL STRATEGIES FOR EMOTIONAL REGULATION (CBT)

You've learned to identify and challenge the distorted thoughts that often trigger and intensify emotional responses, equipping yourself with a powerful cognitive tool for emotional regulation. This internal dialogue intervention is crucial, but it's only half the equation. Now, we're shifting our focus to **behavioral strategies** – the practical, tangible actions you can take to directly influence your emotional state. While thoughts profoundly impact feelings, what you *do* in a given moment, how you move, or what you engage with, can also significantly alter how you feel, especially for the ADHD brain which often responds remarkably well to external action, physical change, and tangible shifts in its immediate environment or internal state.

For men with ADHD, emotional surges can be overwhelming, erupting rapidly and leading to impulsive actions, regrettable words, or prolonged periods of intense distress that feel impossible to escape. The brain's natural "stop and think" mechanism, which involves the inhibitory control of the prefrontal cortex, can be slower or less effective when emotions run high, leading to a shorter fuse and less time for considered responses. This is where behavioral strategies become your proactive toolkit, your first line of defense, and a powerful means of self-soothing. Instead of passively waiting for your thoughts to shift or for the overwhelming emotion to eventually pass, you actively engage in behaviors that can calm your nervous system, strategically change your focus, or provide a healthy, constructive outlet for intense feelings, preventing them from spiraling out of control.

Think of it like this: if your car's engine is overheating due to intense emotional build-up, challenging distorted thoughts is like checking the thermostat or diagnosing the problem with a diagnostic scan. It's essential for understanding the root cause. But behavioral strategies are like pulling over immediately, turning on the fan at full blast, adding coolant, or even temporarily shutting off the engine to prevent permanent damage. They are direct, actionable interventions designed to either reduce the immediate intensity of the emotion or shift your physiological and psychological state to a more regulated one. They give you concrete steps to take when your internal system is in overdrive.

Proactive Approaches: Building Your Emotional Toolkit

These strategies are most effective when practiced regularly and integrated into your daily routine. By proactively building these skills when you are calm, they become more readily available and effective when emotions become overwhelming. Think of this as preventative maintenance for your emotional well-being.

Mindful Movement:

We touched on this in Book 2 for sharpening focus, but it's equally, if not more, powerful for emotional regulation. Physical activity, even a brisk walk, stretching, a few minutes of jumping jacks, or dancing to a favorite song, can provide immediate relief from emotional intensity.

- **Discharge Energy:** Movement provides a healthy, physical outlet for releasing pent-up emotional energy, which is especially useful for managing anger, anxiety, restlessness, or frustration that often manifests physically in ADHD. It's a physiological "reset button."

- **Change Physiology:** Engaging in physical activity directly influences your body's state, shifting it from a "fight or flight" stress response to a more relaxed, parasympathetic state. It can reduce stress hormones like cortisol and increase feel-good neurotransmitters.
- **Shift Focus:** By concentrating on bodily sensations (your breathing, muscles, the feeling of your feet on the ground), movement redirects your attention away from obsessive or spiraling thoughts, grounding you in the present moment.
- **Action:** When you feel an emotion building, or you're stuck in rumination, take a quick, vigorous walk (even just around the block), do 20 push-ups, run up and down a flight of stairs a few times, or simply stand up and stretch powerfully. Don't overthink it; just move.

Scheduled Relaxation/Downtime:

For the ADHD brain, which is constantly processing stimuli and often running on high alert, the persistent internal activity can be profoundly exhausting, leading to emotional overload and burnout. Proactively scheduling genuine, restorative downtime is not a luxury; it's essential maintenance for your emotional well-being and a preventative measure against emotional dysregulation.

- **Action:** Block out specific, non-negotiable times in your day or week for activities that genuinely relax and recharge you. These are not "productive" tasks, but activities chosen purely for their restorative quality. This could be reading a physical book, listening to calming music, engaging in a non-demanding hobby (e.g., drawing, light gardening), spending time in nature, practicing a simple breathing exercise, or simply sitting quietly with a warm beverage. Treat this scheduled downtime with the same importance as a work meeting. This intentional emotional rest prevents your emotional "battery" from running completely flat, making you more resilient when stressors arise.

Sensory Grounding:

When emotions feel overwhelming, intense, or you feel disconnected and "in your head," engaging your senses can rapidly bring you back to the present moment, anchoring you to physical reality and interrupting the emotional spiral.

- **Action:** Use the **5-4-3-2-1 method** as a quick, portable reset: identify **5** things you can *see*, **4** things you can *feel* (e.g., your feet on the floor, the texture of your clothes), **3** things you can *hear*, **2** things you can *smell*, and **1** thing you can *taste*. This exercise forces your attention outwards. Alternatively, keep a "sensory kit" nearby: a stress ball for squeezing, a strong-smelling essential oil (e.g., peppermint, lavender) to inhale, a smooth stone or a textured fabric to touch, a piece of hard candy to taste. Engaging your senses provides immediate, tangible input that can override the intense internal emotional experience.

Structured Problem-Solving:

A pervasive sense of overwhelm often stems from feeling like problems are too big, too numerous, or too ill-defined to tackle. This can lead to emotional paralysis and increased anxiety. A structured approach to problem-solving can directly reduce emotional distress by providing clarity, a sense of control, and a pathway to action.

- **Action:** When a problem arises, instead of ruminating on it or allowing it to trigger a feeling of helplessness, take a few minutes to engage in structured problem-solving. Write down:
    1. **What is the specific problem?** (Define it clearly, concisely, and factually).
    2. **Brainstorm *all* possible solutions.** Don't judge them at this stage; just list everything that comes to mind, no matter how outlandish.
    3. **Evaluate the pros and cons of each solution.** Consider feasibility, resources, and potential outcomes.
    4. **Pick the best (or "good enough") solution.** Don't aim for perfect.
    5. **Create a specific, actionable plan** for implementing that solution (breaking it down into tiny steps, as discussed in Book 3, Chapter 2).
    6. **Set a specific time** to implement the action plan. This process shifts you from emotional reactivity and rumination to proactive, logical problem-solving, which is incredibly empowering and reduces the emotional burden.

In-the-Moment Interventions: When Emotions Run High

These strategies are for when you feel an emotional storm brewing, or you're already in the midst of one. They are designed for immediate, often rapid, application to de-escalate intensity and regain control.

The "STOP" Skill:

A powerful acronym from Dialectical Behavior Therapy (DBT), a close cousin of CBT, designed to create a vital pause between impulse and action, especially when emotions are overwhelming.

- **S - Stop:** Freeze immediately. Do not act on the impulse or say the first thing that comes to mind. Physically stop what you are doing.
- **T - Take a Step Back:** Mentally (and if possible, physically) detach from the immediate situation. Get some perspective. Take a deep breath.
- **O - Observe:** Notice what's happening internally (thoughts, feelings, bodily sensations like tension, racing heart) and externally (what are others doing, what are the facts of the situation). Be a curious observer, not a judge.
- **P - Proceed with Awareness:** After this pause, *choose* a deliberate action that aligns with your values or goals, rather than an impulsive, reactive one.
- **Action:** Practice using STOP whenever you feel a strong urge to react impulsively (e.g., interrupt, lash out, immediately buy something online) or when intense emotions unexpectedly flare up. The more you practice, the more automatic this pause becomes, giving your prefrontal cortex time to engage.

Distraction (Healthy Kind):

Sometimes, when emotions are too intense to process rationally or regulate directly, a temporary, healthy distraction can be incredibly helpful to prevent escalation and give your nervous system time to cool down. This is not avoidance in the long term, but a strategic, short-term pause to change your emotional trajectory.

- **Action:** Engage in a highly absorbing, short-term, and relatively neutral activity that pulls your attention away from the intense emotion: a quick, intense video game level, solving a simple puzzle, listening to a favorite upbeat song, watching a short, funny video clip, doing a quick, absorbing household chore (like washing dishes), or engaging in a brief, engaging conversation that is unrelated to the emotional trigger. The goal is to shift your brain's focus for 5-15 minutes until the emotional intensity drops to a manageable level, allowing you to then apply more direct problem-solving or emotional processing.

Radical Acceptance:

Some situations, and some intense emotions, simply *are*. Fighting reality or trying to force a different emotional response only increases suffering and perpetuates distress. Radical acceptance is acknowledging the reality of a situation or emotion without judgment, even if you don't like it or wish it were different. It's letting go of the struggle against what *is*.

- **Action:** When faced with an unchangeable situation (e.g., a past mistake, someone else's unchangeable behavior, an unavoidable outcome) or an intense, unwanted emotion, internally (or even aloud) say: "It is what it is," or "This is happening," or "I accept that I feel X emotion right now, even though I don't like it." This is not approval of the situation or emotion, but a release of the mental and emotional fight against reality, which paradoxically can significantly reduce distress and free up energy for more constructive actions.

Self-Soothing Through Senses:

Consciously and deliberately engage one or more of your senses in a comforting, calming, and pleasant way. This provides direct, physiological input to your nervous system, helping to de-escalate emotional arousal.

- **Action:**
    - **Sight:** Look at a comforting picture, watch something beautiful (a nature video, calming scenery).
    - **Sound:** Listen to calming music, nature sounds, or a soothing podcast.
    - **Smell:** Light a scented candle, use an essential oil diffuser, or simply smell a comforting scent (e.g., fresh laundry, coffee).
    - **Taste:** Drink a warm, soothing beverage (herbal tea, hot chocolate); eat a small piece of something comforting and savory; savor a piece of hard candy.

- **Touch:** Take a hot shower or bath; wrap yourself in a soft blanket; pet an animal; put on comfortable clothing; hold a smooth stone. These are physical, tangible ways to calm your nervous system, directly impacting your emotional state.

Seek Support/Connect:

Don't isolate yourself when emotions are high or when you're struggling. Connecting with a trusted friend, family member, mentor, or therapist can provide perspective, comfort, validation, and a safe space to process intense emotions.

- **Action:** Reach out. A quick call, a text message, or even just being in the same room as a supportive person (without necessarily needing to talk about the problem) can help ground you, co-regulate your nervous system, and provide a sense of connection that reduces feelings of isolation and overwhelming emotion. Expressing your feelings to a non-judgmental listener can often help to diffuse their intensity and gain clarity.

By integrating these behavioral strategies into your daily life and having them ready for moments of emotional intensity, you build a powerful, proactive capacity for emotional regulation. This isn't about becoming emotionless or suppressing who you are, but about giving your guiding hand more control over your inner landscape, allowing you to respond to life's challenges with greater intention, resilience, and effectiveness. You are transforming your emotional rollercoaster into a vehicle you can confidently steer.

CHAPTER 4

BUILDING EMOTIONAL RESILIENCE AND DISTRESS TOLERANCE (CBT)

You've learned to identify the thoughts that fuel your emotional responses and the immediate actions you can take to regulate intense feelings. Now, we're going to build on that foundation by focusing on **emotional resilience** and **distress tolerance**. These are crucial skills for men with ADHD, as the inherent challenges of ADHD—like managing daily tasks, social interactions, and professional demands—can often lead to chronic stress and emotional sensitivity.

Emotional resilience is your ability to bounce back from adversity, to adapt well in the face of stress, trauma, tragedy, threats, or significant sources of conflict. It's not about avoiding pain or never feeling negative emotions; it's about navigating them effectively and emerging stronger.

Distress tolerance is the capacity to endure and cope with uncomfortable or painful emotional states without resorting to impulsive, unhelpful, or destructive behaviors. For the ADHD brain, which often seeks immediate gratification or relief from discomfort, learning to "sit with" strong emotions is a powerful act of self-mastery. Instead of reacting to the intense urge to escape discomfort (e.g., procrastinating, self-medicating, lashing out), you develop the ability to ride out the emotional wave.

Think of it like building a mental and emotional immune system. You're not just treating the symptoms (intense emotions); you're strengthening your overall capacity to handle life's inevitable stressors and emotional challenges. This is particularly vital for managing the unique emotional landscape of ADHD, which can feel like living with an overactive internal alarm system.

Building Your Emotional "Immune System": Strategies for Resilience

Resilience is cultivated through consistent practice and a shift in perspective.

1. **Cultivate a Growth Mindset:** Instead of seeing setbacks or emotional struggles as proof of inadequacy, view them as opportunities for learning and growth. Understand that your brain can adapt and that challenges are a chance to strengthen your coping skills.
    - *Action:* After a difficult emotional experience, ask yourself: "What can I learn from this? What could I do differently next time? How did I handle this well, even if imperfectly?"
2. **Practice Self-Compassion:** For men with ADHD, harsh self-criticism often accompanies emotional distress. Self-compassion is treating yourself with the same kindness, understanding, and support you would offer a good friend in a similar situation. It's acknowledging your suffering and offering comfort, rather than judgment.
    - *Action:* When you're struggling, place a hand over your heart and say to yourself (mentally or aloud): "This is a moment of suffering. Suffering is a part of life. May I be kind to myself in this moment."
3. **Build Your "Mastery" List:** Regularly engage in activities that give you a sense of accomplishment, competence, or pleasure, even small ones. This builds self-efficacy and a positive self-image, which are crucial for resilience.

- o *Action:* Make a list of enjoyable or mastery-building activities (e.g., solving a puzzle, learning a new skill, completing a household chore, exercising). Schedule time for these, especially when feeling down or stressed.

4. **Strengthen Your Support Network:** Isolation amplifies distress. Connecting with others provides perspective, empathy, and practical help.
   - o *Action:* Nurture relationships with people who genuinely support you. Don't be afraid to reach out when you're struggling. Consider joining a support group or community focused on ADHD.
5. **Identify and Lean into Your Values:** When you act in alignment with your core values (e.g., honesty, creativity, connection, courage), you build a deeper sense of meaning and resilience, even when things are tough.
   - o *Action:* Reflect on what truly matters to you. When faced with a difficult decision or emotional challenge, ask: "What would my values guide me to do here?"

Riding the Wave: Strategies for Distress Tolerance

These are "crisis survival" skills – techniques to get through acute, intense emotional moments without making things worse. They are about enduring, not necessarily solving the problem in that moment.

1. **Distract Wisely:** As mentioned in Chapter 3, healthy distraction can be a lifeline when emotions are overwhelming. It's about shifting your attention away from the distress until it subsides.
   - o *Action:* Engage in absorbing activities: solve a Sudoku, play a complex video game, watch a captivating movie, do intense physical exercise, or perform a quick, focused chore like cleaning.
2. **Self-Soothe with Senses (Revisited):** Consciously using your five senses to comfort yourself can calm an activated nervous system.
   - o *Action:* Listen to calming music, take a hot bath, use an aromatherapy diffuser, savor a comforting food, wrap yourself in a soft blanket, or focus on a beautiful image.
3. **Improve the Moment:** Find ways to make the present moment more bearable, even if the underlying situation hasn't changed.

    - *Action:* Imagine a calming scene. Find meaning in the suffering (e.g., "This difficult experience is teaching me patience."). Focus on gratitude for something, however small. Take a few deep, slow breaths.
4. **Pros and Cons of Acting on Urges:** When you feel a strong urge to engage in an unhelpful behavior (e.g., yell, withdraw, impulsively spend), quickly list the short-term and long-term pros and cons of *acting* on the urge, and the pros and cons of *resisting* the urge.
    - *Action:* Write down a quick T-chart. Seeing the consequences laid out can often create the necessary pause for wiser choice.
5. **TIP Skills (for Intense Physical Arousal):** These are rapid physical interventions to quickly change your body's chemistry and calm intense emotions.
    - **T**emperature change: Splash cold water on your face, or hold an ice pack on your wrists/neck. This activates the dive reflex, slowing your heart rate.
    - **I**ntense Exercise: Engage in brief, intense physical activity (e.g., sprinting in place, jumping jacks, burpees) for 5-10 minutes to burn off excess energy.
    - **P**aced Breathing: Slow your breathing. Inhale slowly for 4 counts, hold for 2, exhale slowly for 6 counts. This directly impacts your nervous system.
    - **P**aired Muscle Relaxation: Tense a muscle group very tightly for 5-10 seconds, then completely relax it, noticing the difference. Work through different muscle groups.

Building emotional resilience and distress tolerance is a dynamic process. It's about learning to lean into discomfort with courage, knowing that you have a growing toolkit of strategies to navigate challenges without being swept away. By consistently applying these CBT-based tools, you are not just managing your ADHD; you are fundamentally transforming your relationship with your emotions, leading to greater stability, inner strength, and a profound sense of self-mastery.

CHAPTER 5

COMPASSIONATE SELF-TALK AND INNER DIALOGUE

You've explored the emotional landscape of ADHD, learned to challenge distorted thoughts, and acquired powerful behavioral strategies for emotional regulation and distress tolerance. Now, we arrive at a critical, often underestimated, aspect of emotional mastery: **compassionate self-talk and your inner dialogue**. For many men with ADHD, the voice inside their head can be their harshest critic, amplifying anxieties, dismissing achievements, and reinforcing feelings of inadequacy. This internal monologue significantly shapes your emotional experience and your capacity for resilience.

Think of your inner dialogue as a constant conversation you're having with yourself. Is it a supportive coach, offering encouragement and guidance? Or is it a relentless drill sergeant, barking criticisms and fueling self-doubt? For men with ADHD, who often contend with a lifetime of perceived failures, missed deadlines, and impulsive mistakes, the inner critic can be particularly loud and punitive. This harsh self-talk is often a response to external criticism or internal frustration with ADHD symptoms, leading to:

- **Increased shame and guilt:** "I'm so stupid for forgetting that."
- **Reduced motivation:** "Why bother? I'll just mess it up anyway."
- **Heightened anxiety and depression:** Constantly reliving past mistakes or anticipating future failures.
- **Difficulty accepting compliments or successes:** "That was just luck."
- **Self-sabotage:** Unconsciously undermining efforts because of a belief that you don't deserve success.

The good news is that this inner voice is not fixed. Just as you can identify and challenge external negativity, you can learn to reframe your internal narrative, replacing harsh judgment with understanding and encouragement. Cultivating compassionate self-talk is not about being "soft" or ignoring your challenges; it's about building an inner ally who supports your growth, resilience, and emotional well-being.

Transforming Your Inner Critic into an Inner Ally

The goal is to shift from automatic self-criticism to conscious, supportive self-talk.

1. **Become Aware of Your Inner Critic's Voice:** The first step is simply noticing. When you feel a strong negative emotion or make a mistake, pause. What are you saying to yourself? What words, tones, or phrases does your inner critic use? Is it shaming? Demanding? Dismissive?
   - *Action:* Keep a small notepad or use a voice memo to quickly jot down or record critical thoughts as they arise. This externalizes the voice and helps you observe it without judgment.
2. **Identify the Core Beliefs:** Often, repeated critical thoughts stem from deeper, underlying beliefs about yourself (e.g., "I'm not good enough," "I'm lazy," "I'll always fail"). Recognizing these core beliefs allows you to target them more directly.
   - *Action:* Ask yourself: "If this thought were true, what would it say about me as a person?" "What's the deepest fear or insecurity this thought touches upon?"

3. **Challenge the Inner Critic (Applying CBT from Chapter 2):** Use the same questioning techniques you learned for challenging distorted thoughts:
    - "Is this thought 100% true, or is my ADHD brain exaggerating?"
    - "What's the evidence *for* this thought? What's the evidence *against* it?"
    - "What would a compassionate friend say to me right now?"
    - "Is this thought helping me solve the problem or making me feel worse?"
    - *Action:* Write down the critical thought, then write down several compassionate, evidence-based counter-statements.
4. **Practice Self-Compassionate Rephrasing:** Once you've challenged a harsh thought, consciously rephrase it in a kinder, more understanding, and more helpful way.
    - *Original Harsh Thought:* "I can't believe I procrastinated again. I'm so lazy and useless."
    - *Compassionate Rephrasing:* "Okay, I procrastinated on this. That's a common ADHD struggle. What made this task particularly hard? What small step can I take now, or what strategy can I try next time?"
    - *Original Harsh Thought:* "I totally screwed up that presentation. Everyone thinks I'm incompetent."
    - *Compassionate Rephrasing:* "That presentation was tough, and I felt like I struggled. It's okay to feel disappointed. What were my strengths in it? What's one thing I can learn for the next time?"
5. **Use Mindful Awareness to Create Space:** When the inner critic gets loud, practice mindfulness to observe the thoughts without getting entangled.
    - *Action:* Acknowledge the thought ("There's my inner critic again, saying I'm not good enough"). Imagine putting it on a leaf and letting it float down a stream, or observing it like a cloud passing by. This creates mental distance.

6. **Develop a Compassionate Inner Voice:** Actively cultivate a different voice.
    - **Use Positive Affirmations (that resonate):** Find short, truthful, and empowering phrases that counter your common critical thoughts. "I am capable of learning and growing." "My effort is enough." "I can handle this one step at a time."
    - **Imagine a Supportive Figure:** If it's hard to be kind to yourself, imagine what a wise mentor, a loving parent, or a supportive friend would say to you in that moment. Then, "speak" those words to yourself.
    - **Acknowledge Effort, Not Just Outcome:** Praise yourself for trying, for showing up, for taking action, even if the outcome isn't perfect. This is especially important for ADHD brains that can struggle with consistent output.
7. **Practice Gratitude for Your Brain:** Even with its challenges, your ADHD brain offers unique strengths: creativity, quick thinking, hyperfocus, resilience. Acknowledge these.
    - *Action:* Regularly remind yourself of the positive traits that come with your neurotype. This balances the narrative.

Cultivating compassionate self-talk is a continuous practice that slowly rewires your brain's default emotional responses. It builds a powerful internal resource for emotional resilience, allowing you to navigate the ups and downs of life with greater inner stability and self-acceptance. By transforming your inner dialogue, you transform your entire emotional landscape, becoming your own most reliable guiding hand.

CONCLUSION

YOUR EMOTIONAL STRENGTH

You've now completed Book 4, "Mastering Your Emotions with CBT Tools: Navigating the Inner Landscape," and in doing so, you've equipped yourself with a profound understanding and powerful toolkit for managing the often intense emotional experiences that come with ADHD. This journey has not been about suppressing your feelings, but about developing a guiding hand to lead you through your inner world with greater awareness and control.

We've explored the unique **emotional landscape of adult ADHD**, recognizing that rapid mood shifts, low frustration tolerance (including Rejection Sensitive Dysphoria), and impulsive emotional reactions are neurological differences, not character flaws. This understanding is the bedrock of compassionate self-management.

You've then delved into the core CBT principles, learning to:

- **Identify and challenge distorted thoughts**, recognizing that your interpretations shape your reality and can be a source of significant emotional distress. You've gained the ability to question negative self-talk and reframe situations for a more balanced perspective.
- Implement powerful **behavioral strategies for emotional regulation**, from mindful movement and strategic relaxation to sensory grounding and the "STOP" skill, providing you with active ways to shift your emotional state in the moment.
- Build **emotional resilience and distress tolerance**, equipping you with the capacity to bounce back from adversity and to skillfully endure uncomfortable emotions without resorting to unhelpful behaviors.
- Cultivate **compassionate self-talk and a supportive inner dialogue**, transforming your harshest critic into a powerful inner ally who champions your growth and well-being.

The mastery of your emotions is not a destination, but a continuous practice. There will be days when the emotional rollercoaster feels more intense, and old thought patterns might resurface. This is normal. The true strength lies in your commitment to consistently apply these tools, to observe without judgment, and to choose a more intentional response.

You now have a clearer understanding of the interplay between your thoughts, feelings, and actions. You possess a robust set of CBT-based strategies to navigate intense emotions, build inner resilience, and foster a kinder, more supportive relationship with yourself. This emotional strength is a cornerstone of your overall well-being, enhancing your executive function, improving your focus, and profoundly impacting your ability to achieve sustained productivity and build meaningful relationships.

As you move forward, carry these insights and tools with you. Practice regularly. Celebrate your progress, however small. Your capacity for emotional mastery is growing, and with it, your ability to live a more balanced, fulfilling, and empowered life.

Let's pause for a moment and reflect on what you've just read. What resonates with you? What are the strategies you feel you can apply to work and life now versus those that seem more challenging or daunting?

BOOK FIVE

ORGANIZATION, TIME MANAGEMENT, AND RELATIONSHIPS: CRAFTING A BALANCED LIFE

CHAPTER 1

ORGANIZING YOUR PHYSICAL AND DIGITAL WORLD

You've put in significant work strengthening your executive functions, sharpening your focus, and developing emotional resilience. Now, it's time to integrate these hard-won skills into the practical realities of daily living: specifically, how you manage your surroundings, your time, and your connections with others. This final book, "Organization, Time Management, and Relationships," is about **crafting a balanced life** that genuinely works for the man with ADHD, moving beyond merely coping to truly thriving.

We start with **organization**. For many men with ADHD, the physical and digital world can feel like a constant battleground. Piles of papers, overflowing inboxes, scattered notes, and forgotten files are common culprits. This isn't a sign of laziness or a lack of care; it's a direct consequence of challenges with working memory, planning, and task initiation. Your brain's tendency to prioritize novelty over routine, and its difficulty with sustained focus on less stimulating tasks, can make maintaining order feel like pushing a boulder uphill.

The impact of disorganization extends far beyond aesthetics:

- **Lost time and increased frustration:** Constantly searching for misplaced items or information.
- **Missed opportunities and deadlines:** Important documents or emails getting buried.
- **Mental clutter and overwhelm:** A disorganized external environment often mirrors a disorganized internal one, adding to cognitive load.
- **Impact on relationships:** Frustration from partners or family members who struggle with the chaos.
- **Reduced productivity:** Inability to find what you need when you need it, leading to procrastination and delays.

The goal of this chapter is not to turn you into a minimalist guru overnight, but to help you establish **functional organizational systems** that reduce friction, support your executive functions, and free up valuable mental energy. It's about creating order that serves *your* brain, not a rigid system that you'll quickly abandon.

Taming the Physical Chaos: Strategies for Your Space

Your physical environment is a powerful cue. A cluttered space can signal "chaos" to your brain, while an organized one can prompt "clarity" and "focus."

1. **Start Small: The "Hot Spot" Method:** Don't try to organize your entire house at once. Pick one "hot spot" that causes you frequent frustration (e.g., your desk, the kitchen counter, the entryway table). Dedicate 15-30 minutes to *only* that area. This makes the task feel manageable and provides a quick win.
2. **The "One In, One Out" Rule:** For every new item you bring into your home (e.g., a new shirt, a new gadget), commit to removing an old one. This prevents accumulation and forces conscious decision-making.
3. **Give Everything a Home:** Clutter often arises because items don't have a designated place. Assign a specific, logical "home" for every item you own. If it doesn't have a home, it's more likely to end up in a random pile.

4. **Containers and Labels:** Use clear containers, drawers, and baskets to group similar items. Label everything clearly. Labels reduce the mental effort of remembering where things belong and make it easier to put things away.
5. **Vertical Space is Your Friend:** Use shelves, wall organizers, and multi-tiered trays to maximize vertical space, especially on desks or counters. This clears horizontal surfaces, which tend to become dumping grounds.
6. **Regular "Reset" Sessions:** For the ADHD brain, consistent daily tidying can be tough. Instead, schedule short, regular "reset" sessions. This could be 15 minutes at the end of each workday to clear your desk, or 30 minutes on a Saturday morning to tidy common areas. This prevents small messes from becoming overwhelming.
7. **The "Landing Strip" Concept:** Create a designated "landing strip" near your entryway for essential items like keys, wallet, phone, and mail. This prevents frantic searches and ensures critical items are always in a predictable place.

Conquering the Digital Deluge: Strategies for Your Online World

Your digital life can be even more chaotic than your physical one, with endless files, emails, and notifications.

1. **Email Triage: The "4 D's" System:** Don't let your inbox become a to-do list or a storage unit. When you open an email, immediately decide:
    - **Delete:** If it's junk or irrelevant.
    - **Do:** If it takes less than 2 minutes to respond or action.
    - **Delegate:** If someone else needs to handle it.
    - **Defer:** If it requires more time or attention, move it to a specific "To Do" folder or add it to your task manager.
    - *Action:* Aim for Inbox Zero at least once a day, or at minimum, once a week.
2. **Strategic Folder Structure (Less is More):** Resist the urge to create endless nested folders. Keep your main folders broad (e.g., "Projects," "Clients," "Personal," "Archive"). Use a consistent naming convention. Rely on the search function for specific files; your brain is better at remembering keywords than specific folder paths.

3. **Cloud Storage for Accessibility:** Utilize cloud services (Google Drive, Dropbox, OneDrive) for important documents. This allows you to access files from anywhere and reduces the risk of losing them if a device fails.
4. **Desktop Declutter:** Your computer desktop should not be a holding pen for every downloaded file. Clear it regularly. Move temporary files to a "To Sort" folder, and permanent files into your organized folder structure. A clean desktop reduces visual noise and cognitive load.
5. **Digital Note-Taking and Capture:** Invest in one reliable digital note-taking system (e.g., Evernote, Notion, OneNote, Obsidian) to capture ideas, meeting notes, articles, and references. The key is to have *one* trusted place where you put everything, rather than scattering notes across different apps or physical scraps of paper.
6. **Regular Digital Backups:** Prevent the emotional distress of lost data by regularly backing up your important files. Use automated cloud backups or external hard drives.
7. **App Management and Notification Control:** Regularly review the apps on your phone and computer. Delete those you don't use. Turn off all non-essential notifications that constantly pull your attention.

By systematically applying these strategies to both your physical and digital worlds, you will create a more supportive and less distracting environment. This isn't just about tidiness; it's about reducing mental friction, making it easier to find what you need, and freeing up your precious executive function for more productive and fulfilling endeavors. An organized external world becomes a calm anchor for your often-busy internal world.

CHAPTER 2

TIME MANAGEMENT STRATEGIES FOR THE ADHD BRAIN

You've begun to bring order to your physical and digital spaces, reducing external chaos. Now, we turn to an equally vital, and often more elusive, challenge for men with ADHD: **time management**. For many, time can feel like a slippery concept, an abstract idea that constantly eludes grasp. This isn't a failure of willpower; it's often a direct consequence of **time perception challenges (commonly referred to as 'time blindness')**. While 'time blindness' is a widely recognized descriptive term and a hallmark experience for many with ADHD, it's important to understand it's **not a formal diagnostic term**. Instead, it reflects a difficulty in accurately perceiving the passage of time, estimating how long tasks will take, or understanding the immediacy of future events. This neurocognitive difference makes traditional time management particularly challenging.

The impact of poor time management for men with ADHD is profound:

- **Chronic lateness:** Constantly rushing, missing appointments, or underestimating travel times.
- **Missed deadlines:** Leading to stress, poor performance reviews, and damaged reputation.
- **Procrastination loops:** "Plenty of time" quickly turns into "no time at all."
- **Over-scheduling:** Enthusiastically committing to too much, leading to overwhelm and failure to deliver.
- **Inability to prioritize effectively:** Everything feels equally urgent, creating a constant state of reactivity.
- **Increased anxiety and stress:** The perpetual feeling of being behind or out of control.

Effective time management for the ADHD brain isn't about rigid adherence to a minute-by-minute schedule. It's about developing strategies that make time more **tangible, predictable, and manageable** by leveraging your strengths and accommodating your challenges. It's about building awareness and creating external structures that compensate for internal time perception difficulties.

Making Time Tangible: Building Awareness and Estimation Skills

Your internal clock may be off, so let's rely on external cues and conscious practice.

1. **Use External Timers Liberally:** Don't rely on your internal sense of time. Use visual timers (like the Time Timer), phone alarms, or desktop timers for *everything*.
   - **Pomodoro Technique (Revisited):** As discussed in Book 2, using 25-minute focused work intervals followed by 5-minute breaks is an excellent way to structure time.
   - **Time Blocking:** Dedicate specific blocks of time in your calendar for specific tasks or types of work. Treat these blocks as non-negotiable appointments with yourself.
   - **Transition Timers:** Set a 5 or 10-minute alarm *before* you need to leave for an appointment or switch tasks. This provides a crucial buffer and reduces rushing.
2. **Practice "Time Travel" (Mental Rehearsal):** Before starting a task or leaving for an appointment, mentally walk through the steps involved and estimate how long each will take.

- *Action:* For an appointment: "Okay, it's 10:00 AM. I need 5 minutes to grab my keys and jacket, 10 minutes to walk to the car, 20 minutes to drive, and 5 minutes to park and get inside. So, I need to leave by 9:20 AM." Compare this to your initial gut feeling.

3. **The "Actual Time vs. Estimated Time" Log:** For a week or two, keep a simple log. For every task, write down how long you *thought* it would take, and then how long it *actually* took. This builds crucial data about your personal time estimation errors and highlights patterns. You'll likely discover you consistently underestimate certain types of tasks.
4. **Visualize Time:** Use a large wall calendar or a visual planner where you can physically see your week or month laid out. Color-coding different types of activities (work, appointments, personal time) can further enhance this visual understanding of how your time is allocated.

Structuring Your Day: Optimizing Your Schedule

Once you have a better grasp on time, you can build a schedule that works for your unique brain.

1. **Identify Your Peak Productivity Times:** When are you naturally most alert, focused, and energetic? For many with ADHD, this is often in the morning, before stimulants wear off or before too many daily demands accumulate. Schedule your most challenging or important tasks during these "prime time" hours.
2. **Schedule Everything (Even Breaks and Transitions):** Don't just schedule meetings and work tasks. Block out time for breaks, exercise, lunch, deep work, shallow work (email, administrative tasks), and even travel. This creates a realistic view of your day and prevents over-scheduling.
3. **Build in Buffers (The ADHD Tax):** Always add extra time. If you think a meeting will be 30 minutes, block 45. If a task takes 1 hour, block 1.5 hours. This "ADHD tax" on time acknowledges your tendency to underestimate and provides crucial breathing room, reducing stress from constant rushing.
4. **The "Rule of 3":** At the start of each day, identify the top 3 most important tasks you *must* accomplish. Focus on these before anything else. This prevents getting bogged down in less important activities and ensures you move the needle on your priorities.

5. **Leverage External Accountability:** If you struggle to stick to a schedule, find ways to add external accountability. This could be a scheduled check-in with a colleague, a virtual body doubling session, or even just telling a friend your plan for the day.
6. **Review Your Schedule Daily:** Take 5-10 minutes each morning or evening to review your schedule for the next day. Adjust as needed, anticipate potential time conflicts, and mentally prepare for transitions.

Flexible Systems: Adapting to the ADHD Brain

Rigidity often leads to abandonment. Your systems need to be adaptable.

1. **Use Technology Wisely:** Utilize digital calendars (Google Calendar, Outlook Calendar) with alerts and reminders. Set multiple reminders for important appointments. Use task managers that integrate with your calendar.
2. **The "Park It" Place:** If you're in the middle of a task and a new idea or thought pops into your head, don't follow it. Immediately write it down in your designated "capture system" (from Book 3) and then return to your current task. This prevents derailment while ensuring the idea isn't lost.
3. **Prioritize by Energy, Not Just Urgency:** Don't just tackle the most urgent tasks. Consider your current energy levels. If you're feeling low-energy, tackle a less demanding task that still moves you forward. Save your high-energy tasks for when you're at your best.
4. **Forgive Yourself and Adjust:** You will have "off" days. You will misestimate. You will get distracted. When this happens, don't beat yourself up. Acknowledge it, learn from it, and adjust your plan for the next hour or day. The goal is progress, not perfection.

By implementing these time management strategies, you're not just organizing your schedule; you're building a stronger, more reliable internal clock and a more realistic understanding of how you actually use your time. This mastery over time is a crucial component of reducing stress, increasing productivity, and ultimately, crafting a more balanced and fulfilling life.

CHAPTER 3

NURTURING RELATIONSHIPS AND COMMUNICATION

You've made significant strides in organizing your environment and managing your time, two foundational elements for a more balanced life. Now, we turn to perhaps the most sensitive and profoundly impactful area: **nurturing relationships and communication**. For men with ADHD, the very traits that make you creative, spontaneous, and exciting can also present unique challenges in interpersonal dynamics.

The impact of ADHD on relationships is often underestimated, yet it can be a source of significant friction and misunderstanding. Common challenges include:

- **Difficulty with active listening:** Your mind might wander during conversations, leading to missed details or appearing disengaged.
- **Impulsive interruptions:** Blurt out thoughts or finish sentences, often without meaning to be rude.

- **Emotional intensity and reactivity (RSD):** Overreacting to perceived criticism or minor disagreements, leading to arguments.
- **Forgetfulness:** Missing appointments, forgetting important dates, or failing to follow through on promises.
- **Time blindness impacting others:** Chronic lateness or underestimating time for shared activities, causing frustration for partners or friends.
- **Task initiation in shared responsibilities:** Struggling to start or complete chores or shared projects, leading to resentment.
- **Hyperfocus on hobbies/interests:** Becoming so engrossed in your passions that you inadvertently neglect your partner or family.

These challenges aren't about a lack of caring; they're symptoms of a neurobiological difference. However, left unaddressed, they can lead to partners feeling unheard, unprioritized, or overwhelmed. The good news is that with awareness, specific strategies, and open communication, you can significantly strengthen your relationships and foster deeper connections.

Building Bridges: Strategies for Effective Communication

Communication is the bedrock of any healthy relationship. For ADHD, it's about being more intentional and strategic.

1. **Practice Active and Mindful Listening:** This is paramount. When someone is speaking to you, consciously turn off distractions (put down your phone, close your laptop). Make eye contact. Internally paraphrase what they are saying to ensure comprehension.
   - *Action:* Use the "Listen, Summarize, Clarify" technique: Listen carefully, then say, "So, if I'm hearing you right, you're saying [summary of what they said]. Is that correct?" This shows you're engaged and helps avoid misunderstandings.
   - *Action:* If your mind wanders, gently bring it back to their words. It's a "rep" for your attention, as discussed in Book 2.
2. **Delay Your Response (The "Pause Button"):** Combat impulsive interruptions or emotional outbursts by creating a deliberate pause.

- *Action:* When you feel an urge to interrupt or react, try taking a deep breath before speaking. You can even silently count to three. Or, if you absolutely have to say something, preface it with, "That sparks a thought, can I quickly mention it before I forget, then you can continue?" (Use sparingly).

3. **Use "I" Statements:** When discussing difficult topics or expressing emotions, focus on your feelings and experiences rather than blaming.
   - *Instead of:* "You never listen to me!"
   - *Try:* "I feel unheard when I'm speaking and you're looking at your phone."
4. **Schedule Important Conversations:** For sensitive or important topics, don't rely on spontaneous moments. ADHD brains can benefit from knowing when a difficult conversation is coming.
   - *Action:* Say, "I'd like to talk about [topic] tonight after dinner. Does that work for you?" This allows both parties to prepare emotionally and mentally.
5. **Externalize Your Thoughts (Respectfully):** Sometimes, your brain is just moving too fast. Learn to externalize without overwhelming your listener.
   - *Action:* "My thoughts are a bit scattered right now, but what I'm trying to say is..." or "I have several ideas popping up, let me try to walk through them one by one." This manages expectations.

Building Connection: Strategies for Relationship Nurturing

Beyond communication, specific actions strengthen the bonds in your relationships.

1. **"Time In" for Connection:** Schedule quality, distraction-free time with your partner, children, or close friends. This could be a regular "date night," a dedicated family activity, or just 15 minutes of uninterrupted conversation each day.
   - *Action:* Put these "connection times" into your calendar and treat them as non-negotiable appointments.
2. **Acknowledge and Validate Emotions (Especially for RSD):** When your partner or friend expresses an emotion, practice validating their feeling before offering solutions or explanations.

    - *Action:* "I can see why you'd feel frustrated about that," or "It sounds like you're really disappointed." This is crucial for navigating perceived criticism (RSD) from both sides – for you to validate their feelings, and for them to validate yours.
3. **Proactive Problem-Solving for Shared Responsibilities:** Don't wait for resentment to build over forgotten chores or shared tasks.
    - *Action:* Use visual aids for shared tasks (e.g., a whiteboard chore chart). Break down larger tasks into smaller, manageable steps. Schedule specific times for joint tasks, and use reminders. Communicate openly about what you can realistically commit to.
4. **The "5-Minute Burst of Appreciation":** Take brief moments throughout the day to show appreciation or affection. This could be a quick text, a genuine compliment, or a spontaneous hug. These small gestures add up.
    - *Action:* Make it a habit to verbally express gratitude or appreciation to your partner or family members at least once a day.
5. **Educate Your Loved Ones About ADHD (Gently):** Help your close relationships understand how ADHD impacts you, without making excuses.
    - *Action:* Share resources (like this book!). Explain *why* you might forget things or interrupt, and discuss strategies you're trying. This fosters empathy and can help them adapt their expectations or communication style.
6. **Manage Hyperfocus (Consciously):** If you're prone to hyperfocusing on hobbies or work, proactively communicate your boundaries or set timers.
    - *Action:* Tell your partner, "I'm going to work on this project for the next hour, and then I'll be done and focused on you." Use a timer to pull yourself out.

Nurturing relationships and improving communication for men with ADHD is an ongoing process of self-awareness, intentional action, and open dialogue. By applying these strategies, you'll not only reduce friction and misunderstanding but also build deeper, more resilient connections that enrich your life and provide invaluable support on your journey to a balanced existence.

CHAPTER 4

SELF-CARE AND PREVENTING BURNOUT IN A DEMANDING WORLD

You've been diligently working on organizing your life, managing your time, and strengthening your relationships. This is significant progress! However, the very effort required to implement these strategies, coupled with the inherent demands of living with ADHD in a neurotypical world, can lead to a critical, often overlooked, challenge: **burnout**. For men with ADHD, the constant mental energy expended to focus, initiate, regulate emotions, and manage daily tasks makes you particularly susceptible to exhaustion, cynicism, and a reduced sense of accomplishment.

Burnout isn't just about feeling tired; it's a state of chronic physical, emotional, and mental exhaustion. It's often accompanied by:

- **Emotional depletion:** Feeling empty, numb, or overwhelmed.
- **Cynicism and detachment:** A growing sense of negativity towards your work, responsibilities, or even people.
- **Reduced efficacy:** Feeling less capable and productive, even if you're trying harder.
- **Increased irritability:** A shorter fuse and less patience with others.
- **Physical symptoms:** Headaches, fatigue, sleep disturbances, or increased susceptibility to illness.

For men with ADHD, these symptoms can sometimes be mistaken for worsening ADHD, leading to further frustration. The reality is that the constant effort to compensate for executive function challenges, navigate sensory sensitivities, and manage emotional dysregulation drains your internal resources at a faster rate. This is why **self-care** is not a luxury; it's a fundamental necessity for sustainable productivity and emotional well-being. It's the fuel that keeps your engine running.

This chapter will guide you through understanding the signs of burnout and implementing proactive self-care strategies that are specifically tailored to the needs of the ADHD brain, ensuring you can maintain your momentum and enjoy a truly balanced and fulfilling life.

Recognizing the Red Flags: Signs of Impending Burnout

Becoming attuned to your own unique burnout signals is the first step toward prevention.

1. **Increased Procrastination and Apathy:** You might find yourself avoiding tasks you once found manageable or even enjoyable. A general feeling of "I just don't care" sets in.
2. **Heightened Irritability or Emotional Blunting:** Small annoyances trigger disproportionate anger, or conversely, you feel a general numbness and difficulty experiencing joy or enthusiasm.
3. **Chronic Fatigue and Sleep Disturbances:** You're constantly tired, even after adequate sleep. Sleep patterns might become erratic, making it harder to fall asleep or stay asleep.
4. **Physical Manifestations:** Frequent headaches, muscle tension, digestive issues, or a weakened immune system (getting sick more often) can all be signs of chronic stress.
5. **Cynicism and Negative Self-Talk:** A pervasive sense of negativity about your work, colleagues, or even your own capabilities. The inner critic becomes louder and more relentless.

6. **Difficulty with Focus and Memory (Worsening ADHD Symptoms):** Your core ADHD symptoms might feel amplified – more distractibility, greater difficulty with task initiation, increased forgetfulness. This is your brain signalling it's overloaded.
7. **Increased Desire to Isolate:** Pulling away from social interactions or activities you typically enjoy.

If you recognize several of these signs, it's a clear signal that it's time to intentionally integrate more self-care into your routine.

Proactive Self-Care: Fueling Your ADHD Brain

Self-care isn't a one-size-fits-all solution; it's about finding what genuinely recharges *you*. For the ADHD brain, novelty and stimulation can be both a lure and a drain, so the right balance is crucial.

1. **Schedule True Downtime (The "Non-Negotiable Recharge"):** This is paramount. Just as you schedule work and appointments, schedule blocks of time for genuine rest and rejuvenation. This means *unplugging* from work, social media, and demanding tasks.
   - **Action:** Experiment with what truly recharges you: quiet reading, nature walks, playing with a pet, listening to music, engaging in a non-productive hobby (e.g., doodling, tinkering), or simply sitting quietly. Put these in your calendar.
2. **Prioritize Sleep Hygiene:** As discussed in Book 2, quality sleep is non-negotiable for ADHD brains. It directly impacts emotional regulation, focus, and energy.
   - **Action:** Establish a consistent bedtime and wake-up time (even on weekends). Create a relaxing pre-sleep routine (e.g., dim lights, warm bath, no screens 1 hour before bed). Optimize your sleep environment (dark, cool, quiet).
3. **Nourish Your Body and Brain:** Consistent energy levels are crucial for sustained effort.
   - **Action:** Focus on balanced meals with protein, healthy fats, and complex carbohydrates. Stay well-hydrated throughout the day. Be mindful of caffeine and sugar intake, as they can lead to energy crashes that exacerbate ADHD symptoms.

4. **Incorporate Movement Daily:** Physical activity is a powerful antidote to stress and mental fatigue. It helps regulate dopamine, reduces restlessness, and improves mood.
    - **Action:** Find an activity you enjoy and can stick with, even if it's just 20-30 minutes of brisk walking most days. Vary your activities to maintain interest.
5. **Set Realistic Boundaries:** The ADHD brain can struggle with saying "no" due to impulsivity or a desire to please. Overcommitment is a fast track to burnout.
    - **Action:** Learn to identify your capacity and politely decline requests that will overwhelm you. Protect your scheduled downtime and deep work blocks from intrusions.
6. **Delegate and Automate:** If possible, offload tasks that drain you or are highly repetitive.
    - **Action:** Delegate tasks at work or home where feasible. Explore automation tools for recurring digital tasks (e.g., bill payments, email filters). This frees up mental energy.
7. **Practice Mindful Breaks and Transitions:** Integrate short moments of mindfulness throughout your day to reset your nervous system.
    - **Action:** Use the "One-Minute Mindfulness Break" (from Book 2) between tasks. Before transitioning from work to home life, take 5 minutes to decompress – listen to a song, sit in silence, or do a quick stretch.
8. **Connect with Your Support System:** Social connection is a powerful buffer against stress and loneliness.
    - **Action:** Regularly connect with trusted friends, family, or a therapist who understands your experiences. Don't isolate yourself when feeling overwhelmed.
9. **Engage in "Flow State" Activities:** Activities that fully absorb you and provide a sense of timeless enjoyment are incredibly restorative.
    - **Action:** Identify hobbies or interests where you lose track of time (e.g., playing music, painting, gardening, specific video games, building models). Intentionally schedule time for these.

Preventing burnout is an ongoing, proactive commitment to yourself. It's about recognizing that your ADHD brain requires deliberate care and intelligent energy management. By consistently integrating these self-care strategies, you're not just avoiding exhaustion; you're building a foundation of sustainable well-being that will allow you to leverage your strengths, manage your challenges, and ultimately craft a truly balanced and fulfilling life.

CONCLUSION

YOUR BALANCED LIFE, REDEFINED

You've now reached the conclusion of Book 5, "Organization, Time Management, and Relationships: Crafting a Balanced Life," and in doing so, you've integrated all the tools and insights from the previous books into a holistic framework for thriving with ADHD. This journey has been about much more than just managing symptoms; it's been about proactively designing a life that leverages your strengths, accommodates your challenges, and brings you a profound sense of equilibrium and fulfillment.

We started this book by addressing the practical, yet often overwhelming, aspects of daily living:

- **Organizing your physical and digital world:** You've learned to transform chaos into functional order, creating clear spaces that reduce mental clutter and support your focus.
- **Mastering time management:** By confronting "time blindness" and implementing tangible strategies, you've gained greater control over your schedule, reducing lateness and increasing predictability.
- **Nurturing relationships and communication:** You've acquired essential skills to listen actively, communicate effectively, and build stronger, more empathetic connections with your loved ones.
- And finally, in this last chapter, you've understood the critical importance of **self-care and preventing burnout**, recognizing that sustained well-being is the bedrock upon which all other successes are built.

The true essence of this book, and indeed this entire series, is the idea of **redefining success on your own terms**. For the man with ADHD, a "balanced life" isn't about achieving neurotypical perfection or adhering to rigid ideals. It's about:

- **Awareness:** Deeply understanding how your unique brain works and how it impacts your experiences.
- **Acceptance:** Embracing your neurodiversity, recognizing that your ADHD is a part of who you are, with both challenges and

remarkable strengths.

- **Adaptation:** Continuously learning, experimenting, and refining strategies that genuinely support *your* specific needs and goals.
- **Action:** Translating insights into consistent, manageable steps that move you forward.
- **Compassion:** Treating yourself with kindness, understanding, and forgiveness throughout the journey.

You now have a comprehensive toolkit covering executive functions, focus, productivity, emotional regulation, organization, time management, relationships, and self-care. This is not a static manual but a dynamic guide. There will be days when strategies click, and days when you feel off-kilter. This is the human experience, amplified sometimes by ADHD. The power lies in your ability to **review, adapt, and iterate**, as you learned in Book 3.

As you step forward, carry the confidence that comes from knowledge and practical application. You are not just managing ADHD; you are actively *crafting* a life that allows you to flourish. Your unique blend of creativity, spontaneity, and energy, when supported by these learned skills, becomes a powerful force for innovation and connection.

Embrace the ongoing journey. Celebrate your resilience. Trust in your growing capacity for self-mastery. Your balanced life, redefined and purposefully built, awaits.

Let's pause for a moment and reflect on what you've just read. What resonates with you? What are the strategies you feel you can apply to work and life now versus those that seem more challenging or daunting?

OVERALL CONCLUSION

THE EMPOWERED MAN WITH ADHD

You've journeyed through this comprehensive five-book series, dedicating yourself to understanding, adapting, and ultimately thriving with ADHD. This isn't just a collection of strategies; it's a profound transformation of how you relate to your own neurobiology and engage with the world around you.

From the foundational executive functions, through the intricacies of focus and productivity, navigating your emotional landscape, and finally, crafting a balanced life — you've actively built a robust framework for success on your own terms. You've come to understand that **ADHD isn't a deficit to be cured, but a unique operating system to be mastered.**

This series has armed you with:

- **Self-Awareness:** A deep understanding of how your brain works, its strengths, its challenges, and its unique rhythms. This insight is the foundation of all effective self-management.
- **Actionable Strategies:** Concrete, practical tools across all vital areas of life, designed to work *with* your ADHD brain, not against it.
- **Emotional Resilience:** The capacity to navigate intense feelings, challenge distorted thoughts, and cultivate an inner dialogue that supports, rather than sabotages, your well-being.
- **System Building:** The ability to create external structures that compensate for internal challenges, reducing friction and freeing up mental energy for what truly matters.
- **Self-Compassion:** The crucial understanding that progress, not perfection, is the goal, and that kindness toward yourself is the most powerful catalyst for sustainable change.

You are no longer merely coping with ADHD; you are actively **crafting a life that is aligned with your unique strengths and values.** You are becoming the architect of your own experience, making intentional choices rather than being swept away by distraction, procrastination, or emotional turbulence.

The journey continues, of course. Life is dynamic, and so are the demands placed upon you. There will be new challenges, moments of overwhelm, and times when you may temporarily fall back on old habits. This is normal. The true power lies in your newfound ability to:

- **Recognize** when you're struggling.
- **Refer** back to your toolkit.
- **Re-engage** with the strategies that work for you.
- **Review, Adapt, and Iterate** your approach, always learning and evolving.

You are now an **Empowered Man with ADHD.** You possess the knowledge, the skills, and the mindset to navigate your world with greater clarity, purpose, and peace. Embrace your neurodiversity, celebrate your unique gifts, and continue to build the extraordinary life you are capable of living.

- *An additional note: Although this book is titled as being geared towards the needs of men with ADHD, it can be used by women too.*

PART 2: ADHD ORGANIZATION AND CLEANING 5-IN-1

Get Organized and Stay Consistent with Easy Routines and Systems for Organizing and Keeping Your Home and Life Clean

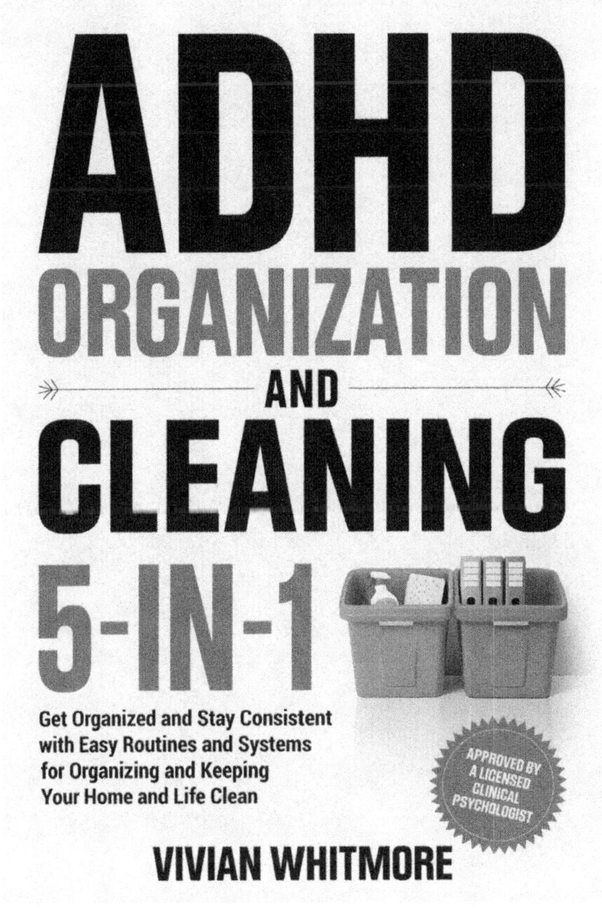

FOREWORD BY CAROLINA ESTEVEZ, PSY.D.

As a psychologist, I found *ADHD Organization and Cleaning 5-in-1: Get Organized and Stay Consistent with Easy Routines and Systems for Organizing and Keeping Your Home and Life Clean* by Vivian Whitmore to be both practical and deeply validating for individuals with ADHD. This excellent resource bridges neuroscience, behavioral strategies, and compassionate guidance, making it an invaluable tool for anyone struggling to create order in their environment and their mind.

The opening chapters on routines, habits, and the effects of clutter establish a realistic framework. Rather than framing clutter as moral failure, the author presents it as an executive functioning challenge that can be resolved by being broken down into achievable steps. This approach aligns with cognitive-behavioral strategies I have recommended in therapy—reducing shame and highlighting personal strengths and skill-building.

I particularly appreciated the chapter on how progress beats perfection, which reframes productivity as a continuum. ADHD brains are prone to all-or-nothing thinking, so emphasizing incremental improvement is not only motivational, but also protective against discouragement.

ADHD Organization and Cleaning 5-in-1: Get Organized and Stay Consistent with Easy Routines and Systems for Organizing and Keeping Your Home and Life Clean provides several strategies that are effective in aiding people with ADHD in achieving a more organized and structured daily life. For instance, the 10-minute tidy illustrates this beautifully in the first chapter. It is a time-limited task that generates momentum and provides a "small win," which in turn reinforces positive behavior.

The sections on energy mapping and environmental anchors demonstrate psychological insight into how context shapes behavior. By aligning tasks with natural energy peaks and using visual cues in the environment, the book harnesses principles of behavioral psychology in a way that is accessible and actionable.

From a clinical perspective, I was also impressed by the exploration of routines, habits, and time management. The discussion of time blocking and seasonal routines shows sensitivity to the cyclical patterns many clients with ADHD experience. The inclusion of a cleaning toolkit provides a concrete, sensory-friendly entry point to tasks that often feel abstract or overwhelming.

ADHD Organization and Cleaning 5-in-1: Get Organized and Stay Consistent with Easy Routines and Systems for Organizing and Keeping Your Home and Life Clean does not shy away from the emotional dimension of organization. The chapters on why a clean space calms the brain and on bouncing back after setbacks underscore the role of environment in emotional regulation. These insights mirror research showing that reduced visual clutter can lower cognitive load and support attentional control.

As a psychologist, I value the inclusion of reflection questions and quizzes, as these tools transform the book from a passive guide into an interactive self-help tool. This promotes metacognition—a key therapeutic goal in ADHD management—by encouraging readers to notice patterns, strengths, and areas of growth.

ADHD Organization and Cleaning 5-in-1: Get Organized and Stay Consistent with Easy Routines and Systems for Organizing and Keeping Your Home and Life Clean is both scientifically informed and practically grounded. I am confident that it will offer readers with ADHD—and those supporting them—an empowering roadmap for creating environments that foster focus, calm, and sustainable routines. I will be recommending it in my clinical practice.

Carolina Estevez, Psy.D.

Licensed Psychologist

INTRODUCTION

WELCOME TO YOUR ORGANIZED LIFE

The idea of "getting organized" can feel like a mountain to climb, especially for those of us with an ADHD brain. The world often seems built for neurotypical minds, a place where to-do lists are linear, focus is constant, and "just do it" is considered helpful advice. Let's be honest: that's not our reality. The well-intentioned advice of "just make a list" or "stick to a schedule" often rings hollow, creating a cycle of aspiration, frustration, and eventual shame. We know what we "should" do, but the bridge between intention and action can feel impossible to cross. This persistent friction, the energy spent trying to force ourselves into a system that simply doesn't fit, is a silent but exhausting tax on our mental and emotional well-being.

This book is a guide for a different kind of reality. It's not about forcing yourself into a system that doesn't fit; it's about building one that does. It's for the person who starts cleaning the kitchen and ends up organizing the entire garage because **hyperfocus** takes over. It's for the person who feels overwhelmed by a single messy drawer and a person who can't find their keys for the tenth time this week. It's for you. This is an invitation to stop fighting your brain and start working with it. Instead of trying to become someone you're not, we will focus on designing a life that celebrates who you are.

This is a 5-in-1 guide that focuses on tangible, flexible, and sustainable strategies. You won't find any one-size-fits-all solutions here, because your brain is unique. Instead, you'll find a **toolkit** of concepts and systems that you can adapt to your life, your home, and your unique way of thinking. We'll show you how to work with your brain's natural tendencies, like harnessing hyperfocus for deep cleaning, rather than constantly fighting against them. This is not a journey to a perfectly sterile, minimalist space; it's a journey to a peaceful, functional home that supports your passions and allows you to thrive.

Understanding the "ADHD Tax"

Before we can build a new system, we must first acknowledge the one we've been living with: the **"ADHD Tax."** This is the mental, emotional, and even financial cost of living with executive dysfunction in a world that doesn't account for it. It's the anxiety of a late bill, the shame of a messy house when guests are coming over, the frustration of a project that never gets finished, and the lost time spent searching for misplaced items. It's the constant, low-level stress that comes from feeling like you're always playing catch-up.

This volume is designed to help you start recouping that tax. We will do this not by forcing you into a rigid mold, but by building **external systems** that compensate for your internal challenges. Our goal is to reduce the friction in your daily life, freeing up your mental energy for what truly matters. We'll show you how a simple routine can save you hours of anxiety and how a small reward can be the difference between a task being done or remaining abandoned indefinitely.

The 5 Pillars of Your New Toolkit

This book is divided into five core sections, each a pillar of your new organizational toolkit. They are designed to be read in order, as each concept builds upon the last.

- **Pillar 1: The Foundations of a Flexible Routine.** We'll begin by challenging the very idea of a "perfect" routine. You'll learn to redefine your relationship with clutter, embrace the **"good enough" mindset**, and harness the **power of small wins**. This is a chapter about unlearning old, shaming habits and embracing a compassionate, realistic perspective. We will lay the groundwork for a routine that works *with* your fluctuating energy levels, not against them.
- **Pillar 2: Mastering Routines and Habit Formation.** With the right mindset in place, we'll dive into the practical application of building routines. You'll learn how to implement a **Morning Reset** to start your day with intention, an **Evening Routine** to calm your mind and prepare for the next day, and a **Weekend Deep Dive** that transforms overwhelming tasks into manageable projects. We'll use concepts like **micro-habits** and **habit stacking** to build these routines with minimal effort.
- **Pillar 3: Decluttering and Organizing Made Easy.** Decluttering can feel like an impossible task, but it doesn't have to be. We'll introduce you to a simple, guilt-free method for getting started. You'll learn to identify and conquer your personal **"chaos hotspots,"** using the **"Keep, Toss, Donate"** method to make swift, confident decisions. This chapter is about creating a functional, peaceful home without having to get rid of everything you own.

- **Pillar 4: The Cleaning Toolkit and Time Management.** We'll shift our focus from organizing to cleaning, but with a twist. You'll learn how to build a simple, effective **"cleaning toolkit"** that is always at the ready. We'll also explore **time-management hacks** and **gamification techniques** like the **"Beat the Clock"** method that turn tedious chores into fun, engaging challenges. This is about making chores less of a burden and more of a game you can win.
- **Pillar 5: Staying Consistent and Bouncing Back.** This is the most critical chapter of the book. Consistency is the ultimate goal, but for the ADHD brain, it can feel impossible. You'll learn the **"Don't Break the Chain"** method to build momentum and the **"Art of the Rebound"** to get back on track without judgment. This chapter is about building a system that is resilient enough to handle the inevitable moments when life gets in the way.

A Note on Neurodiversity

Neurodiversity is the idea that differences in brain function are just that, differences, and not deficits. Your ADHD brain is a powerful engine with incredible potential. It is creative, energetic, empathetic, and often capable of intense, focused problem-solving. This book isn't about "fixing" your ADHD; it's about empowering you to navigate life's challenges with confidence and **self-compassion**. The strategies you'll find here are designed to work for you, not against you. They are about creating a sense of peace and control without sacrificing who you are.

We will not talk about your brain as being "broken." Instead, we will talk about its unique wiring and how to build a life that is perfectly suited to it. Think of your ADHD brain not as a faulty machine, but as a high-performance sports car with a unique set of controls. You wouldn't try to drive a sports car like a family sedan. Similarly, you shouldn't try to force your brain into a neurotypical mold. This book will give you the manual for that sports car—the tools and the understanding to drive it with skill and confidence.

The Power of Self-Compassion

This entire book is built on a foundation of **self-compassion**. We will not talk about "shoulds" or "failures." We will talk about **learning opportunities** and **systems that don't fit**. The voice in your head that tells you you're not good enough is a powerful enemy of progress. The most important tool you will learn is how to silence that voice with kindness.

Self-compassion is not an excuse for inaction; it is the engine for sustainable change. When you fall off the wagon, self-compassion is the voice that says, "It's okay, let's try again tomorrow," instead of "You've ruined everything." This single shift in perspective is often the difference between a temporary slip-up and a permanent derailment. It is the core principle that will allow you to build a life that is not just organized, but also forgiving and kind.

To All Readers

While this book is titled "ADHD Organization and Cleaning 5-in-1," the principles and strategies within are valuable for anyone seeking to bring more order and calm into their life. The challenges of motivation, task initiation, and maintaining routines are universal human experiences, even if they are more pronounced for those with ADHD.

- **For the student** struggling to manage their assignments and keep their dorm room tidy.
- **For the professional** who feels overwhelmed by a mountain of emails and a cluttered desk.
- **For the parent** who wants to create a more peaceful home for their family.

This book is for you. Inclusivity is at the heart of this book, and the goal is to provide a guide that is welcoming and helpful to all. The strategies are designed to be accessible and low-friction, because we believe that the best systems are the ones that are easy to use.

So, let's begin this journey. Let's redefine what it means to be organized, and create a space and a life that truly works for you. This isn't a race to the finish line; it's a marathon of small, intentional steps. Your organized future is not a destination to be reached, but a life to be lived. And it begins right now.

BOOK ONE

THE FOUNDATIONS OF A FLEXIBLE ROUTINE

CHAPTER 1

FROM OVERWHELMED TO EMPOWERED
REDEFINING YOUR RELATIONSHIP WITH CLUTTER SO IT NO LONGER CONTROLS YOU.

For many with ADHD, clutter isn't just a mess; it's a source of shame, anxiety, and overwhelm. We look at a disorganized space and see a reflection of our own perceived failures. The endless piles of clothes, the stacks of mail, the overflowing countertops—each item feels like a judgment. The constant visual noise creates a persistent cognitive burden, much like having a dozen browser tabs open in your mind at all times. It's an energy drain that makes it harder to focus, think clearly, and feel at peace in your own home.

What if we could change that narrative? This chapter is about shifting your perspective. Instead of viewing clutter as a moral failing, let's see it as a puzzle to be solved. Let's redefine our relationship with our things and our space.

The Problem with "Getting Rid of Everything"

Conventional wisdom often suggests ruthless decluttering, throwing out everything that doesn't "spark joy" or serve an immediate purpose. For the ADHD brain, this can be a recipe for disaster. **Decision fatigue** is a real and powerful force. Faced with a mountain of choices about what to keep and what to discard, many of us become paralyzed and abandon the task entirely. The result? The clutter remains, and the feeling of failure intensifies. For a brain that already struggles with executive functions like prioritization and sustained attention, a task that demands hundreds of micro-decisions is a system designed to fail.

The first step isn't to get rid of things; it's to understand them. What purpose do these items serve, even if they're not in their "right" place? The stack of books on your nightstand might be a reminder of your passion for reading. The pile of mail could be a sign that you're an active, engaged person with a lot going on. Acknowledging this can lessen the shame and allow you to approach the task with a clearer mind. The goal is to move past the judgment and see the objects for what they are.

The Power of Small Shifts

Instead of a complete overhaul, we'll start with small, manageable shifts. The goal is to move from being overwhelmed by your space to feeling in control of it. We'll introduce a new vocabulary and a new mindset.

- **From "Mess" to "Opportunity":** Every cluttered surface is an opportunity to create a system that works for you. Instead of a daunting mountain, you see a series of small, solvable problems.
- **From "Should" to "Could":** Instead of "I *should* clean this room," try "I *could* spend ten minutes on this one corner." This simple word change lowers the pressure and makes the task feel optional, which can make it easier to start.
- **From "All at Once" to "One at a Time":** Focus on a single item, a single drawer, or a single surface. This breaks the cycle of overwhelm and allows you to build momentum. This is the core of **micro-decluttering**, a powerful technique that delivers a quick win and a small dose of dopamine, encouraging you to continue.

By redefining your relationship with clutter, you're healing your mindset. You're acknowledging that your brain works differently, and that's okay. You're giving yourself permission to find a new, more compassionate way forward. You are taking back control, one small shift at a time.

CHAPTER 2

THE MYTH OF "NORMAL" & THE POWER OF "ENOUGH": HOW PROGRESS BEATS PERFECTION EVERY TIME.

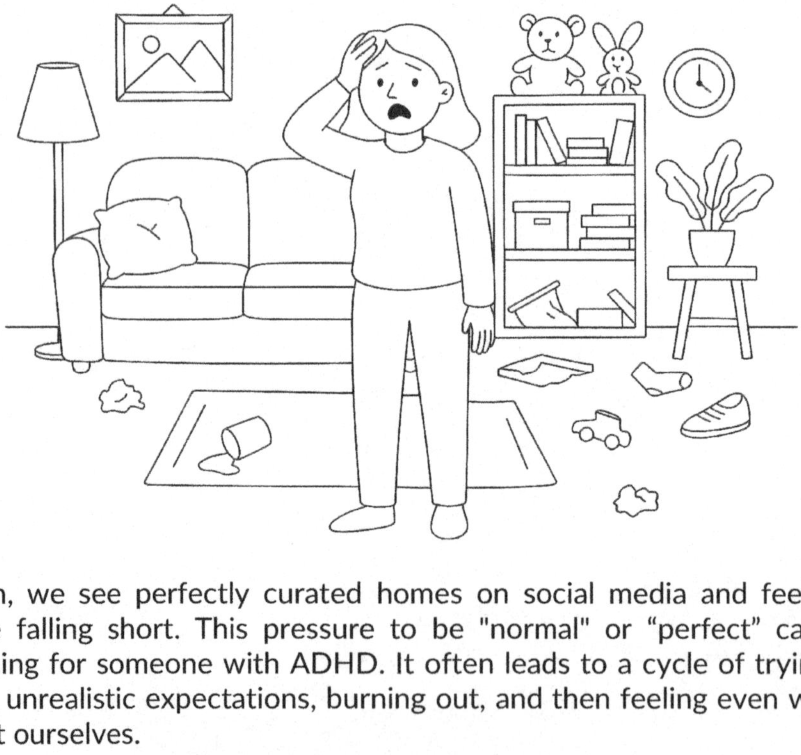

Often, we see perfectly curated homes on social media and feel like we're falling short. This pressure to be "normal" or "perfect" can be crushing for someone with ADHD. It often leads to a cycle of trying to meet unrealistic expectations, burning out, and then feeling even worse about ourselves.

This chapter is a permission slip to embrace imperfection. It's about letting go of the myth of normal and finding the power in "enough." The constant pressure to meet an impossible standard of "normal" is a self-defeating game. "Normal" for a neurotypical person might involve a structured, linear approach to tasks, but for the ADHD brain, that path is often a source of frustration, not success. By shedding the expectation of conforming to a norm that doesn't fit, you can begin to build a system that works with your brain, not against it.

Progress Over Perfection

The idea of "**progress over perfection**" is a cornerstone of a flexible routine. For the ADHD brain, perfectionism is often a form of procrastination. We often don't start a task because we're afraid we can't do it perfectly, so we don't do it at all. The goal isn't to have a spotless, show-ready home every single day. The goal is to make small, consistent improvements that make your life easier and less stressful. This is about embracing the messy, incremental nature of real life.

Think of it like a game: you're not aiming for a perfect score on the first try. You're simply trying to get to the next level. This mindset shift is crucial. It gives you permission to make mistakes, to have a bad day, and to keep going anyway. It's the difference between seeing a day without cleaning as a total failure and seeing it as a temporary pause.

Here are a few examples of what "good enough" looks like in practice:

- **A "Good Enough" Kitchen:** Your kitchen doesn't have to look like a magazine cover. If the counters are clear enough to prepare a meal and the dishes are done enough to not attract pests, that's a win.
- **A "Functional" Closet:** Instead of a color-coded, perfectly folded closet, aim for one where you can find what you need without a search party.
- **A "Manageable" Routine:** A routine that you can stick to 80% of the time is far more valuable than a "perfect" routine you abandon after a week.

This approach acknowledges that life is dynamic and that a rigid routine will inevitably fail. A flexible routine, however, can bend without breaking.

The Power of "Enough"

Knowing what "**enough**" looks like is a superpower for the ADHD brain. It prevents the all-or-nothing thinking that often derails our efforts. When you can define what "enough" means for a specific task, you can complete it and move on without the pressure of having to make it flawless. This is a powerful tool against the "I'll just do it all later" mentality. It provides a clear finish line, which is essential for a brain that struggles with sustaining attention on a single task.

For example, "enough" might mean:

- Doing laundry is "enough" when you have clean clothes to wear for the week, not when every last sock is folded and put away.
- A clean living room is "enough" when the floor is clear of obstacles and you have a comfortable place to sit, not when the couch cushions are perfectly fluffed.

This chapter is about giving yourself grace. Your brain is wired for creativity, quick thinking, and dynamic problem-solving. It's not wired for the monotonous, rigid systems that society often promotes. By embracing "enough," you're not lowering your standards—you're setting **realistic ones that allow you to thrive**.

This is not a license to give up; it's a license to succeed on your own terms. It's a fundamental shift from a mindset of self-criticism to one of self-compassion. The goal is to create a peaceful, functional life, not a perfectly staged one. This approach honors your unique strengths and acknowledges your challenges without judgment. When you can let go of the pressure to be "normal," you can start living a life that is authentically yours. You are enough, and so is your effort.

CHAPTER 3

THE 10-MINUTE TIDY: SMALL, ADHD-FRIENDLY WINS THAT CREATE BIG MOMENTUM.

The greatest enemy of an organized life is **overwhelm**. When a task seems too big, our brains tend to shut down, and we do nothing at all. This phenomenon is particularly acute for the ADHD brain, which struggles with task initiation and prioritization. A large, unstructured task like "clean the living room" is a perfect trigger for analysis paralysis. The key to breaking this cycle is to start small. This chapter is dedicated to the power of tiny, achievable actions that build momentum and make a noticeable difference without triggering decision fatigue.

The 10-Minute Tidy

This is a simple, yet profoundly effective, strategy. The goal is to bypass the internal debate and just start. Set a timer for 10 minutes and focus on a single, small area. The rules are simple and designed to remove mental roadblocks:

- **Don't plan; just start.** Pick a surface (a countertop, a coffee table, a section of the floor) and begin putting things away. The act of starting, even without a perfect plan, is the most critical step.
- **Focus on "home."** Put items where they belong. If an item doesn't have a home, don't worry about it for now. Just put it in a temporary "to-sort" bin. This single rule prevents you from getting bogged down in the minutiae of where to store something, allowing you to maintain focus on the task at hand.
- **Stop when the timer goes off.** When the ten minutes are up, you're done. No matter how much you've accomplished, you can walk away with a win. The hard stop provides a sense of closure and prevents a 10-minute tidy from spiraling into an exhaustive, multi-hour ordeal.

The genius of this method is that it bypasses the planning phase, which is often a major roadblock for the ADHD brain. The difficulty with the planning phase of a task for those with ADHD is rooted in the brain's executive functions. The prefrontal cortex (PFC), the part of the brain responsible for these functions, is crucial for skills like:

- **Task initiation:** The ability to start a task.
- **Planning and prioritization:** Breaking down a large task into manageable steps and deciding which to do first.
- **Working memory:** Holding and manipulating information in your mind.

In the ADHD brain, there is a **dysregulation of dopamine and norepinephrine** in the PFC. These neurotransmitters are essential for communication between brain cells and are directly involved in motivation, reward, and attention. When a task requires significant planning, the PFC needs a lot of dopamine to function effectively. A large, unstructured task like "clean the living room" demands a high level of executive function, but the ADHD brain struggles to produce the necessary dopamine to activate this process. This results in **analysis paralysis**—a state where the brain is overwhelmed by the number of steps required and never sends the signal to start.

How the Method Works

The "10-minute tidy" works because it circumvents this neurobiological roadblock. Instead of relying on a high-demand planning process, it turns the task into a low-demand, immediate action.

1. **Reduces Cognitive Load:** By setting a short timer and focusing on a single, small area, the method dramatically reduces the cognitive load on the PFC. The brain doesn't have to plan a whole-room cleaning; it just has to focus on one simple instruction: "tidy for 10 minutes."
2. **Triggers Action, Not Planning:** The simplicity of the instruction moves the task from the realm of complex executive function to the realm of simple habit formation. The act of setting a timer serves as a powerful external cue that overrides the internal struggle to initiate.
3. **Provides an Immediate Reward:** The quick, visible progress made in just 10 minutes provides a fast dopamine hit, which is a powerful motivator for the ADHD brain. This positive feedback loop makes it much easier to start the task again next time, slowly building a new, more effective neural pathway.

In short, the method doesn't try to "fix" the brain's challenges with planning; it simply finds a brilliant way to go around them.

Other Small Wins

The 10-minute tidy is just one example. There are countless other small, manageable steps you can integrate into your day to build a habit of proactive organization:

- **The "One-Thing" Rule:** Before leaving a room, find one thing to put away. It can be a mug, a book, a stray sock. Just one thing. This is a subtle yet powerful trick that turns a mindless transition into a moment of intentionality, preventing small messes from accumulating into large ones.
- **The "Micro-Clean":** While waiting for your coffee to brew or a pot to boil, wipe down a small section of the counter. These short, otherwise "dead" moments in your day can be repurposed for a small, productive task.
- **The "Two-Minute Rule":** If a task takes less than two minutes to complete, do it immediately. This could be putting a dish in the dishwasher, responding to a quick email, or taking out a small bag of trash. This rule is a direct counter to procrastination, as it leverages the principle that it takes more mental energy to put off a small task than it does to simply do it.

- **The "Landing Strip Reset":** Before bed, take just two minutes to clear your main "landing strip", the entry table, kitchen counter, or coffee table where things tend to pile up. This ensures you wake up to a clear, calm space, which sets a positive tone for the entire day.

These small wins may seem insignificant on their own, but their cumulative effect is profound. They build confidence, establish new neural pathways, and, most importantly, show you that you are capable of creating order in your life. By celebrating these small victories, you're retraining your brain to associate cleaning and organizing with a sense of accomplishment, not with dread or overwhelm.

CHAPTER 4

WHY A CLEAN SPACE CALMS YOUR BRAIN

THE NEURO-PSYCHOLOGY BEHIND YOUR ENVIRONMENT AND FOCUS.

Our brains are constantly processing information from our environment. For the ADHD brain, this can be an overwhelming flood of sensory input. A cluttered space isn't just visually unappealing; it's a **cognitive drain**. This chapter explores the psychological link between your physical environment and your mental state, revealing how a cleaner, more organized space can lead to a calmer, more focused mind.

The Cognitive Load of Clutter

Every object in your field of vision demands a tiny amount of your brain's attention. A stack of papers on a table, a pile of clothes on a chair, a jumble of items on a counter, each is a silent distraction. For a brain that already struggles with filtering out irrelevant stimuli, this creates a significant cognitive load. The prefrontal cortex (PFC), the brain's executive control center, is responsible for tasks like filtering out distractions and sustaining attention. Research shows that in the ADHD brain, the PFC can have reduced activity and dysregulation of key neurotransmitters, making this filtering process much more difficult.

A cluttered environment essentially bombards the brain with a constant stream of visual data that it cannot easily ignore. It's like a computer with dozens of unnecessary programs running in the background, consuming valuable processing power. This persistent visual noise forces the brain to constantly make micro-decisions: "What is that item? Where should it be? Do I need to deal with it?" This perpetual state of low-grade mental effort leads to **decision fatigue** and, eventually, a feeling of being completely overwhelmed. A clean and organized space, by contrast, reduces this cognitive load. It provides a sense of visual calm, allowing your brain to allocate its limited resources to what's truly important. It's not about an empty room, but about creating a functional, peaceful environment where your mind can finally rest and focus.

The Link Between Order and Emotion

The connection between your physical surroundings and your emotional state is a well-documented psychological phenomenon. For the ADHD brain, a tidy space can have a direct and positive impact on your emotions and motivation. The act of cleaning or organizing, even in small doses, can be a powerful form of mindfulness. It grounds you in the present moment and gives you a tangible sense of control over your immediate surroundings. This feeling of control is particularly important for people with ADHD who often feel a lack of control over their thoughts, impulses, and routines.

Furthermore, a messy environment is a potent source of stress. Studies have shown a correlation between high levels of household clutter and elevated **cortisol** levels, the body's primary stress hormone. A cluttered space is a constant, physical reminder of uncompleted tasks and disorganized thoughts, which can trigger a continuous, low-grade stress response.

The Brain's Need for a Predictive Environment

Beyond just visual clutter, the brain's need for order is deeply tied to its desire for predictability. The lack of a dedicated "home" for an object creates a constant need for the brain to categorize and remember where things are. This is another significant source of cognitive load. An organized space is one that is predictable; every item has a place, and you don't have to expend mental energy searching for your keys or wallet. This predictability frees up your working memory for creative thought and problem-solving. It also reduces "future anxiety", the dread of a task you know you have to do but haven't started.

CHAPTER 5

SYSTEMS BUILT FOR YOU: CREATING A CUSTOM APPROACH THAT WORKS WITH YOUR BRAIN, NOT AGAINST IT.

Traditional organization advice often fails the ADHD community because it's built on a foundation of rigid rules and systems that demand a level of sustained focus and routine that many of us simply don't have. This final chapter of Book 1 is about rejecting that rigid rulebook and empowering you to build a custom-built system that works with your unique brain.

From "Should" to "What If?"

Instead of asking, "What should a clean home look like?" start asking, "What if I organized my life in a way that feels natural to me?" This is about experimenting and finding what works.

- What if I didn't fold my clothes perfectly, but instead created a simple "toss and go" system for my drawers?
- What if I didn't file every piece of paper, but instead created a single "action" box for everything that needs my attention?
- What if my daily routine isn't the same every day, but instead I have a flexible set of micro-habits that I can adapt to my energy levels?

Custom-Building Your Tools

Your organizational system should be a reflection of you, not a reflection of a Pinterest board. Think about what your brain needs to function well.

- **Out of Sight, Out of Mind? Or Out of Mind, Out of Sight?** Some people with ADHD need to have things out where they can see them. For others, visual clutter is a huge distraction. Figure out which one you are and design your storage accordingly.
- **Use Visual Cues:** Use clear containers, labels with pictures, and open shelving to make it easy for your brain to see where things belong.
- **Embrace Your Strengths:** Use your hyperfocus to do a deep-clean on a specific day of the month. Use your creativity to come up with new, fun ways to organize.

CHAPTER 6

ENERGY MAPPING: ORGANIZING AROUND YOUR NATURAL RHYTHMS

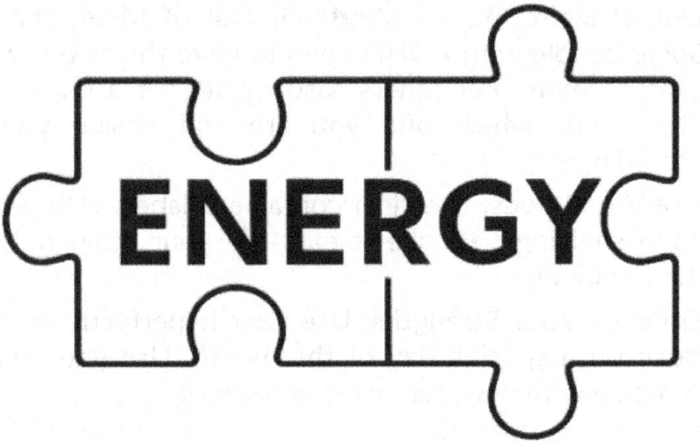

The ADHD Energy Puzzle

If you live with ADHD, you already know this: your energy levels don't run in neat, predictable lines. Some days, you wake up brimming with enthusiasm and dive headfirst into projects you've been putting off for months. Other days, even brushing your teeth feels like scaling a mountain. This inconsistency is not laziness or lack of discipline, it's neurobiology. The ADHD brain processes dopamine differently, which affects not only focus but also motivation and energy regulation.

Understanding your unique energy rhythms is like finding a secret map of your brain. Instead of pushing against your dips or wasting your peaks, you can align your tasks with your natural flow. That's what **energy mapping** is about: noticing when you're sharp, sluggish, restless, or calm, and using that awareness to work *with* your brain, not against it.

Why Energy Matters More Than Time

Most productivity systems tell you to "manage your time." For ADHD, time is slippery. You may intend to clean for "just 15 minutes" but suddenly two hours have vanished, or you may underestimate a task so much that it snowballs into overwhelm.

But energy? Energy is tangible. You *feel* it. You know the difference between the morning when your brain is buzzing with ideas versus the afternoon crash where you can't remember what you walked into the room for.

Managing energy instead of time is a game-changer because:

- **Energy is the fuel**: If the tank is empty, no amount of scheduling will move you forward.
- **Energy impacts focus**: Higher energy often means better executive functioning.
- **Energy determines sustainability**: Matching tasks to your natural rhythm reduces burnout.

By learning to observe your patterns, you stop asking, *"What should I be doing at 3 PM?"* and start asking, *"What kind of energy do I have right now, and what tasks fit that?"*

Step 1: Discover Your Energy Peaks and Valleys

Energy mapping starts with awareness. For one week, try this simple exercise:

1. **Create an "Energy Journal".** Divide the day into blocks (morning, mid-morning, afternoon, evening, night).
2. **Rate your energy.** Use a simple 1–5 scale (1 = drained, 5 = high-energy)
3. **Notice the patterns.** Are mornings clear but afternoons foggy? Do you get a second wind at night?

Over time, you'll see trends. Maybe you consistently struggle with focus after lunch but come alive around 7 PM. Or maybe your best mental clarity is in the early morning before distractions pile up.

This awareness alone can transform your routines. Instead of forcing yourself into "morning productivity" because everyone says it's best, you learn to design your schedule around *your* truth.

Step 2: Assign "Energy-Friendly" Tasks

Once you've mapped your rhythms, match them with the right type of tasks. Think of your energy like a spectrum:

- **High-Energy / High-Focus Times:**
  - Decluttering sessions
  - Paying bills or handling paperwork
  - Tackling chaos hotspots (kitchen, closet, garage)
  - Deep-cleaning tasks that require sustained attention
- **Medium-Energy / Moderate-Focus Times:**
  - Tidying (10-minute resets)
  - Folding laundry
  - Prepping meals
  - Doing "batch tasks" like responding to emails
- **Low-Energy / Low-Focus Times:**
  - Brain dumps
  - Listening to podcasts while wiping counters
  - Sorting small items into bins
  - Reflection or light planning for the next day

The point isn't to always be productive, it's to **choose wisely**. If you try to do your taxes during a low-energy crash, you'll get stuck and feel frustrated. But if you pair that same slump with a mindless task like folding towels, you'll keep momentum without burning out.

Step 3: Build "Energy Anchors"

Energy naturally fluctuates, but you can create anchors that help stabilize your flow:

- **Hydration & Snacks:** The ADHD brain is extra sensitive to dips in blood sugar. Keep protein-rich snacks nearby.
- **Movement Breaks:** Physical activity boosts dopamine and norepinephrine, both critical for focus. A 5-minute walk can reset a slump.
- **Sensory Cues:** Music, scents (peppermint or citrus), or even lighting changes can refresh your energy.
- **Mini Routines:** Rituals like the "5-Minute Reset" after lunch can act as anchors, signaling your brain it's time to shift gears.

These don't eliminate energy dips, but they soften the crash and give you reliable tools to re-engage.

Step 4: Respect the ADHD "Second Wind"

Many with ADHD experience bursts of energy late at night, what some call the "ADHD second wind". While the world says you should be winding down, your brain suddenly wants to reorganize the bookshelf or deep-clean the fridge.

Instead of fighting this, learn to channel it responsibly:

- Use it for **quiet tasks** (organizing digital files, folding laundry, prepping for tomorrow).
- Protect your sleep by setting a **wind-down timer**, an alarm that signals "wrap up in 20 minutes."
- Keep a "night box" or tray: a place where you can toss items you want to handle tomorrow instead of spiraling into a midnight project.

This honors your rhythm without letting it sabotage your rest.

Step 5: Plan with "Flexible Blocks"

Forget rigid hour-by-hour scheduling. Use flexible blocks based on energy:

- **Morning Boost Block (High Energy):** Big projects, paperwork, creative work.
- **Afternoon Slump Block (Low/Medium Energy):** Tidying, chores, low-brain tasks.
- **Evening Reset Block (Medium Energy):** Launchpad prep, quick cleanup, self-care.
- **Late-Night Burst Block (Optional High Energy):** Quiet, contained projects.

By labeling blocks by energy instead of time, you give yourself grace and freedom. If your "boost" shows up later than expected, you can shift tasks accordingly without guilt.

ADHD-Friendly Hacks for Energy Management

1. **Use Visual Energy Trackers:** Color-coded stickers or charts to mark high/low energy times each day.
2. **Task-Swap Lists:** Keep two lists—"high-focus" tasks and "low-focus" tasks. Choose based on your current state.
3. **Pair Energy with Rewards:** After using a peak to tackle something hard, reward yourself immediately (snack, 5 minutes scrolling, or a victory dance).

4. **Micro-Rest Stations:** Set up cozy nooks with blankets, water, and low-stim activities so recovery doesn't become avoidance.

Common Pitfalls (and Fixes)

- **Pitfall:** "I planned to do paperwork in my high-energy block, but I wasted it scrolling."
    - **Fix:** Remove distractions in advance; pair paperwork with a motivating playlist or co-working session.
- **Pitfall:** "I get frustrated when my energy map doesn't match every day."
    - **Fix:** Remember, it's a *map*, not a guarantee. Energy shifts with sleep, stress, and hormones. The goal is awareness, not control.
- **Pitfall:** "I try to force big tasks into my low-energy slumps."
    - **Fix:** Redefine "success." Use slumps for resets, brain dumps, or light chores instead of expecting peak performance.

Real-Life Example: Emily's Laundry Dilemma

Emily dreaded laundry. By the time she faced the overflowing basket, she was always in her 3 PM slump. She'd start folding, lose steam, and leave half-finished piles everywhere.

Through energy mapping, she discovered her **highest energy was 9–11 AM**. So instead of saving laundry for later, she made it her **morning focus task** twice a week. By pairing folding with an upbeat playlist, she finished loads with ease. For her **slump block**, she reassigned easier tasks like matching socks or putting folded clothes away.

The result? A routine that fit her rhythms, not one that fought against them.

CHAPTER 7

ENVIRONMENTAL ANCHORS
DESIGNING SPACES THAT CUE ACTION

Why Your Environment Matters More Than You Think

Living with ADHD often feels like you're carrying your to-do list in your head ... but the list has holes in it, and items keep falling out. You intend to take out the recycling, but by the time you pass the kitchen bin, your brain has already jumped to something else. You want to clean your desk, but your mind gets hijacked by the pile of unopened mail.

The truth is, your environment is a *partner*. Every object around you sends a message, consciously or unconsciously. The trick is to design your spaces so they **cue the behaviors you want** instead of constantly derailing you. This is what I call **environmental anchors**: intentional, visible, and supportive cues in your space that make routines easier to start and habits easier to keep.

The Science of Environmental Cues

ADHD brains struggle with working memory and self-directed recall. In plain language: "out of sight, out of mind" is brutally real. If something isn't right in front of you, it might as well not exist. That's why bills get forgotten once tucked in a drawer, why half-finished laundry sits in the machine until it smells, and why a planner buried in your bag never gets used.

Research on habit formation shows that **environmental design** often has a bigger impact than willpower. Psychologist Kurt Lewin described behavior as a function of both the person *and* the environment. Change the environment, and the behavior often follows.

For ADHD, this means we need to make **the desired action the easiest, most obvious choice**, and remove friction for starting. Environmental anchors reduce the reliance on memory and motivation and instead use **visual and physical prompts** to guide behavior.

Step 1: Identify Your "Forgetting Zones"

Before you start adding anchors, notice where your environment is currently *working against you*. Ask yourself:

- Where do I often forget steps in routines?
- Which spaces feel overwhelming or chaotic?
- Where does clutter pile up, no matter how often I tidy?
- What do I avoid doing because it feels too far away, too hidden, or too complicated?

These are the prime spots for anchors. For example:

- If shoes pile by the door, maybe your current shoe storage is too hidden or inconvenient.
- If you constantly forget to take vitamins, maybe they're stuck in a closed cupboard.
- If mail stacks up unopened, maybe you don't have a landing spot for it.

Awareness is the first step to creating better support.

Step 2: Make the Invisible Visible

ADHD-friendly environments thrive on **visibility**. When you can see it, you remember it. When you hide it, it disappears.

Examples of visibility anchors:

- Clear bins instead of opaque boxes.
- Hooks instead of drawers (for keys, bags, coats).
- Open shelving for frequently used items.
- Labels, even if obvious, so your brain doesn't have to think.

Think of visibility as removing the mental step of recall. Instead of your brain needing to remember "*where did I put my scissors?*", the scissors live in a jar on your desk, easy to spot.

Step 3: Create "Behavior Triggers"

The most powerful anchors are ones that directly cue the action you want.

- **Water Cue:** Keep a water bottle on your desk to trigger hydration.
- **Launchpad Cue:** Place your packed bag, shoes, and keys by the door so leaving the house feels automatic.
- **Cleaning Cue:** Store wipes in every room so a quick counter swipe doesn't require a trip to the supply closet.
- **Bedtime Cue:** Place your book and lamp within arm's reach to make reading instead of scrolling the default.

These are not just convenience hacks. They're **friction removers**, each anchor lowers the effort needed to start the action.

Step 4: Shrink the Distance

One of the biggest ADHD roadblocks is "activation energy": the invisible effort it takes to *start*. If supplies are far away, packed too tightly, or hidden in containers, your brain is more likely to give up.

Anchors reduce activation energy by shrinking the distance between the impulse and the action:

- Keep laundry baskets in multiple rooms.
- Place trash bins wherever clutter tends to collect.
- Have cleaning kits in the bathroom, kitchen, and living room.
- Store art supplies on the table if you want to draw more often.

Remember: the easier it is to start, the more likely it is you'll follow through.

Step 5: Use Color and Contrast

The ADHD brain responds strongly to novelty and stimulation. You can use **color and contrast** as anchors:

- Brightly colored bins for categories (blue = tech cords, red = first aid).
- A neon sticky note on the front door as a reminder to grab lunch.
- A cheerful rug in the entryway to visually anchor the "drop zone."
- Contrasting folders so paperwork categories are instantly recognizable.

Visual pop acts like a mental spotlight, directing your attention where it's needed most.

Step 6: Anchor Habits to Spaces

Every room can have a purpose, and your environment can remind you of it.

- **Kitchen:** Clear counters = meal prep anchor. Put a fruit bowl front-and-center.
- **Living Room:** Remote stored in a tray = cue to reset space after TV time.
- **Bedroom:** Hamper near the bed = clothes don't end up on the floor.
- **Bathroom:** Skincare products laid out in order = visual routine guide.

The point is not to make spaces picture-perfect, but to **make them functional prompts** for the habits you care about.

ADHD-Friendly Environmental Hacks

1. **Double Up:** Keep duplicates of frequently used items (scissors, chargers, cleaning wipes) in multiple locations. It's cheaper than the stress of losing them.
2. **Drop Zones Everywhere:** Trays, baskets, or hooks where items naturally land. Better to contain than constantly fight habits.
3. **See-Through Storage:** Use transparent containers so nothing becomes "invisible clutter."
4. **Label Everything:** Even if it feels silly, labels reinforce memory. "Pens" on the pen jar. "Snacks" on the pantry bin.
5. **Portable Kits:** A cleaning caddy, art kit, or office box that can move room-to-room keeps tasks flexible.

Common Pitfalls (and Fixes)

- **Pitfall:** "I set up anchors, but now it just feels like clutter."
  - **Fix:** Anchors must be intentional. Choose visible *but limited* items. Rotate or reset monthly.
- **Pitfall:** "I forget the anchor exists after a while."
  - **Fix:** Refresh anchors by changing their color, position, or style to re-capture attention.
- **Pitfall:** "My family doesn't use the anchors."
  - **Fix:** Involve them in setup. If they help design the drop zone or choose the bin colors, they're more likely to engage.

Real-Life Example: Jason's Entryway Chaos

Jason's mornings were a mess. Every day, he lost precious minutes searching for his keys, wallet, or work badge. He'd leave the house frazzled, often forgetting something important.

His fix was an **entryway anchor system**: a tray for wallet and keys, a hook for the badge, and a basket for outgoing mail. He even added a sticky note on the door that read: "Keys. Wallet. Badge."

Within a week, his mornings felt calmer. The anchor system didn't change his ADHD, it changed his environment so his ADHD brain didn't have to remember everything.

Step 7: Refresh Regularly

ADHD brains crave novelty. Anchors that work today may fade into the background in a few months. That's normal.

To keep them effective:

- Rotate bins or swap their colors.
- Move anchors slightly to make them noticeable again.
- Do a quick monthly reset of your hotspots (entryway, desk, kitchen counter).

Think of it as *updating your environment to keep up with your brain.*

Closing Thought

Environmental anchors aren't about perfection. They're about **partnership**—letting your space support your brain instead of sabotaging it. By turning your environment into a silent coach, you lower the mental load, reduce forgotten steps, and make routines feel almost automatic.

You don't have to fight your ADHD in the abstract. You can build homes, systems, and cues that quietly whisper: *"Do this next."* And when your space is on your side, consistency becomes possible, not because you forced it, but because it's built right into the world around you.

Reflection Questions:

- *We've gone over a lot in these first few chapters, so if it feels a bit overwhelming, that's okay. Let's pause for a moment and reflect. Which one of the core principles from Book 1, redefining your relationship with clutter, embracing a "good enough" mindset, or the power of small wins, resonates with you the most, and why?*
- *Now, let's put it into practice. What is one specific, tiny change you can make today to begin building your own custom-built system? This could be a 10-minute tidy in one small area or using the two-minute rule for a single task.*
- *In the spirit of embracing a "good enough" mindset, what is one area of your home that you can stop striving for perfection in, and what would a "good enough" version of that space look like for you this week?*
- *Think about the concept of "cognitive load". What is one visual "chaos hotspot" in your home that you know is silently draining your mental energy? What is one single item you can remove or put away from that space to reduce that load?*
- *We discussed redefining our relationship with clutter from a "mess" to an "opportunity." What is one item you've been avoiding or feeling shame about that you can now look at as an opportunity to create a system that works for you?*

This chapter, and this entire book, is a toolkit for a journey of discovery. By giving yourself permission to be imperfect, to be flexible, and to be yourself, you are building a foundation for a life that is not just organized, but also authentic and joyful.

BOOK TWO

MASTERING ROUTINES AND HABIT FORMATION

CHAPTER 1

MORNINGS THAT WORK FOR YOUR BRAIN STARTING THE DAY WITH ENERGY AND FOCUS.

For many with ADHD, mornings can feel like a chaotic race against the clock. The brain fog, the forgotten items, the impulsive detours, it's a recipe for a stressful start to the day. This is a direct result of **executive dysfunction**, a core feature of ADHD that impairs the brain's ability to plan, prioritize, and initiate tasks. The prefrontal cortex (PFC), the brain's "command center" responsible for these skills, relies heavily on neurotransmitters like dopamine and norepinephrine. In the ADHD brain, the dysregulation of these chemicals makes it difficult for the PFC to function optimally, especially after a night of sleep when motivation and focus are at their lowest.

The purpose of a morning routine, therefore, isn't to create a rigid, military-style schedule. Instead, it's to build a predictable, supportive structure that acts as an **external brain**, reducing friction and freeing up mental energy for the day ahead. By automating low-effort habits, you bypass the need for constant, deliberate decision-making, which is a major source of morning stress. The goal is to move from a place of frantic reaction to one of intentional action.

Combatting Brain Fog

The feeling of "brain fog" is a common morning symptom of ADHD, characterized by a sluggish mind and difficulty concentrating. This sensation is directly linked to low levels of dopamine and sluggish blood flow to the brain upon waking. A simple solution is to get your body moving. Physical activity is one of the most effective and accessible ways to stimulate the brain.

Start with something simple that gets your body moving. This could be a five-minute stretch, a glass of water, or a short walk. The physical activity helps to increase blood flow to the brain, which in turn stimulates the release of key neurotransmitters. **Dopamine**, the "feel-good" and "motivation" chemical, gets a boost, as does **norepinephrine**, which helps with focus and arousal. This neurochemical kickstart is a proactive way to reduce brain fog and improve cognitive function before your day even begins.

Consider making these small movements part of your routine: a quick yoga flow, a few minutes of jumping jacks, or even just dancing to a favorite song while you get ready. The key is that the activity is low-effort and enjoyable enough that you'll actually do it. Pairing this with a glass of water also helps to rehydrate your brain and body, which have been without fluids all night.

Preventing Forgotten Items: The "Launchpad"

Forgetting keys, a wallet, or a packed lunch is a classic ADHD challenge, and it's deeply connected to issues with working memory and object permanence. The brain struggles to consistently hold onto the location of objects over time. When you're rushing in the morning, a forgotten item can lead to a frantic, last-minute search that completely derails your calm start.

The solution is to create a physical, non-negotiable external system: the **Launchpad**. This is a designated spot, a small table, a hook, a basket, near your front door where you place everything you need for the day (keys, wallet, phone, bag, lunch). By making this a habit the night before, you completely eliminate the frantic morning search. You are offloading the mental task of remembering where your things are to a reliable, physical system. This strategy works because it removes the reliance on an inconsistent internal system (your working memory) and replaces it with a simple, visual cue. When you wake up, everything is exactly where it should be.

Make it a part of your evening routine to place your items on the Launchpad before you wind down for the night. This is a simple, two-minute habit that pays dividends in reduced morning anxiety and a smoother transition out the door.

Simplifying Decisions

Every decision, no matter how small, depletes mental energy and contributes to **decision fatigue**. For the ADHD brain, which already has a limited supply of this energy, a morning full of choices can be incredibly draining. The act of choosing what to wear, what to eat, or what to do first is a silent burden on the brain's executive functions.

The key to a peaceful morning is to structure your routine so that you're making as few decisions as possible. This involves front-loading the decision-making process into the previous evening when you have less time pressure and more cognitive energy.

- **Lay Out Your Clothes:** A simple act like picking out your clothes the night before removes one major decision from your morning.
- **Pre-Pack Your Lunch:** Packing your lunch after dinner means you don't have to think about it in the morning, saving you time and mental energy.
- **Ready-to-Go Coffee:** Have your coffee machine pre-set and ready to brew with the press of a button.

The less you have to think about, the smoother your morning will be. This isn't about being a robot; it's about intentionally removing low-stakes decisions from a time when your brain is least equipped to handle them. This proactive approach allows you to conserve your precious mental resources for the more complex challenges and tasks that await you later in the day.

Remember, a routine doesn't have to be perfect. The goal is progress, not perfection. If you can only manage two or three of these steps on a given day, that's still a win. The consistency of these small wins will build a foundation for more peaceful, productive mornings and, ultimately, a more organized and less chaotic life.

CHAPTER 2

THE EVENING RESET: WAKING UP TO A HOME (AND MIND) THAT'S ALREADY READY.

Just as a morning routine sets you up for the day, an evening routine sets you up for a successful tomorrow. For many with ADHD, evenings can be a time of heightened distraction, where the mental energy used for executive functioning throughout the day is depleted. This leads to what some researchers call the **"rebound effect,"** where the brain, tired from a day of constant effort to stay on task, seeks immediate gratification and falls prey to distractions like social media, television, or impulsive projects. A simple task like putting away dishes can turn into an hour-long scroll through social media, leaving you feeling more disorganized and stressed than before.

An evening reset is a series of simple habits designed to bring a sense of closure to the day and proactively prepare your mind and space for the next one. It's a low-effort, high-impact routine that creates a crucial buffer between the chaos of the day and the restorative power of sleep. By engaging in these intentional actions, you are essentially telling your future self, "I've got you covered."

The "Five-Minute Tidy"

The first step in an evening reset is the **"Five-Minute Tidy."** This is a quick, concentrated burst of activity designed to combat the buildup of visual clutter that accumulates throughout the day. Set a timer for five minutes and quickly put away anything that's out of place in your main living areas. The rules are simple:

1. **Don't get sidetracked:** The goal is not a deep clean, but a quick surface reset.
2. **Focus on high-traffic areas:** Prioritize the kitchen counter, living room coffee table, or entryway. These are the spaces that will have the biggest impact on your morning mindset.
3. **Use the "home" principle:** Put items back where they belong, and don't get bogged down in finding new storage solutions.

The psychological power of this small habit is immense. Waking up to a clear, calm space, rather than a messy one, significantly reduces morning anxiety and decision fatigue. A cluttered environment acts as a constant, low-grade stressor, and eliminating it before bed ensures that your brain isn't starting the day in a state of overwhelm. It's an act of compassion for your future self, providing a sense of order before the day's challenges even begin.

The Launchpad Check

Building on the morning routine, the next crucial step is the **"Launchpad Check."** This simple act of preparation is one of the most powerful things you can do to reduce morning stress, which is often a direct result of the ADHD brain's challenges with working memory. After a long day, your brain's ability to hold onto key information is at its lowest. This is why a simple task like remembering your wallet can feel impossible in the morning rush.

The Launchpad, a designated spot near your front door, becomes a physical "external brain." During your evening reset, take a moment to place everything you'll need for the next day on this spot. This includes keys, wallet, phone, work bag, and anything else essential. By consistently doing this, you are offloading the mental burden of remembering these items from your working memory to a simple, visual, and physical system. This not only prevents the frantic morning search but also frees up mental energy for more important tasks.

The Mindful Transition

For many with ADHD, the end of the day is when our minds race the most. The brain, now without the structured stimulation of work or daily tasks, can get caught in a whirlwind of thoughts, worries, and to-do lists, making it difficult to fall asleep. This is because the **sympathetic nervous system** (the "fight or flight" response) is still active, and you need to engage the **parasympathetic nervous system** (the "rest and digest" response) to wind down.

The mindful transition is a series of calming activities that help to quiet your mind and signal to your brain that it's time to rest. This is not about being productive; it's about being intentional.

- **Journaling:** A quick brain dump of all the thoughts swirling in your head can be a powerful way to externalize worries and clear your mind.
- **Reading:** Picking up a physical book (not on a screen) for just 10-15 minutes can help to shift your focus away from the day's stressors.
- **Mindful Listening:** Listening to a calming podcast or a guided meditation can gently redirect your attention and soothe your nervous system.

This evening transition is an act of self-care that tells your brain it's okay to let go. By consistently preparing for the next day and intentionally winding down, you're not just organizing your home, you're organizing your peace of mind and investing in a more restorative night's sleep.

CHAPTER 3

WEEKEND POWER HOURS: TACKLING BIGGER TASKS WITHOUT THE BURNOUT.

The idea of tackling a "weekend deep dive" can sound exhausting, especially if you're already feeling overwhelmed. For the ADHD brain, a whole day dedicated to cleaning can be a trap. It's a task so big and unstructured that it often triggers **task paralysis**, where the sheer scale of the project prevents it from ever being started. This is due to executive function challenges, particularly with task initiation and the ability to maintain sustained attention. The brain looks at the monumental task, sees no clear starting or stopping point, and simply shuts down.

This chapter is about reframing the deep dive not as a marathon, but as a series of targeted sprints. It's a strategy for tackling large, overwhelming projects by breaking them into manageable, rewarding chunks. The goal is to make significant progress without burning out or abandoning the project entirely.

The Key to Success: Planning and Chunking

The key to a successful weekend deep dive is to proactively create a plan that works with your brain, not against it. This involves two core principles: **Themed Days** and **Time-Chunking**.

Themed Days Instead of a general "cleaning day," which is a recipe for decision fatigue, try a "Kitchen Day" or a "Bedroom Day." This simple act of pre-planning reduces the number of decisions you have to make on the day itself. When you wake up, you don't have to ask, "What should I clean first?" The answer is already decided. This focuses all your energy on a single area, allowing for a more streamlined and less overwhelming experience.

For example, a "Kitchen Day" could involve a series of smaller, themed sprints: "Pantry Organization," "Refrigerator Deep Clean," and "Countertop Declutter." By grouping similar tasks together, you minimize the mental switching costs and can build a productive rhythm.

Time-Chunking This is where you turn your deep dive from a marathon into a series of short, manageable sprints. The **Pomodoro Technique**, a well-known time-management method, is highly effective for the ADHD brain. The technique involves breaking work into 25-minute intervals, separated by short breaks. For a weekend deep dive, you can modify this slightly: break your deep dive into 20-30 minute sprints with built-in breaks.

- Use a timer to stay on task, and when the timer goes off, get up and do something completely different for 10-15 minutes. This honors your brain's need for novelty and helps to replenish your mental energy.
- The structured intervals provide a clear finish line for each task, which gives you a small, immediate sense of accomplishment and a crucial **dopamine hit**. This positive feedback loop is a powerful motivator for the ADHD brain.
- By taking a break, you are preventing the burnout that comes from prolonged focus. This ensures that you can sustain your effort over a longer period without losing momentum.

The Power of an Accountability Partner

Trying to tackle a big project alone can be a major source of procrastination. The ADHD brain thrives on external motivation and social engagement. Having an accountability partner can be a game-changer. The simple act of telling someone your plan, and knowing they'll check in on you, creates a powerful sense of obligation. This is rooted in social psychology, where the desire to not disappoint another person can be a stronger motivator than our own internal desires.

Ask a friend or family member to help you for a few hours, or simply ask them to check in on your progress. Having someone else involved can be a huge motivator.

- **Co-working:** If you have the option, ask a friend or family member to physically help you. The social aspect can make a tedious task feel more like a fun activity.
- **Virtual Check-ins:** If that's not possible, a simple text exchange can be a powerful tool. Let them know what you're working on, and have them send you a quick "How's it going?" text at the end of a sprint.

The All-or-Nothing Trap

It's crucial to remember the goal isn't to clean the entire house in one weekend. The goal is to make significant progress in one or two key areas. By reframing the deep dive as a series of manageable chunks with built-in breaks and support, you can make a weekend deep dive feel less like a chore and more like a productive, achievable project.

This approach directly counters the **all-or-nothing thinking** that so often derails the ADHD brain. The feeling of "I didn't finish everything, so I failed" is replaced with, "I completed my two sprints today, and that's a win." This focus on progress, not perfection, is the foundation for a sustainable, compassionate approach to organization. You're not fighting against your brain; you're working with it to create a system that allows you to succeed.

CHAPTER 4

THE "BRAIN DUMP" RESET: CLEARING MENTAL CLUTTER SO YOU CAN ACTUALLY RELAX.

Our brains are not designed to be filing cabinets. For those with ADHD, a brain full of to-do lists, ideas, and worries can feel like a crowded, noisy room. This constant internal chatter is a major source of anxiety and a significant barrier to focus. The "brain dump" is a simple yet revolutionary tool for capturing these mental fragments and clearing your mind. It's a proactive strategy to externalize your thoughts, which is a core skill for managing ADHD symptoms.

The concept is rooted in the neurobiology of **working memory**. Working memory is the system in the brain that holds and processes information needed to carry out complex cognitive tasks. For the ADHD brain, working memory is often a limited resource. Every uncompleted task, every looming worry, every fleeting idea consumes a portion of this limited capacity. It's like having too many programs running at once on a computer; everything slows down, and eventually, the system crashes. A brain dump is a way to close those mental tabs and free up your working memory for the task at hand.

How to Perform a Brain Dump

A brain dump is the process of writing down every thought, idea, and task that is swirling in your head. It's about externalizing, not organizing. The process is quick, unfiltered, and designed to minimize the cognitive effort required to start.

1. **Find a Dedicated Space:** The tool itself doesn't matter; the consistency does. Use a notebook, a blank document on your computer, or a notes app on your phone. Having a dedicated space ensures you always know where to go when you feel overwhelmed. This removes the decision of "where do I write this down?" and streamlines the process.
2. **Set a Timer:** Give yourself 5-10 minutes to write down everything that comes to mind. The time limit is crucial for the ADHD brain. It prevents you from getting bogged down in trying to make the dump perfect. It creates a sense of urgency that helps you overcome the initial inertia of starting.
3. **Don't Filter:** Write down everything, no matter how big or small. This could include tasks, worries, creative ideas, grocery lists, or things you need to remember to buy. The key is to suspend judgment and just let the thoughts flow from your brain to the page. There are no bad ideas or trivial worries in a brain dump. The goal is to get it out, not to evaluate it. This unfiltered approach is what truly allows you to clear your mind.
4. **Put It Away:** Once the timer goes off, close the notebook or minimize the window. The goal is to clear your mind, not to immediately start working on everything you wrote down. By closing the document, you are physically signaling to your brain that the information has been captured and it is now safe to forget about it. This is a powerful act of trust in your external system.

The Neuro-Psychological Benefits

The beauty of the brain dump is that it allows you to let go of a thought without having to act on it immediately. You know it's been captured, so your brain can stop looping it in the background. This frees up working memory and reduces the mental clutter that prevents you from focusing on the task at hand.

For the ADHD brain, which struggles with object permanence (the idea that things continue to exist even when they cannot be perceived), a brain dump provides a sense of certainty. When a thought is on the page, you can trust that it is "safe" and will be there when you need it. This reduces the low-grade anxiety of feeling like you might forget something important.

The act of writing is also a powerful tool for grounding the mind. The physical act of putting pen to paper can be a form of mindfulness, helping you to slow down and connect with your thoughts in a more deliberate way. It moves your thoughts from the abstract, chaotic space of your mind into a concrete, organized form on a page. This externalization is the first and most critical step toward bringing order to your internal world.

In summary, a brain dump is not just an organizational tool; it's a mental health practice. It's a way to give your overworked brain a break, to offload its burdens, and to create the mental space you need to focus, create, and live with less anxiety.

CHAPTER 5

HARNESSING HYPERFOCUS: TURNING YOUR ADHD SUPERPOWER INTO A DEEP-CLEANING TOOL.

Hyperfocus is one of the most powerful and misunderstood aspects of ADHD. It's the ability to lock onto a task with intense concentration, often for hours at a time, to the exclusion of everything else. While hyperfocus is often associated with playing video games or diving deep into a new hobby, it can be a superpower for organization and cleaning. This unique ability is a direct result of the ADHD brain's dopamine-seeking nature. When a task is novel, challenging, and engaging, it provides a powerful dopamine hit that allows for an extraordinary level of sustained attention. Instead of viewing hyperfocus as a flaw, this chapter is about learning to intentionally trigger and harness it to your advantage.

The Conditions for Hyperfocus

Hyperfocus is a phenomenon you can't force, but you can actively create the conditions that make it more likely to occur. It is often triggered by a combination of interest, challenge, and a sense of urgency. By intentionally cultivating these conditions, you can transform a daunting cleaning task into a rewarding project.

- **Interest:** Choose a task that is genuinely interesting to you. This might be organizing a collection, rearranging furniture, or tackling a complex digital filing system. The key is to find the angle that sparks curiosity. If you love history, maybe you organize your old family photos. If you're a tech enthusiast, perhaps you focus on re-wiring and organizing all the cables behind your entertainment center.
- **Challenge:** Turn the task into a game. Can you organize your entire closet in one hour? Can you make your pantry look like a professional grocery store in 45 minutes? By introducing a time limit or a specific, measurable goal, you're tapping into the brain's desire for a challenge. This activates the reward system, releasing dopamine and making the task more engaging.
- **Urgency:** Create a soft deadline to add a sense of importance. Tell a friend you're going to show them your organized closet in two hours. Having an external commitment, even a small one, provides the kind of social pressure that can be a powerful motivator for the ADHD brain.

The Activation Phase

Don't wait for hyperfocus to strike; actively seek it out. This is where the strategies from earlier chapters come into play, particularly the concept of lowering the barrier to entry. The biggest hurdle is often the activation energy required to start.

Start by eliminating all distractions. Put your phone in another room, turn off non-essential notifications, and turn on some music (without lyrics if they're distracting). Music is an incredibly powerful tool for the ADHD brain, as it can act as a form of "auditory scaffolding," providing a consistent external stimulus that helps to focus the mind and override the constant internal chatter.

Commit to just starting the task for five minutes. This small, non-threatening commitment is often enough to trigger the hyperfocus. The act of starting, even without a perfect plan, can quickly become an immersive experience. This is a crucial neuro-psychological trick: the initial effort is a small, low-risk investment that often pays off with a burst of high-reward, focused activity.

The Landing Pad and Post-Hyperfocus Care

The downside of hyperfocus is that when it ends, you can feel utterly exhausted and overwhelmed. The intense concentration required for a hyperfocused state can deplete key neurotransmitters like dopamine and serotonin, leading to a sudden "crash" or feeling of burnout. In this state, the mess you created in your wake can feel like a new, even more daunting problem.

To prepare for this, set up a **"landing pad"** for when your hyperfocus ends. This is a small, clear space, a box, a corner of a table, or a simple basket, where you can put down any tools, half-organized items, or general clutter. This simple act of pre-planning prevents the post-hyperfocus crash from creating a new mess. It gives you a safe, designated spot to drop everything without creating a new source of visual clutter. When you're ready, you can come back to it.

Furthermore, it's essential to plan for your recovery. After a deep hyperfocus session, your brain is exhausted.

- **Rehydrate and refuel:** You may have forgotten to eat or drink.
- **Take a planned rest:** Lie down, take a walk, or do something completely non-demanding for at least 30 minutes to give your brain a chance to reset.
- **Acknowledge your effort:** Give yourself a moment to acknowledge the significant work you just completed. This conscious celebration provides a final dopamine reward that reinforces the positive behavior.

By learning to harness this unique strength, you can turn a daunting cleaning project into a productive and even enjoyable experience. You're not fighting against your brain's nature; you're using it as a powerful tool to build the life you want.

CHAPTER 6

THE TWO-MINUTE CONTAINER RULE KEEPING CLUTTER IN CHECK AUTOMATICALLY

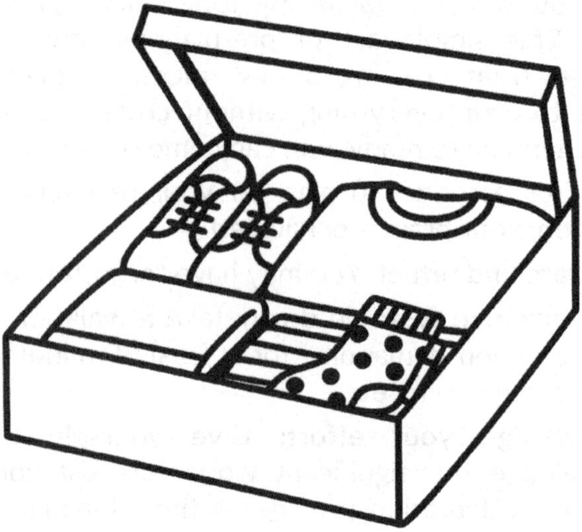

Why Containers Are Secretly Powerful

If you live with ADHD, clutter often feels like a sneaky enemy. You don't set out to pile things on the counter, but suddenly there's a stack of unopened mail, a few receipts, a random pen, and yesterday's coffee mug. Multiply that across your home and it can feel like chaos spreads faster than you can ever clean it up.

Here's the good news: clutter is not a moral failing. It's simply **stuff without a clear home**. And when your brain has to make endless micro-decisions about where to put each item ("Does this go in the drawer? On the desk? Back in the bag?"), it gets overwhelmed and defaults to dropping things wherever.

Enter the **container**. A container is an *external system* that does the thinking for you. It tells your brain, "This is where this type of thing lives." Even better, it puts a natural limit on how much of something you can keep before it needs attention.

The **Two-Minute Container Rule** builds on this concept. It's a simple, ADHD-friendly system:

1. **Designate containers for recurring clutter categories.**
2. **When a container is full, take two minutes to reset it.**

That's it. No overwhelming deep-clean, no endless decision fatigue. Containers act as boundaries, and the two-minute reset keeps clutter from turning into chaos.

Why ADHD Brains Love Containers

To see why this works so well, let's look at what containers *actually do* for your brain:

- **Reduce decision fatigue:** You don't have to wonder where mail goes, it goes in the mail basket.
- **Create visual boundaries:** A container makes it obvious when a category has reached its limit.
- **Shrink activation energy:** Tossing keys into a bowl is faster than putting them in a drawer.
- **Anchor habits:** The physical presence of a container becomes a behavioral cue.

In other words, containers externalize memory and reduce friction, two things the ADHD brain desperately needs.

Step 1: Spot Your "Clutter Categories"

Before you start buying bins, pause. You don't need containers for *everything*. The most powerful ones target recurring clutter categories, the items that constantly trip you up.

Look around your home and ask:

- What always piles up on counters?
- What never seems to have a home?
- What do I constantly misplace?

Common ADHD clutter categories include:

- Mail and paperwork
- Keys, wallet, phone, chargers
- Receipts

- Random small items (lip balm, coins, pens)
- Laundry (dirty, clean-but-not-folded, mismatched socks)
- Dishes that migrate to non-kitchen spaces

Each of these deserves its own container.

Step 2: Choose ADHD-Friendly Containers

Not all containers are created equal. If it takes too much effort to use them, your brain will ignore them. Choose containers that:

- **Are open and easy to access.** Lids create friction.
- **Are visible.** Clear bins or open trays beat opaque boxes.
- **Are sized appropriately.** Too big = a black hole. Too small = constant overflow.
- **Match your natural habits.** If you always drop mail by the door, put the mail basket *there*, not across the room.

Examples:

- A wide, shallow tray for keys and wallet.
- A wire basket for incoming mail.
- A small laundry hamper in the bedroom *and* bathroom.
- A pretty bowl on the coffee table for remotes.

The goal isn't Pinterest-perfect aesthetics, it's usability.

Step 3: The Two-Minute Reset

Here's where the magic happens. The **Two-Minute Container Rule** is simple:

- When a container fills up, don't panic.
- Set a timer for two minutes.
- Empty or reset the container.

That's it.

The time limit matters. It reframes the task from "ugh, I have to clean all this" to "I only need two minutes." Even if you don't finish, two minutes is enough to make a dent and prevent the build-up from spiraling.

Examples:

- Mail basket full? Spend two minutes recycling junk mail and pulling out bills.
- Laundry hamper overflowing? Two minutes to start a load.
- Toy bin full? Two minutes to toss broken toys and reset.

By making it short and non-threatening, you sidestep the ADHD trap of perfectionism and procrastination.

Step 4: Use Containers as "Pause Points"

Here's a powerful mindset shift: containers don't have to be permanent homes. They can be **pause points**, temporary holding spots until you have energy to finish.

- A basket on the stairs for items that need to go upstairs.
- A tray on your desk for papers you'll sort later.
- A bin by the door for things to return to friends or stores.

This removes the pressure of "I have to finish this right now" and instead creates a gentle system that moves clutter along in stages.

Step 5: Rotate and Refresh

ADHD brains crave novelty, so containers can fade into the background if they stay the same forever. To keep them effective:

- Change the color or style seasonally.
- Re-label bins every few months.
- Swap positions to make them noticeable again.

This refresh re-engages your attention and keeps the system working long-term.

Real-Life Example: Maya's Mail Mountain

Maya dreaded her mail. She'd toss it on the kitchen counter, where it snowballed into intimidating stacks. She'd avoid it for weeks, then panic when bills were overdue.

Her fix? A **mail basket by the door**. Every piece of mail went in immediately. Twice a week, she set a timer for two minutes and sorted: recycle junk, put bills in a "to pay" folder, file the rest.

Suddenly, mail wasn't a mountain. It was a five-minute task spread across the week.

Step 6: Pair Containers with Routines

Containers work best when linked to small, regular habits.

- Empty the entryway tray while your coffee brews.
- Sort the mail basket every Tuesday and Friday.
- Reset the laundry hamper every Saturday morning.
- Clear the "miscellaneous" basket before bedtime.

These mini-routines take minutes but prevent weeks of stress later.

ADHD-Friendly Hacks for Containers

1. **Label Everything.** Even obvious bins. Labels remove the micro-step of thinking.
2. **Double Up.** If clutter piles in multiple spots, put containers in *each* one.
3. **Match Flow, Not Theory.** Place containers where the clutter naturally happens, not where you wish it would.
4. **Use Pretty Ones (If You Care).** A container you like looking at is one you'll actually use.
5. **Don't Over-Organize.** Categories can be broad. "Mail." "Tech." "Random stuff." Keep it simple.

Common Pitfalls (and Fixes)

- **Pitfall:** "My containers just became more clutter."
    - **Fix:** Remember the Two-Minute Reset. Containers are holding spots, not dumping grounds.
- **Pitfall:** "I forget to empty the containers."
    - **Fix:** Add container resets to your Reminder Web (see Chapter 7). Use phone alarms or sticky notes.
- **Pitfall:** "I made my system too complicated."
    - **Fix:** Simplify categories. Broad bins are better than micro-sorted chaos.

The Psychology of "Enough"

Containers also teach a subtle but important lesson: the power of *enough*. If your book basket is full, maybe it's time to stop buying new ones until you read the old ones. If your snack bin is overflowing, maybe it's time to finish what you have.

This isn't about restriction, it's about creating natural, external boundaries so your brain doesn't have to constantly police your behavior. The container does it for you.

Closing Thought

The **Two-Minute Container Rule** isn't glamorous. It won't make your home look like a magazine. But that's not the goal. The goal is to make your environment easier to live in, one basket, one tray, one boundary at a time.

When you externalize memory into containers and pair them with tiny resets, you take the pressure off your brain and let your space work for you. Over time, these little systems add up to something powerful: a home that stays livable, not because you forced yourself to be perfect, but because you designed it to support your ADHD brain.

And that's the beauty of external systems. They don't demand discipline—they create ease.

CHAPTER 7

THE REMINDER WEB: BUILDING A NETWORK OF SUPPORTS THAT REMEMBER FOR YOU

Why a Single Reminder Isn't Enough

You've probably experienced this: you set one phone alarm to remind you to take your medication at 8 AM. The alarm goes off. You silence it. You tell yourself you'll get up in a minute. Then three hours later, you realize you never took the medication.

This isn't laziness, it's ADHD neurology. Our brains are **brilliant at responding to novelty and stimulation** but **terrible at holding future intentions in working memory**. A single reminder is fragile. If you miss it, get distracted, or override it, the whole system collapses.

That's why you need a **Reminder Web**. Instead of one fragile thread, you create a *network of cues* that catch you from multiple angles. If you ignore one, another is waiting. If you miss the second, the third picks up the slack. The web doesn't rely on your memory, it holds you gently but firmly in place.

The ADHD Problem with "Just Remembering"

Psychologists call ADHD an **executive functioning disorder**, meaning the brain struggles with self-management skills like planning, sequencing, and remembering. For many of us, intentions are like soap bubbles, they're beautiful for a moment, then they vanish.

That's why you can genuinely *mean* to pay the bill, fold the laundry, or take the trash out, and still not do it. Memory alone is too leaky to trust.

External reminders are not a crutch. They are a **prosthetic for working memory**. Just as someone with weak eyesight uses glasses, someone with ADHD can use reminders to strengthen recall.

What Is the Reminder Web?

The Reminder Web is a layered system of **redundant reminders** that:

1. **Externalize memory.** The web holds the task so your brain doesn't have to.
2. **Reduce failure points.** If you miss one reminder, another catches you.
3. **Work across modalities.** Visual, auditory, physical, and social cues all reinforce each other.
4. **Create momentum.** Repeated nudges gently guide you toward action instead of demanding discipline.

Think of it like having safety nets under a trapeze. One net is risky. A whole web of nets? Much safer.

Step 1: Map Your "Memory Leaks"

Before you build your web, notice where tasks currently slip through the cracks.

Ask yourself:

- What do I *always* forget?
- When during the day do I get derailed?
- Which reminders have failed me before (and why)?

Examples:

- Forgetting meds because the pill bottle is in a closed cabinet.
- Forgetting laundry because it's out of sight in the basement.
- Forgetting appointments because one phone alert wasn't loud enough.

These leaks are the places your web needs to be strongest.

Step 2: Layer Your Reminders

A Reminder Web works because it layers cues. Instead of hoping one will stick, you create **redundancy**.

Example: Morning Medication

- Phone alarm at 8:00 AM.
- Pill bottle on the nightstand (visual cue).
- Post-it note on the bathroom mirror ("Take meds").
- Smart speaker reminder at 8:15 if you haven't logged it.
- Accountability text from a friend once a week.

Now, missing your meds would require ignoring *five* reminders, not just one.

Step 3: Use Multiple Modalities

Different types of reminders work on different brain pathways. A strong web uses a mix:

- **Visual:** Sticky notes, wall calendars, whiteboards, color-coded bins.
- **Auditory:** Phone alarms, smart speakers, kitchen timers, music cues.
- **Physical:** Placing items in your path (trash bag on the doorknob).
- **Digital:** Calendar notifications, task apps, recurring checklists.
- **Social:** Accountability buddies, shared family reminders, coworking groups.

The more modalities you use, the more resilient your web becomes.

Step 4: Make Reminders Unignorable

ADHD brains are experts at tuning out background noise. The trick is to make reminders stand out.

- Use novelty: Rotate alarm sounds or sticky note colors.
- Use location: Place cues in spots you literally can't miss.
- Use humor: Write silly or exaggerated notes ("Hey genius, water the plants!").
- Use redundancy: Pair alarms with physical cues so it's harder to ignore.

Unignorable doesn't mean overwhelming. It means designing reminders that cut through the fog in ways that feel supportive, not nagging.

Step 5: Automate Wherever Possible

One of the best parts of the Reminder Web is automation. The less effort you spend remembering to remind yourself, the better.

- **Digital automation:** Set recurring calendar alerts, auto-bill pay, and recurring grocery orders.
- **Smart home automation:** Lights that dim at bedtime, plugs that turn off appliances, thermostats that adjust.
- **Physical automation:** Drop zones (keys always in the bowl, mail always in the basket).

Automation creates a background structure that runs without you having to constantly think about it.

Step 6: Pair Reminders with Routines

Reminders work best when anchored to existing habits.

- Put your vitamin bottle next to your coffee maker (cue = morning coffee).
- Put your gym shoes by the front door (cue = leaving the house).
- Add a calendar alert to check the mail on the same day you take out the trash.

The Reminder Web isn't just about nudges, it's about weaving them into the natural flow of your day.

Step 7: Refresh Your Web Regularly

Here's the catch: ADHD brains adapt quickly. What feels novel today becomes invisible in a few weeks. That's why you need to refresh your web:

- Change alarm tones monthly.
- Rotate sticky note colors or locations.
- Swap your whiteboard for a chalkboard or digital screen.
- Update accountability partners or groups.

Refreshing keeps your web visible and effective long-term.

Real-Life Example: Sarah's Laundry Loop

Sarah constantly forgot her laundry in the washer. Clothes would sit for days, start to smell, and need rewashing.

She built a Reminder Web:

- Phone alarm labeled "Switch Laundry" whenever she started a load.
- A sticky note on the washing machine lid: "Don't forget me!"
- A smart plug set to turn off the washer light after 90 minutes.
- A text check-in with her roommate once a week.

Within a month, she stopped re-washing loads. Her web caught her before the task slipped away.

ADHD-Friendly Reminder Hacks

1. **Name Your Alarms.** Instead of "8:00 AM," label it "Take Meds" or "Start Dishwasher."
2. **Use Visual Landmines.** Place items in your way so you literally can't forget.
3. **Double-Cue Important Tasks.** Always pair a digital reminder with a physical cue.
4. **Leverage Other People's Brains.** Ask friends or family for gentle nudges.
5. **Stack Reminders with Rewards.** Pair reminders with something pleasant (music, coffee, small break).

Common Pitfalls (and Fixes)

- **Pitfall:** "I ignore my reminders after a week."
  - **Fix:** Refresh regularly with new sounds, colors, or placements.
- **Pitfall:** "I feel nagged by my own systems."
  - **Fix:** Keep tone playful and kind. Reminders should feel like support, not shame.
- **Pitfall:** "Too many reminders make me overwhelmed."
  - **Fix:** Start with one strong web for your biggest pain point, then expand gradually.

The Psychology of Redundancy

You might worry that needing multiple reminders makes you "weak" or "childish." Let's flip that.

Airplanes have multiple backup systems. Doctors use checklists. Athletes have coaches. Professionals in every field use redundancy because it *works*.

For ADHD, redundancy isn't overkill—it's wisdom. The Reminder Web is how you build consistency without relying on unreliable memory or discipline.

Closing Thought

A single reminder is like a single thread—fragile, easy to snap. But a web of reminders? That's strong, resilient, forgiving. It doesn't demand perfection. It doesn't punish you for forgetting. It simply catches you, gently, again and again.

When you build a Reminder Web, you stop relying on shaky memory and start relying on systems. And that's the true power of external supports: they let your environment, your technology, and your community carry what your brain was never designed to hold alone.

You don't have to "just remember." You can build a web that remembers *for you*.

Reflection Questions:

- *In Book 2, we discussed several strategies for creating routines and habits. Which of these, either the morning routine, the evening reset, or the weekend deep dive, do you think would have the most immediate positive impact on your life? What is one specific, tiny action you can take this week to begin implementing it?*
- *This book also introduced the "Brain Dump" and the idea of harnessing hyperfocus. What is one specific task, either a small cleaning project or an organizational challenge, that you feel you could use a "Brain Dump" on, or intentionally engage your hyperfocus to complete this week?*
- *Think about the concept of the **"evening reset"**. What is one item or uncompleted task that, when left undone at the end of the day, consistently causes you stress or anxiety the next morning? How could a simple, five-minute evening habit prevent this?*
- *We discussed how to **harness hyperfocus**. What is a hobby or activity you've hyperfocused on in the past? What were the conditions of that experience (music, a challenge, no distractions) and how could you intentionally replicate those conditions for a productive task this week?*

- *The purpose of these routines isn't just to clean, but to create a specific feeling. What is the feeling or mental state you're hoping to achieve with a more consistent routine (e.g., peace, calm, control)?*

BOOK THREE

DECLUTTERING AND ORGANIZING MADE EASY

CHAPTER 1

KEEP, TOSS, DONATE SIMPLIFIED: A NO-DRAMA FRAMEWORK FOR FAST DECISIONS.

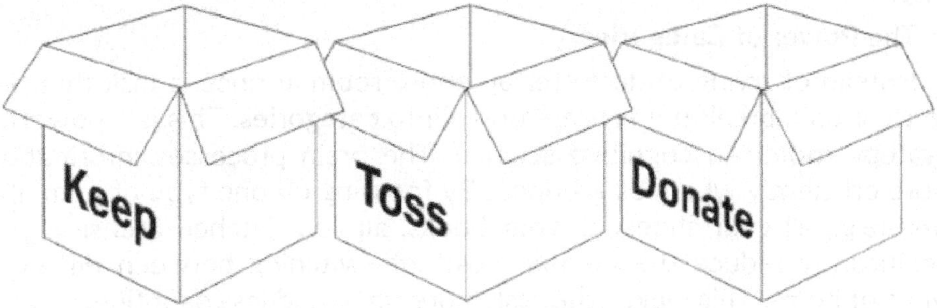

Traditional decluttering methods often fail the ADHD brain because they rely on a single, prolonged session of decision-making. The sheer volume of choices (such as Should I keep this? Will I need it later? Is this still good?) is a surefire recipe for **decision fatigue**. When faced with this cognitive overload, the prefrontal cortex, which is already working overtime to manage focus and attention, becomes exhausted, leading to paralysis and the complete abandonment of the task.

The **"Keep, Toss, Donate"** method is a more manageable and less overwhelming approach that simplifies the process into a clear, three-part framework. It's designed to combat decision fatigue and keep you moving forward by turning a monumental task into a series of small, rapid-fire choices.

The Three Bins: A Simple Framework

To start, you need to set up your decluttering station. Grab three containers:

- A **"Keep"** box for items you want to put in their proper place. This is not their final destination; it's a temporary holding zone. The goal is to get things off the cluttered surface and into a designated box, which is a significant win.

- A **"Toss"** bag for things that are broken, expired, or have no use. This category should be for items that require zero thought. If it's a broken gadget, a holey sock, or an expired condiment, it goes in the bag without a second thought.
- A **"Donate/Sell"** box for items that are still useful but no longer serve you. This re-frames the action. You're not losing something; you're giving it a new life and helping someone else. This positive mental reframing can make the decision much easier.

This three-bin system is a physical representation of the decisions you'll be making, which is a powerful tool for a brain that relies on visual cues.

The Power of Categories

Instead of trying to declutter an entire room at once, a task that has no clear end, break the process down into **categories**. This is a powerful strategy rooted in cognitive science. The brain processes information more efficiently when it's grouped. By focusing on one type of item at a time (e.g., all your shoes, all your books, all your kitchen utensils), you significantly reduce the mental "cost" of switching between different types of items. This makes the task more finite and less daunting.

As you pick up each item, make a quick, intuitive decision: Keep, Toss, or Donate? Don't overthink it. The goal is to make a rapid decision and move on. The first instinct is often the right one. This is a direct counter to analysis paralysis, as it prioritizes momentum over perfect judgment. By the end of a category session, you'll have a clear sense of accomplishment, which provides a crucial **dopamine** hit and motivates you for the next round.

The "Maybe" Box is a Trap

You may be tempted to create a "Maybe" box for items you're unsure about. Avoid this at all costs. A "Maybe" box is a trap for the ADHD brain. It doesn't solve the problem; it simply delays the decision and creates a new form of clutter. It becomes a graveyard of indecision, a physical manifestation of your fear of making the "wrong" choice. This feeds into the very anxiety you're trying to escape.

If you're truly on the fence, lean towards donating. The item will be more useful to someone else than it is collecting dust in your home. If a "Maybe" box is absolutely necessary for your peace of mind, make it a temporary system with a hard deadline. For example, "I'll keep this box for three months, and if I haven't opened it by then, everything inside gets donated." This structure turns a vague, endless "maybe" into a concrete, time-limited decision.

A Practical Application: The Decluttering Sprint

To make this method even more effective, combine it with the **"10-Minute Tidy"** concept from Book 2. This is the **"Decluttering Sprint."**

1. **Set a Timer:** Set a timer for 10-15 minutes. This creates a clear start and a clear end.
2. **Grab Your Bins:** Have your "Keep," "Toss," and "Donate" containers ready.
3. **Choose a Category:** Pick a single, small category to work on, like "all the mugs in the cupboard" or "all the pens on my desk."
4. **Rapid-Fire Decisions:** Work through the items as quickly as you can, making a quick decision for each.
5. **Stop When the Timer Goes Off:** When the timer dings, you're done.

The "Keep, Toss, Donate" method provides a simple, clear-cut framework that turns a huge, overwhelming task into a series of small, rapid-fire decisions. It's not about being perfect; it's about being decisive and making progress. By building this momentum, you can reclaim your space and your peace of mind, one small decision at a time.

CHAPTER 2

PAPERWORK & DIGITAL CHAOS: SYSTEMS TO CONTROL YOUR INBOX, DESK, AND FILES.

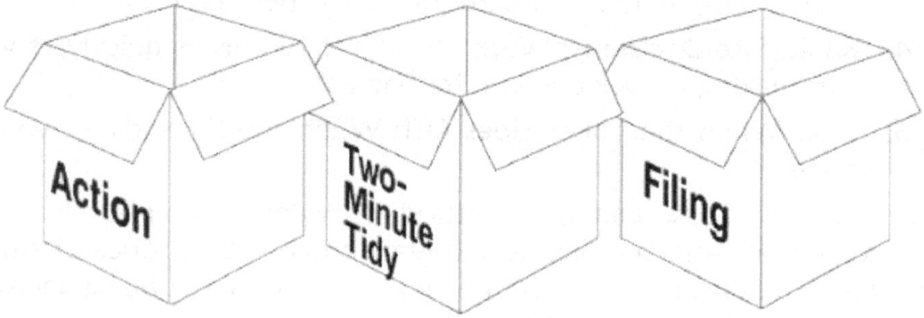

Paperwork and digital files can be a constant source of stress for the ADHD brain. They multiply with seemingly no effort, and the thought of organizing them can feel impossible. This is because both physical and digital clutter trigger the same executive function challenges that make physical clutter so draining: task initiation, prioritization, and working memory. The endless stream of emails, files, and documents competes for your attention, creating a significant **cognitive load** and contributing to a pervasive sense of overwhelm. This chapter provides simple, actionable strategies to create a system that works for the modern, busy individual, turning chaos into order one simple step at a time.

Taming Paperwork

The key to managing paper clutter is to have a simple, visible system that doesn't require a complex mental map. The reason piles form on every available surface is a neuro-psychological one: the brain struggles with object permanence. If an item is in a drawer or a folder, it's easily forgotten. A visible system acts as an external brain, providing a clear, non-negotiable home for every piece of paper that enters your life.

- **The "Action" Box:** All incoming mail and papers go into a single, designated box. This prevents piles from forming on every surface. This "Action" box is not for storage; it is a temporary holding zone. By funnelling all new papers into one spot, you're containing the chaos and creating a single point of entry for all paperwork. This is a fundamental step in reducing the visual clutter that drains your mental energy.

- **The "Two-Minute Tidy":** Once a week, go through the "Action" box. If a piece of paper takes less than two minutes to deal with (e.g., paying a bill online, scheduling an appointment, or signing a form), do it immediately. This is a direct application of the "Two-Minute Rule" from Book 2, which leverages the fact that the mental energy required to put off a simple task is often greater than the energy required to complete it. For items that will take longer, move them to a separate "To Do" file to be scheduled into a longer work block.
- **A Simple Filing System:** For papers you need to keep, create a filing system with broad, easy-to-remember categories. Avoid micro-filing with folders for every single type of document. Instead, use broad categories like **"Medical," "Financial," "Home,"** and **"Important Documents."** The fewer folders you have, the easier it is to maintain, and the less cognitive effort is required to file a new document. A simple box or a hanging file system with clear, large labels works best. The goal is retrieval, not perfection.

Conquering Digital Clutter

Digital clutter can be just as overwhelming and anxiety-inducing as physical clutter. An inbox with thousands of unread emails, a desktop covered in icons, or a downloads folder full of unorganized files is a digital representation of a disorganized mind. It can lead to the same feelings of overwhelm and analysis paralysis.

- **The "Digital Brain Dump":** Just like with physical thoughts, take time to dump all your unorganized files, photos, and digital to-dos into a single, temporary folder. This is a crucial first step that gets everything out of sight and into a single, contained space, reducing visual clutter on your desktop and in your mind. From this folder, you can later organize the files into their proper homes.
- **Email Management:** Your email inbox is a primary source of digital stress. Create a simple **two-folder system**: an "**Action**" folder for emails that need a response and an "**Archive**" folder

for everything else. The goal is to get your inbox to zero as often as possible. Once you've read an email and completed any necessary actions, archive it. This simple system, combined with unsubscribing from unnecessary mailing lists, makes managing your inbox a proactive task instead of a reactive one.

- **Desktop Declutter:** Your desktop is your digital workspace. A cluttered desktop makes it difficult to find files and is a constant visual distraction. Keep it clean and use a few folders to group similar items. For example, have a folder for "Current Projects" and another for "Downloads." The principle of a clean workspace from Book 1 applies here just as much as it does to a physical desk.

By creating a simple, easy-to-maintain system for both physical and digital clutter, you can significantly reduce the mental load and anxiety associated with them. The goal is not a pristine, perfect system but a functional one that supports your unique brain.

CHAPTER 3

TAMING THE CHAOS HOTSPOTS: ADHD-FRIENDLY STRATEGIES FOR KITCHENS, CLOSETS, AND MORE.

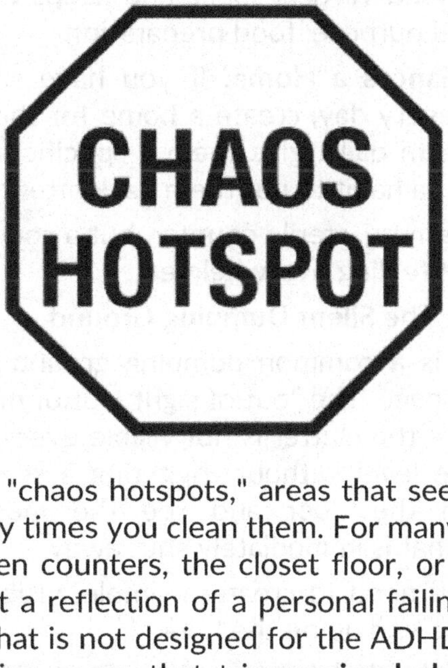

Every home has its "chaos hotspots," areas that seem to attract clutter no matter how many times you clean them. For many with ADHD, these are often the kitchen counters, the closet floor, or the bathroom sink. These spots are not a reflection of a personal failing; they are a direct result of a system that is not designed for the ADHD brain. These areas are low-effort landing zones that trigger **visual clutter**, which in turn creates a constant cognitive drain. This chapter provides specific, actionable strategies for taming these trouble spots and creating systems that are intuitive and easy to maintain. The key is to design a system that works *with* your brain's natural tendencies, not against them.

The Kitchen Counter: The Primary Landing Strip

The kitchen counter is often the home's primary landing strip. It's the first place we put down keys, mail, groceries, and miscellaneous items. For a brain that struggles with object permanence (the ability to remember that an item exists even when it's not in sight), the counter becomes a perfect short-term memory substitute. Everything is visible, but the sheer volume of visual information creates a significant **cognitive load**.

To combat this, the goal is to get as much off the counter as possible.

- **Create a Designated Launchpad:** Use a decorative tray or bowl for high-value, high-use items like keys, wallet, and sunglasses. This corrals the clutter into a single, defined space.
- **Go Vertical:** Use magnetic strips on the wall for knives and other metal utensils. Mount a small corkboard or a hanging file on the wall to hold important papers, notes, or bills. This utilizes unused vertical space and keeps the counter clear for its intended purpose: food preparation.
- **Give Appliances a Home:** If you have small appliances you don't use every day, create a home for them in a cupboard. If you use them daily, give them a specific spot on the counter and make it a habit to put them back after each use.

The goal isn't an empty, sterile counter, but a counter clear enough to make dinner without feeling overwhelmed.

The Closet Floor: The Silent Dumping Ground

The closet floor is a common dumping ground because it's a low-effort, out-of-sight space. The "out of sight, out of mind" principle works here in reverse: since the clutter is not visible every day, it can build up to an unmanageable level without triggering a sense of urgency. The moment you open the door and see the mess, it becomes an overwhelming task that is immediately shut away.

To solve this, you need to create a simple, visible system for items that would otherwise end up on the floor.

- **Install Simple Shelving or a Shoe Rack:** This provides a clear, designated home for shoes, which are a major culprit of floor clutter.
- **Utilize Cubbies or Bins:** Use cubbies or labeled bins to create a home for clothes you haven't decided on, or for seasonal items. The visual boundaries of the cubbies help to contain the clutter.
- **Commit to the "One-In, One-Out" Rule:** For every item of clothing you bring into your home, one must leave. This simple rule prevents the closet from reaching a state of critical mass. Make a commitment to put one item away as soon as you take

it off. This small habit can prevent the closet floor from becoming a major problem.

The Bathroom Sink: The Jumble of Jars

The bathroom sink and counter often become a jumble of bottles, tubes, and containers. This visual clutter is a subtle but persistent stressor. It also makes a simple task like wiping down the counter feel like a massive undertaking.

- **Use Trays or Small Containers:** Use a simple tray or small containers to group similar items (e.g., all your dental care products, all your skincare). This prevents a jumble of bottles and tubes and makes it easy to wipe down the counter.
- **Go Vertical:** Install a wall-mounted toothbrush holder to get items off the counter.
- **The Power of the Drawer:** Use drawer organizers to provide a specific home for items that don't need to be on the counter. This keeps them accessible but out of sight, providing a sense of visual calm.

The Entryway: The Catch-All Zone

A final, common chaos hotspot is the entryway or mudroom. This space is the first and last point of contact with the outside world, making it a natural catch-all for coats, bags, shoes, and mail.

- **Hooks for Everything:** Install a series of hooks at varying heights for coats, bags, and backpacks. This is a low-effort alternative to a closet and provides an immediate home for items as you walk in the door.
- **A Shoe Rack or Mat:** Give shoes a dedicated spot. This prevents them from being scattered across the floor.
- **A Mail Drop Zone:** Place a small basket or box on a nearby table. All incoming mail goes here, preventing it from being scattered throughout the house. This is the first step in the paperwork system from Chapter 2.

The key to taming chaos hotspots is to design a system that works with your brain's natural tendencies. This isn't about being a neat freak; it's about creating a home that is functional and reduces daily friction. By setting up these simple, intuitive systems, you can dramatically reduce the amount of mental energy you spend on managing your physical space and free up your mind for the things that truly matter.

CHAPTER 4

THE ONE-IN, ONE-OUT RULE: A SIMPLE HABIT THAT KEEPS CLUTTER FROM CREEPING BACK.

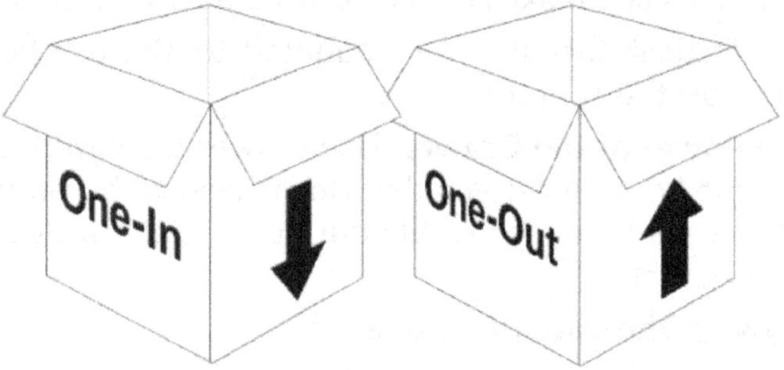

Impulse purchases are a common challenge for those with ADHD, leading to a constant inflow of new items that contribute to clutter. The "One-In, One-Out" rule is a simple, effective method to prevent this cycle and maintain a sense of order in your home. The impulse to acquire new things is often a direct result of the ADHD brain's constant search for **novelty and a dopamine hit**. The excitement of a new purchase provides an immediate, temporary reward that can override a longer-term goal like a tidy home. The "One-In, One-Out" rule is a powerful, proactive strategy that introduces a moment of intentionality, interrupting the impulsive loop and creating a sustainable system for keeping your home organized.

The Rule in Practice

The rule is exactly what it sounds like: for every new item that comes into your home, one similar item must leave. It's a simple, non-negotiable principle that forces you to be mindful of every purchase. This is not about deprivation; it's about conscious acquisition.

- **Clothes:** If you buy a new shirt, you must donate or toss an old one. This forces you to be honest about what you already own and what you actually wear. It transforms a spontaneous trip to the store into a mindful evaluation of your wardrobe. It prevents your closet from overflowing and makes getting dressed in the morning a less overwhelming task.

- **Books:** When you buy a new book, find one on your shelf that you have already read and pass it on to a friend or donate it to a library. This helps you curate a collection of books you truly want to read or reference, rather than a backlog of books that serve as a visual reminder of what you haven't accomplished.
- **Kitchen Gadgets:** If you buy a new kitchen gadget, get rid of an old one you no longer use. This prevents your drawers and cupboards from becoming a graveyard of single-use items you bought with good intentions.
- **Kids' Toys:** When a new toy comes in, one old toy must be passed along. This teaches children the same principle and keeps their play areas manageable.

This method works because it externalizes the decision-making process. The rule is a clear, physical constraint that bypasses the mental gymnastics of whether or not you should make a purchase. It simplifies the decision: "Is this new item worth the cost of getting rid of an old item?"

The Neuro-Psychological Benefits

The "One-In, One-Out" rule is a powerful mental trick. It shifts the focus from the pleasure of a new purchase to the act of mindful exchange. It forces a moment of **intentionality** that can prevent an impulsive buy from becoming a future clutter problem. For a brain that struggles with **impulse control** and long-term planning, this rule provides an essential, built-in filter.

Furthermore, this rule helps to combat the psychological trap of **"out of sight, out of mind."** New items that are not immediately addressed can quickly contribute to a new clutter pile. By forcing an immediate action, removing an old item, you are creating a new habit of maintenance.

The rule also helps you redefine your relationship with your belongings. Instead of seeing them as things you've acquired, you see them as a curated collection that serves a purpose in your life. This mindset shift is crucial for long-term organization.

Addressing Common Challenges

While the rule is simple, implementing it can have its challenges.

- **"What about sentimental items?"** This is a valid concern. The "One-In, One-Out" rule is primarily for everyday, non-sentimental items. For sentimental items, create a small, designated "Memory Box." The rule is that the box has a limited size. Once it's full, you must re-evaluate its contents before adding anything new.
- **"What if I don't have a similar item to get rid of?"** Use a flexible interpretation. The goal is to maintain a balance, not a strict one-to-one ratio. If you buy a new item and can't find a similar one to remove, find something else that is no longer serving you, or commit to a small decluttering sprint to make room.

The "One-In, One-Out" rule is about creating a conscious filter that helps you maintain control over what comes into your home. It's an act of self-care that prevents future overwhelm and supports a calm, organized environment. By embracing this simple habit, you're not lowering your standards; you're setting realistic ones that allow you to thrive.

CHAPTER 5

FURNITURE & STORAGE THAT WORK FOR YOU: DESIGNING SPACES YOUR BRAIN CAN ACTUALLY MAINTAIN.

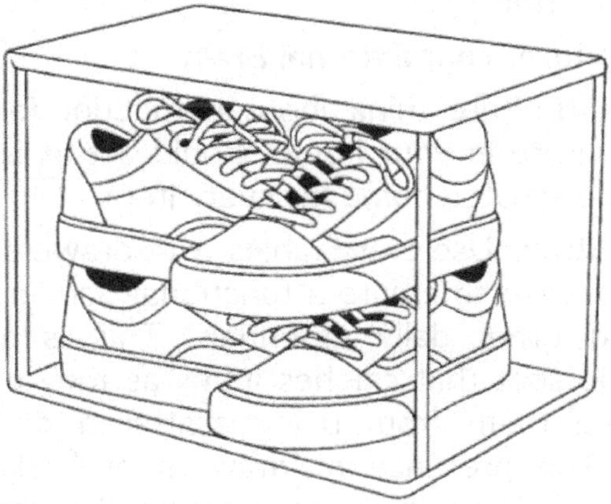

The right furniture and storage solutions can be game-changers for the ADHD brain. They can either support a functional, organized home or create more frustration. This chapter is about making intentional choices that work with your brain's natural tendencies, rather than against them. It's about viewing furniture not just for its aesthetic appeal, but as a tool for organization and a supportive element in your daily life.

The "Out of Sight, Out of Mind" Trap

Traditional storage often relies on putting things away in closed cabinets and drawers. For the ADHD brain, this can be a significant problem. If we can't see an item, we forget it exists. This phenomenon is directly tied to challenges with **working memory** and **object permanence**, core aspects of executive dysfunction. An item in a closed drawer is, for all intents and purposes, a forgotten item until a frantic, last-minute search ensues. This is where the balance between hidden and visible storage becomes a critical strategy.

- **Use Clear Containers:** Clear bins in your pantry, closet, and fridge make it easy to see what you have and where it is. This provides a crucial visual cue that bypasses the need for working memory. You no longer have to remember that the extra box of cereal is on the top shelf; you can see it. This makes it easier to find things and to know when you are running low on supplies.
- **Open Shelving:** For some, open shelving can be a great way to display items they need to remember, such as books, a watch collection, or daily-use kitchen items. This works best when the items are neatly arranged and serve a decorative purpose. By turning necessary items into a visual part of your home's aesthetic, you keep them in your line of sight without adding to visual clutter.

Functional Furniture: Your External Brain

When choosing furniture, think about its function for you, not just its aesthetic. The furniture in your home should act as an external brain, providing a clear, designated home for every item.

- **Landing Strips:** Use entry tables with drawers or a bench with built-in storage to create a functional "landing strip" for keys, mail, and other daily essentials. This is a physical, non-negotiable spot that catches items as they enter your home, preventing them from being scattered on every available surface. The presence of drawers or baskets provides an immediate, low-effort storage solution that reduces the mental energy required to put an item away.
- **Multi-Purpose Furniture:** Ottomans with hidden storage or beds with built-in drawers can be a great way to create extra storage without adding clutter to your space. A storage ottoman, for instance, can serve as a footrest, a coffee table, and a tidy place to store blankets or magazines, all in one. This maximizes space and provides a simple, accessible home for items that would otherwise be left out.

The Power of Accessibility and Zones

The key to a successful storage system is accessibility. If it's difficult to put something away, the ADHD brain will, by default, choose the path of least resistance and leave it out.

- **Hooks vs. Hangers:** Consider the mental effort required. A hook requires one action: hang. A hanger requires multiple actions: open the closet door, find a hanger, put the garment on the hanger, and place it on the rod. For everyday items like coats and purses, a series of decorative hooks near the door is a far more functional and ADHD-friendly solution.
- **The "Zones" Method:** Think about your home in terms of functional "zones." For example, create a "paperwork zone" with a dedicated tray for incoming mail and a small filing box, a "keys and wallet zone" in your entryway, or a "reading zone" in your living room with a basket for books and magazines. This strategy reduces cognitive load by grouping similar items and tasks, which helps your brain locate and engage with what it needs more efficiently.

The goal is to design a home that is a supportive environment—a place where every item has a logical, accessible home that makes it easy for you to stay organized and find what you need. By being intentional with your furniture and storage choices, you're not just decorating your home; you're building a system that allows you to live with greater ease and less anxiety. This is an act of self-care and a foundational strategy for a more peaceful and productive life.

CHAPTER 6

SENSORY-FRIENDLY CLEANING MAKING CHORES LESS OVERWHELMING

Why Cleaning Can Feel Like an Assault

If you've ever put off vacuuming because the noise made your teeth clench, or avoided scrubbing the bathroom because the smell of bleach made you gag, you're not alone. Many people with ADHD also experience heightened **sensory sensitivities**. That means sights, sounds, smells, textures, and even temperatures hit harder than they do for neurotypical people.

This is why cleaning, which already demands executive function skills, can feel doubly punishing. It's not just about remembering steps and following through, it's about enduring a barrage of sensory discomfort. The harsh squeak of a sponge, the chemical tang of cleaners, the scratch of dust against your throat, the sticky feeling of soap residue on your hands, it all stacks up into one overwhelming, unpleasant experience.

For some, it's not even about sensitivity but about **sensory boredom**. Cleaning feels unbearably dull, like your brain is deprived of stimulation and screaming for something else. Both overstimulation and understimulation can make cleaning feel like torture.

The good news? You can design cleaning routines that are **sensory-friendly**, ones that minimize overwhelm and even add comfort, stimulation, or pleasure to the process.

The ADHD–Sensory Connection

ADHD brains process sensory input differently. Some people are **sensory seekers**, craving more stimulation to stay engaged. Others are **sensory avoiders**, feeling overwhelmed by too much input. And many fluctuate between the two, depending on the day, task, or environment.

That means the exact same cleaning task can feel totally different from one person to the next:

- One person might find vacuuming soothing because it's loud and rhythmic.
- Another might find it unbearable, like nails on a chalkboard.
- One might enjoy the smell of lemon cleaner because it feels fresh and stimulating.
- Another might gag at the chemical scent and abandon the whole task.

Understanding your sensory profile is key. Instead of fighting against your brain, you can tailor cleaning to your comfort level, making it less punishing and more sustainable.

Step 1: Identify Your Sensory Triggers

The first step is noticing which parts of cleaning overwhelm or shut you down. Pay attention to the five senses:

- **Sight:** Clutter, bright lights, or visual chaos that makes your brain spiral.
- **Sound:** Loud vacuums, scraping chairs, or the buzz of appliances.
- **Smell:** Harsh cleaners, mildew, garbage odors.
- **Touch:** Sticky residues, slimy sponges, gritty dust, soggy rags.
- **Taste:** Less common, but some people are sensitive to chemical taste in the air.

Ask yourself: Which of these make me dread cleaning? Which are tolerable? Which are secretly enjoyable? Your answers will guide which hacks to adopt.

Step 2: Choose Sensory-Friendly Cleaning Tools

Sometimes the difference between dread and ease is simply using the right tools.

- **Noise Sensitivity:**
  - Use quieter vacuums (many stick vacuums are softer than old uprights).
  - Wear noise-canceling headphones or earplugs while vacuuming.
  - Turn cleaning into a sensory "bubble" by listening to upbeat music or podcasts.
- **Smell Sensitivity:**
  - Switch to unscented cleaners.
  - Use vinegar, baking soda, or mild soap instead of harsh chemicals.
  - Dilute concentrated cleaners more than the bottle suggests.
  - Open windows for fresh air.
- **Texture Sensitivity:**
  - Wear gloves (latex-free if needed) to avoid slimy or sticky textures.
  - Use microfiber cloths (soft, non-scratchy, quick-drying).
  - Replace steel wool or abrasive sponges with gentler scrubbers.
- **Visual Overload:**
  - Break large messes into smaller zones so you don't take in all the chaos at once.
  - Use bins or baskets to contain mess during cleaning so you see progress quickly.

It's not about being fancy. It's about **making cleaning tolerable** so you'll actually do it.

Step 3: Adjust the Environment

You don't have to accept your cleaning environment as-is. Small tweaks can completely change how it feels.

- **Lighting:** Harsh overhead lights can make dirt more visible but also feel oppressive. Try warm-toned bulbs or lamps.
- **Air Quality:** Run an air purifier while dusting, or use fans to move air while cleaning bathrooms.
- **Temperature:** If heat makes you cranky, set a cooler temperature before cleaning. If cold makes you avoid chores, cozy up with socks and a hoodie first.
- **Soundscape:** Create a playlist that energizes you, or listen to white noise to block out unpleasant sounds.

Think of cleaning less as a "task" and more as creating a **sensory setting** that supports your comfort.

Step 4: Add Pleasant Sensory Input

If cleaning is boring or uncomfortable, balance it with input that feels good.

- **Make it Musical:** Blast upbeat songs or calming instrumental tracks, depending on your mood.
- **Gamify It:** Set a timer with a fun sound, or challenge yourself to "beat the buzzer."
- **Scents You Love:** If strong smells overwhelm you, choose a gentle essential oil diffuser while you clean.
- **Movement Boosts:** Dance while sweeping, or stretch while folding laundry.

This doesn't erase the discomfort of certain chores, but it gives your brain positive stimulation to make the experience less punishing.

Step 5: Modify the Task Itself

Sometimes the best solution is to **do the task differently**. ADHD brains thrive when we adapt tasks instead of forcing rigid methods.

- **Vacuum Alternative:** If vacuuming noise is unbearable, use a broom or quiet handheld vacuum for small areas.
- **Dish Dread:** If slimy dishes are a sensory nightmare, rinse them immediately after use or run them through a quick soak before handling.
- **Bathroom Tasks:** Use disposable wipes instead of cloths if scrubbing textures bother you.
- **Dusting:** Use dusters with extendable handles so you don't feel particles on your skin.

Cleaning doesn't have to follow "the right way." It only has to follow **the way you'll actually do it.**

Step 6: Break It Into Micro-Tasks

Sensory overload often comes from trying to endure too much at once. Instead, shrink tasks into tolerable bites.

- Wipe one counter, not the whole kitchen.
- Vacuum one rug, not the whole floor.
- Do one load of laundry, not "all the laundry."

This keeps the sensory input brief and makes it easier to recover between steps.

Step 7: Build Recovery Into Your Routine

Even with hacks, cleaning can still be draining. Plan for **sensory recovery**:

- Rinse your hands with warm water after touching unpleasant textures.
- Step outside for fresh air after using cleaners.
- Take a quiet moment after vacuuming if the noise rattled you.
- Reward yourself with a pleasant sensory experience afterward (tea, a soft blanket, a scented candle you enjoy).

Recovery isn't indulgent, it's part of making the task sustainable.

Case Study 1: Kevin and the Vacuum

Kevin dreaded vacuuming. The roar of the machine made his heart race, and he'd avoid the task for weeks, letting crumbs pile up.

His solution? He bought a quieter stick vacuum, wore noise-canceling headphones, and set a 5-minute timer with his favorite song. He still didn't *love* vacuuming, but it went from intolerable to manageable. He vacuumed weekly instead of monthly, and his space felt lighter as a result.

Case Study 2: Dana and the Dishes

Dana hated doing dishes because the slimy food bits made her gag. She'd let dishes pile until the sink was a mountain.

Her fix: she wore thick dish gloves, added a drop of lemon essential oil to her soap for a pleasant scent, and rinsed dishes immediately after meals to avoid buildup. Suddenly, dishes were no longer torture—they were just part of her routine.

Step 8: Shift From Punishment to Care

For many of us, cleaning feels tied to shame. Maybe you were scolded as a child for not doing chores "right." Maybe you've internalized the idea that a clean house equals moral worth. When you combine shame with sensory overwhelm, no wonder cleaning feels like punishment.

Reframe cleaning as **self-care, not self-punishment.**

- Wiping your counters isn't a chore, it's giving Future You a fresh start.
- Vacuuming isn't torture, it's creating a calmer sensory environment.
- Washing dishes isn't punishment, it's setting up tomorrow's meals with ease.

When you change the narrative, cleaning feels less like suffering and more like kindness.

Step 9: Accept "Good Enough"

Sensory-friendly cleaning is not about spotless perfection. It's about creating a livable space without overwhelming your senses.

If you only wipe half the counter today, that's still better than none. If you vacuum just the high-traffic areas, that's still progress.

ADHD thrives on **permission to be imperfect**. When you accept "good enough," you reduce pressure and make cleaning a task you can return to instead of avoid.

Step 10: Layer Sensory Strategies Together

One hack helps. Three or four together? That's when cleaning becomes sustainable.

Example: Cleaning the bathroom might mean...

- Wearing gloves for textures.
- Opening a window for airflow.
- Playing upbeat music.
- Using mild, unscented cleaners.
- Taking a shower afterward as recovery.

Each layer softens the sensory impact until the task is doable.

Closing Thought

For ADHD brains, cleaning often feels like punishment because it bombards us with sensory input we didn't choose. But you don't have to endure cleaning the way others expect you to. You can adapt it to your needs, softening, customizing, and reframing until it's no longer torture.

A sensory-friendly approach isn't about luxury. It's about practicality. It's about recognizing that your brain and body deserve systems that work *for you*, not against you.

When you reduce sensory overwhelm and add sensory comfort, cleaning stops being an assault and starts being... tolerable. Maybe even enjoyable. And that small shift makes all the difference in creating a home where you can thrive.

CHAPTER 7

CLEANING IN MOTION
TURNING TASKS INTO MOVEMENT BREAKS

Why Cleaning Feels Like a Chore

For most people with ADHD, the hardest part about cleaning isn't the cleaning itself, it's getting started. Sitting still and telling yourself, *"Okay, I have to spend the next three hours scrubbing this house"* is overwhelming before you even pick up a sponge. It feels heavy, boring, and endless.

But here's something important: ADHD brains **love movement**. We crave stimulation. We think more clearly when our bodies are engaged. That's why pacing while talking on the phone feels natural, or why ideas pop into your head when you're walking instead of sitting at your desk. Movement helps regulate dopamine, and dopamine is exactly what's missing when a cleaning task feels impossible.

So what if cleaning wasn't a dreaded block of time, but instead a **series of movement breaks**? What if instead of punishment, cleaning became energy? That's the mindset shift behind "Cleaning in Motion."

The ADHD Brain and Movement

Science has shown that physical activity boosts dopamine and norepinephrine—the very neurotransmitters ADHD brains struggle to regulate. This is why exercise often makes ADHD symptoms feel lighter: focus improves, moods stabilize, and tasks feel more manageable afterward.

Cleaning isn't always thought of as exercise, but many chores qualify as **functional movement**: squatting, reaching, lifting, walking, bending, twisting. The difference is perspective. Instead of seeing chores as something to suffer through, reframing them as opportunities for natural movement can make them more engaging, stimulating, and sustainable.

Step 1: Redefine Cleaning as "Micro-Workouts"

You don't need a treadmill or a gym membership to move your body. Every time you sweep, scrub, or vacuum, you're already doing physical work. The trick is to start noticing, and celebrating, that movement.

- **Vacuuming:** Walking lunges with extra resistance.
- **Wiping counters:** Shoulder and arm workout.
- **Laundry:** Squats from lifting baskets, stretching while folding.
- **Sweeping or mopping:** Core twists and rhythmic cardio.
- **Decluttering:** Carrying items back and forth like weighted steps.

Instead of groaning about having to clean, think: *I'm sneaking in a few minutes of movement that my body and brain will thank me for.*

Step 2: Use Music and Rhythm

Movement becomes easier when it has rhythm. That's why people walk faster to upbeat songs or naturally match their pace to a beat. Music transforms chores into dance.

- Make a playlist with 3–5 high-energy songs. Each track is one "cleaning sprint."
- Match your actions to the beat: wipe to the rhythm, sweep in time, fold clothes on the downbeat.
- Rotate playlists so novelty keeps you engaged.

This approach does two things:

1. It makes cleaning fun instead of flat.
2. It keeps time limited, three songs equals about 10 minutes, which is a manageable micro-cleaning session.

Step 3: Turn Cleaning Into Movement Breaks

Long cleaning marathons are overwhelming. Short bursts feel doable. Instead of "cleaning the kitchen," try:

- Wiping counters for 2 minutes between emails.
- Vacuuming one rug after a phone call.
- Folding laundry during a podcast break.

By reframing chores as **movement breaks**, you satisfy your body's craving for stimulation and avoid the ADHD trap of endless sitting.

Step 4: Gamify the Experience

ADHD brains thrive on novelty, challenge, and reward. Turning cleaning into a game provides that dopamine hit.

- **Beat the Timer:** Can you unload the dishwasher before the song ends?
- **Zone Cleaning:** Race against yourself to see how fast you can reset one area.
- **Step Counter Challenge:** Track steps while cleaning, see how many you rack up.
- **Family Game:** Assign everyone a zone and play "cleaning relay."

Games add playfulness and stimulation, which shifts cleaning from obligation to challenge.

Step 5: Stack Cleaning With Other Stimulation

If cleaning feels too boring, pair it with something else stimulating. This turns cleaning into background movement rather than the sole focus.

- Listen to an audiobook, podcast, or comedy show.
- Call a friend while tidying.
- Watch a TV show while folding laundry.
- Use body doubling, clean on video chat with someone else.

The cleaning becomes secondary to the enjoyable activity, which tricks your brain into getting it done.

Step 6: Break Cleaning Into "Circuits"

Think of your home as a workout circuit. Instead of slogging through one task for an hour, rotate through small sets of chores.

Example circuit:

1. Wipe counters (2 minutes).
2. Sweep kitchen floor (2 minutes).
3. Put laundry in the washer (2 minutes).
4. Declutter the entryway (2 minutes).

Repeat the circuit once or twice, and you'll have tackled multiple zones without burning out. Circuits keep variety high and boredom low, perfect for ADHD brains.

Step 7: Use Movement to Manage Energy

Some days you're buzzing with restlessness. Others, you feel like a slug. Cleaning can meet you where you are.

- **On hyperactive days:** Channel restless energy into high-motion tasks (vacuuming, scrubbing floors, hauling laundry).
- **On low-energy days:** Choose gentler tasks (dusting, folding clothes, wiping mirrors).

The key is to let your body guide which cleaning tasks fit your energy level, rather than forcing a rigid plan.

Step 8: Build "Anchor Routines"

Anchor routines pair a movement with a chore so it becomes automatic.

- After brushing your teeth, wipe the bathroom counter.
- While waiting for your coffee, unload the dishwasher.
- During TV commercials, fold a few pieces of laundry.

Over time, these micro-movements become habitual, like brushing your teeth itself. They're no longer chores, just natural extensions of your day.

Step 9: Celebrate Progress Visibly

One of the best motivators for ADHD brains is **seeing immediate results**. Cleaning in motion offers lots of visual wins: a cleared counter, a vacuumed rug, a tidy shelf.

Instead of focusing on the long road ahead, pause to notice the visible difference you made in just a few minutes of movement. The brain gets a dopamine boost, which fuels motivation to keep going later.

Step 10: Reframe Cleaning as Self-Expression

Here's the deeper shift: Cleaning doesn't have to feel like punishment. It can be a form of self-expression and empowerment.

- Dancing while mopping turns drudgery into performance.
- Choosing tools and products you like (a colorful broom, a lavender-scented spray) makes the process more personal.
- Moving your body with rhythm and intention turns "chores" into an embodied practice of care.

This isn't about pretending cleaning is glamorous, it's about claiming it as something that works *for you* rather than against you.

Case Study 1: Nadia and the Afternoon Slump

Nadia worked from home and hit a wall around 3 PM daily. She'd scroll on her phone, groggy and unproductive. One day, instead of fighting the slump, she tried a 10-minute "cleaning sprint." She blasted two upbeat songs, danced around while sweeping, and wiped the counters. By the time she sat back down, she was energized, and her kitchen was cleaner. Cleaning became her daily "reset ritual" instead of wasted time.

Case Study 2: James and the Family Game

James dreaded family cleaning days. His kids complained, and he'd feel frustrated when nothing got done. He decided to gamify it: each family member had a zone, and they raced to finish before a 15-minute playlist ended. They'd blast music and laugh at each other's goofy dance moves. Suddenly, cleaning wasn't a fight, it was bonding. The house wasn't spotless, but it was livable, and the family enjoyed the process.

Step 11: Lower the Bar to Keep Moving

The trap of perfection kills momentum. If you think, *I need to deep-clean the entire kitchen*, your brain freezes. But if you think, *I'll just dance-wipe this counter for two minutes*, you're more likely to start.

Small motion leads to bigger motion. Once you're moving, you might keep going. But even if you don't, you've already made progress.

Step 12: Link Cleaning to Joyful Movement

If cleaning is dull, link it with movements you *do* enjoy:

- Dance while folding laundry.
- Do squats while picking things off the floor.
- Stretch while wiping windows.
- Put on roller skates to sweep a large room.

Silly? Maybe. Effective? Absolutely. ADHD thrives on novelty and fun, why not make cleaning part of it?

Step 13: Use Cleaning as Transition Rituals

ADHD brains struggle with transitions, switching from one task to another feels jarring. Cleaning in motion can act as a bridge.

- Do a 5-minute cleaning sprint between work and dinner.
- Wipe down a table between study sessions.
- Vacuum one room before moving into relaxation mode.

These rituals mark the end of one activity and prepare your brain for the next.

Step 14: Track Motion, Not Perfection

Instead of tracking spotless rooms, track movement. Did you do 15 minutes of cleaning sprints today? Great. Did you rack up 2,000 steps while decluttering? Amazing.

When you measure motion instead of perfection, cleaning feels less like judgment and more like progress.

Step 15: Create Movement Zones

Design your home with "movement-friendly" cleaning in mind:

- Keep lightweight tools accessible (hand vac, dusting wand).
- Store cleaning supplies in each room to reduce barriers.
- Place baskets where clutter collects so you can tidy with a single movement.

When tools are easy to grab, it's easier to turn small bursts of energy into quick cleaning motions.

Step 16: Respect Your Body's Limits

While cleaning can be reframed as movement, it's not about pushing yourself into exhaustion. ADHD brains often forget to notice physical fatigue until it's too late.

- Pace yourself with short bursts.
- Use ergonomic tools (lightweight vacuums, long-handled dusters).
- Listen to your body, stop before you hit sensory or physical burnout.

Sustainability matters more than intensity.

Closing Thought

Cleaning doesn't have to be a punishment. For ADHD brains, it can be **stimulation, movement, energy, and even joy**. When you reframe chores as opportunities to move, dance, stretch, and reset, you free yourself from the heavy, shame-filled narrative that cleaning must be endless drudgery.

Your home doesn't need perfection, it needs motion. A few steps, a few wipes, a few bursts of energy, that's enough to keep the cycle going. Cleaning in motion is about shifting from stillness and overwhelm into action and rhythm. And once you see it this way, chores stop being punishment and start being part of the vibrant, kinetic life your ADHD brain was built for.

Reflection Questions:

- *Book 3 offered several strategies for tackling clutter in specific areas, such as the kitchen, closets, and paperwork. Which of these "chaos hotspots" in your own home feels the most overwhelming to you, and what is one small, manageable change you can make this week to begin a "Keep, Toss, Donate" session?*
- *We also discussed the "One-In, One-Out" rule and the importance of functional furniture. Reflect on your last few purchases. Was there an item you bought on impulse that could have been handled differently? What is one way you could apply the "One-In, One-Out" rule to a future purchase?*
- *Think about the concept of **"cognitive load"**. Which piece of furniture or storage in your home is not currently working for you, and what small change could you make to a piece of furniture or storage solution to reduce the mental energy you spend on that space?*
- *The **"Keep, Toss, Donate"** method encourages quick decisions. What is one item you've been putting off making a decision about, and what is the one-sentence justification you can use to either keep it, toss it, or donate it?*
- *What is one **"chaos hotspot"** that you feel a sense of shame about? How can you reframe that space from a "mess" to an "opportunity" to create a system that works for your brain, rather than against it?*

BOOK FOUR

THE CLEANING TOOLKIT AND TIME MANAGEMENT

CHAPTER 1

THE ADHD-FRIENDLY CLEANING KIT

ONLY THE ESSENTIALS YOU'LL ACTUALLY USE.

For many people, a trip down the cleaning aisle can be overwhelming. The sheer number of products, each promising a specific, miraculous result, can lead to **decision fatigue** and clutter. For the ADHD brain, a complicated toolkit is a barrier to starting. The mental effort required to decide which product to use for which surface, or where to even find the right tool, can be enough to trigger task paralysis. This chapter is about simplifying your cleaning supplies to the essentials, making the process less daunting and more practical.

The goal isn't to be a minimalist cleaning guru; it's to create a low-friction system that removes the mental roadblocks that prevent you from starting a cleaning task in the first place.

The "Less Is More" Approach

You don't need a different product for every surface. A simple, effective cleaning kit can be built with just a few key items. The neuropsychological benefit of this approach is that it significantly reduces **cognitive load**. When you have one product for most jobs, you eliminate the micro-decision of "Which cleaner should I use?" and can get straight to the task.

The foundational kit includes:

- **All-Purpose Cleaner:** A good all-purpose cleaner can handle most surfaces in your kitchen and bathroom. Look for one that is non-toxic and multi-surface. These cleaners use a combination of **surfactants**, molecules that reduce the surface tension of water, and mild solvents to lift dirt, grease, and grime from surfaces. This single product can effectively replace separate countertop sprays, floor cleaners, and bathroom sprays, thereby drastically reducing the visual clutter under your sink.
- **Microfiber Cloths:** These are highly effective for dusting and wiping without leaving streaks. The magic of microfiber lies in its composition: it's made of tiny synthetic fibers that are split into microscopic hooks and loops. These fibers create a greater surface area and a positive electrostatic charge that attracts and holds onto dirt and dust. Having a separate color for different rooms (e.g., blue for the bathroom, green for the kitchen) can help with **cross-contamination** and keep things organized. This simple **color-coding system** is another external brain strategy that helps you avoid mental mistakes and ensures you're not using the same cloth for your toilet and your kitchen counter.
- **A Solid Vacuum or Broom:** A tool you can easily grab and use is key. Consider a cordless vacuum for quick, low-friction cleanups. For the ADHD brain, the effort of dragging out a heavy, corded vacuum is often a significant barrier to action. A lightweight, cordless option can be a game-changer, making a quick ten-minute vacuum feel less like a chore and more like a simple, spontaneous act.
- **Glass Cleaner:** For windows and mirrors. While an all-purpose cleaner can often work on glass, a dedicated glass cleaner is one of the few exceptions worth making, as it is specifically

formulated to dry quickly and leave no streaks, ensuring a visually calm, satisfying result.

- **Toilet Cleaner and Brush:** A dedicated set for the bathroom is essential for hygiene and should be kept within easy reach of the toilet.
- **Rubber Gloves:** Essential for protecting your hands during deep cleaning, a small but important act of self-care.

By keeping your supplies minimal and accessible, you're reducing the mental hurdle of "Where do I even start?" Your cleaning kit should be a supportive tool, not another source of clutter and overwhelm.

The Cleaning Caddy: Your Portable Command Center

Having a minimal list of supplies is only half the battle; the other half is making them accessible. This is where the **cleaning caddy** comes in. A caddy is a small, portable container, a bucket, a large basket, or a divided box, that holds all your essential cleaning supplies in one place.

The genius of the cleaning caddy is that it completely eliminates the need to hunt for supplies. Instead of wandering from room to room, gathering cloths, sprays, and brushes, you simply grab your caddy, and everything you need is right there. This dramatically lowers the **activation barrier**, the mental effort required to start a task. The caddy transforms a multi-step process ("find the supplies, then clean") into a single-step one ("grab the caddy, then clean").

Your cleaning caddy should contain:

- Your all-purpose cleaner
- Your glass cleaner
- A set of your color-coded microfiber cloths
- A small brush for scrubbing
- Your rubber gloves

Keep this caddy in a central location, like under the kitchen sink, so it's always ready to go. When you need to do a five-minute tidy or a ten-minute sprint, the caddy becomes your portable "command center," allowing you to move quickly and efficiently from one task to the next without losing momentum.

The Power of Scent and Sound

Cleaning is often a monotonous task, and monotony is the Achilles' heel of the ADHD brain. It craves novelty and stimulation, and when a task is repetitive and uninteresting, the brain will seek a dopamine hit elsewhere, leading to distraction. This is where you can intentionally introduce sensory input to make cleaning more engaging.

- **Scent:** The smell of a clean space is a powerful reward in itself, but you can also use scent as a motivator. Choose an all-purpose cleaner with a scent you enjoy. This small sensory detail can make the task more pleasant. You can also use an essential oil diffuser with scents like peppermint or citrus, which have been shown to improve focus and energy.
- **Sound:** Music or a podcast can act as a form of **auditory scaffolding** for the ADHD brain. A good playlist can help you maintain focus by providing a consistent external rhythm that overrides the internal mental chatter. It turns a tedious chore into a small, personal party. Podcasts or audiobooks can also serve this purpose, providing a narrative to follow while your body is engaged in a repetitive task. Just be mindful of your choices: if a podcast is too engaging, it can become a distraction.

Putting It All Together: A Low-Friction Cleaning System

Your essential cleaning supply list is the foundation, but a true system is what makes it work. By keeping your supplies minimal and organizing them in a cleaning caddy, you are creating a system that is easy to start and easy to maintain. By adding sensory elements like music or a pleasant scent, you are making the task more enjoyable and supportive of your brain's natural tendencies. This isn't about fighting your brain; it's about working with it. You are designing a system that respects your energy levels, rewards your efforts, and makes a clean, organized home an achievable and sustainable reality.

CHAPTER 2

TIME-BLOCKING MADE SIMPLE

SCHEDULING HACKS THAT KEEP YOU ON TRACK WITHOUT STRESS.

Time blindness is a common challenge for those with ADHD. It's not a character flaw or a sign of being lazy; it's a neurobiological reality. The ADHD brain often struggles to accurately perceive the passage of time, making it difficult to estimate how long a task will take. This is rooted in a dysfunction of the brain's executive functions, particularly in the prefrontal cortex, which is responsible for temporal reasoning and planning. Tasks that we think will take ten minutes can stretch into hours, and major projects can seem impossible to start because we can't mentally map out the steps. This chapter introduces simple, ADHD-friendly scheduling hacks that help you manage your time effectively without rigid, unrealistic rules.

The purpose of these strategies is to create an **external brain**, a system of cues and structures that compensates for an internal sense of time that is often unreliable.

Time-Blocking with a Twist

Time-blocking is the practice of scheduling specific blocks of time for certain tasks. For the ADHD brain, a full hour of "clean the kitchen" is often a non-starter. It feels vague, overwhelming, and doesn't provide a clear finish line. A flexible, ADHD-friendly approach is needed.

Focus Sprints: The Power of the Pomodoro

Instead of blocking off a full hour, try using **Focus Sprints**. Block off 20-30 minute "sprints" of focused work, followed by a 10-15 minute break. This is a direct application of the **Pomodoro Technique**, a time-management method that has been proven to be highly effective for those with ADHD. The neuroscientific reason this works is twofold:

1. **Reduced Activation Barrier:** A 20-minute task is far less intimidating than a two-hour task. The short duration lowers the mental hurdle to get started, making it easier to overcome procrastination.
2. **Built-In Dopamine:** The built-in break provides a crucial reward. Completing a sprint and taking a break gives your brain a small, immediate dopamine hit, which reinforces the positive behavior and makes you more likely to start the next sprint. This prevents the burnout that comes from trying to maintain prolonged focus.

These breaks are not just a reward; they are an essential part of the process. They allow your mind to wander, to seek the novelty it craves, and to recharge. Sometimes, a sprint can lead you into a state of **hyperfocus** or **"flow,"** where you become so engrossed that you lose track of time. In these moments, it's fine to extend the sprint, but be mindful of a crash afterward. The sprints are a safety net that allows you to work intensely without the fear of getting stuck or burning out.

Task Batching: Reducing Mental Switching Costs

The ADHD brain expends a significant amount of mental energy when it has to switch from one type of task to another. This is known as **"mental switching cost."** The act of putting away dishes, then remembering to pay a bill, then trying to write an email, is a cognitive tax that drains your energy.

Task Batching is a strategy that groups similar tasks together. For example, instead of doing one chore at a time, batch all your "quick tidy" tasks (e.g., wiping counters, putting away clothes, tidying the living room) into one 20-minute sprint. This allows your brain to stay in a single "mode" and conserve precious mental energy. You'll find that you can complete a lot more in a shorter amount of time because you're not constantly fighting against the friction of changing tasks. Other examples include:

- **"Phone Call Batching":** Make all your necessary phone calls (doctor's appointments, customer service) in one block.
- **"Email Batching":** Check and respond to emails only at specific times, like at the start and end of your day.
- **"Errand Batching":** Plan your errands to be in the same geographic area to minimize travel time and mental fatigue.

The Power of the Timer

A timer is one of the most powerful tools in your toolkit. It's a non-judgmental, external cue that helps you stay aware of the passage of time without constant mental effort. It serves as your external brain, helping with both task initiation and task completion.

- **To Get Started:** The timer removes the need for you to "feel" motivated. The simple act of setting a timer for 20 minutes and saying, "I just have to work on this until the timer dings," is often enough to overcome the initial hurdle of starting.
- **To Stay on Track:** The timer provides a constant, external reminder that prevents you from getting lost in a **hyperfocus** loop or a distracting detour.
- **To Stop:** The timer also gives you permission to stop. When the timer goes off, you can walk away with a sense of accomplishment, regardless of how much you've completed. This prevents burnout and reinforces the idea that progress, not perfection, is the goal.

There are many types of timers, each with its own benefits. A simple kitchen timer can work, but for a visual reminder of time, a **visual timer** that shows the time ticking down (like a disappearing colored wedge) can be incredibly effective.

Additional Scheduling Hacks

The "Start-Stop" Method

Instead of just scheduling a task, schedule the **start** and **stop** of it. For example, your calendar entry shouldn't just say "work on report." It should say, "10:00 AM - Start report" and "10:30 AM - Stop report." This makes the task feel finite and less daunting. The explicit "stop" time gives you permission to walk away, which is crucial for a brain that struggles with completion and can feel overwhelmed by an open-ended task.

Body Doubling

Body doubling is the practice of working on a task in the presence of another person, even if they aren't helping. The presence of another person provides a subtle form of accountability and an external anchor for your focus. This is a powerful psychological tool that can help you with task initiation and follow-through. A "body double" could be a friend working in the same room, a partner doing their own chores, or even a virtual "co-working" session with someone on a video call. The social element provides a gentle pressure that can help override procrastination.

The "Parking Lot" or "Distraction Pad"

Distracting thoughts are a normal part of the ADHD brain. During a focus sprint, an unrelated idea or a forgotten task will almost inevitably pop into your head. Instead of following the thought and derailing your current task, use a **"parking lot"** or **"distraction pad."** This is a simple piece of paper or a notes app where you immediately jot down the distracting thought. You are acknowledging the thought, but you are not acting on it. This allows your brain to let go of the thought without the fear of forgetting it, freeing up your mental resources to return to the task at hand.

The Power of Transition

The ADHD brain can find it difficult to switch from one task to another. To make this easier, build in a small, ritualistic action to signal the end of one task and the beginning of the next. This could be a five-minute stretch, making a cup of tea, or a short walk. These **micro-breaks** help the brain reset and create a clear mental boundary between tasks, making the transition smoother and less jarring.

The Role of a "Buffer Zone"

Never schedule tasks back-to-back. Leave 10-15 minute **"buffer zones"** between each scheduled task. This accounts for the unpredictable nature of ADHD time perception and the inevitable delays that occur in daily life. A buffer zone reduces the stress of being late or behind schedule and provides a much-needed moment of breathing room.

By combining these hacks, you can create a robust external system that supports your internal challenges. The goal isn't to be perfect, but to be intentional. You are moving from a feeling of being a victim of time to being an active, intentional manager of it.

CHAPTER 3

MAKE IT FUN OR IT WON'T GET DONE: TURNING CHORES INTO GAMES YOU'LL ACTUALLY PLAY.

The ADHD brain is driven by interest, novelty, and challenge. Monotonous tasks like cleaning are often boring, which makes them incredibly difficult to start and finish. The reason for this is rooted in neurobiology: our brains use a neurotransmitter called **dopamine** to regulate motivation, attention, and reward. Repetitive, low-stimulus tasks like washing dishes or folding laundry produce very little dopamine, so the ADHD brain, which already struggles with dopamine regulation, finds it hard to engage. This is why a simple chore can feel like a monumental, impossible task.

This chapter is about turning boring chores into engaging "games" that hack your brain's reward system and make organization and cleaning feel less like a chore and more like a game. These strategies aren't tricks to fool yourself; they are intentional, neurobiologically-informed approaches to make tasks more appealing by introducing the very elements your brain craves: a clear goal, a sense of urgency, and a tangible reward.

Turning Tasks into Games: Hacking Your Reward System

The key to a successful cleaning game is to pair a low-dopamine task (the chore) with a high-dopamine activity (the game or the reward). This is a process known as **dopamine stacking**, and it's a powerful tool for building habits and overcoming procrastination.

The "Beat the Clock" Game

Set a timer for a short, challenging amount of time (e.g., 5-15 minutes) and see how much you can get done. The time limit creates a sense of urgency and turns a simple task into a race. This works by tapping into your brain's natural desire for a challenge. The clock isn't an enemy; it's a friendly competitor. You're not racing against time, you're racing against your own personal best. This simple act of time-boxing gives the task a clear start and end point, which is crucial for a brain with **time blindness**. The timer becomes an external cue that keeps you focused and prevents you from getting lost in a task that has no clear end. When the timer dings, you can stop, regardless of whether the task is completely finished, and still feel a sense of accomplishment.

This game can be applied to almost any chore:

- "How many dishes can I put away in five minutes?"
- "Can I vacuum the living room in ten minutes?"
- "Can I clear the kitchen counter in three minutes?"

The "Podcast/Music" Game

Only allow yourself to listen to your favorite podcast or music when you are doing a specific chore. This is a classic example of dopamine stacking. You are linking a low-interest activity with a high-interest one. By making your entertainment contingent on your chore, you create a powerful incentive to get started. You can take this a step further by having a specific playlist or podcast that is reserved only for cleaning. This creates a ritual and a mental cue: when the "cleaning playlist" comes on, your brain knows it's time to get to work. The music provides a consistent rhythm and stimulation that helps to override the monotony of the task.

The "Reward System"

Create a simple reward for yourself after you finish a chore. The key to a successful reward system is that the reward must be **immediate, tangible, and not so large that it becomes a distraction.** A delayed or abstract reward is often not enough to motivate the ADHD brain.

- **Small, Immediate Rewards:** 5 minutes of phone time, a square of chocolate, a new episode of your favorite 15-minute show, or a moment of relaxation with a cup of tea.
- **The "Trophy Room" Game:** Create a visible reward system. After completing a chore, you get to place something (a sticker, a checkmark on a list, or a "trophy" item) in a visible spot. This externalizes the reward and provides a powerful visual record of your progress, which is incredibly motivating.

The "One-Song Tidy"

Pick one of your favorite songs and clean for its duration. The length of the song provides a natural time boundary, and the music makes the task more enjoyable. This is a great, low-commitment way to start. It's a non-intimidating way to get started and get a small win. The simplicity of this game is its greatest strength.

Advanced Gamification: Turning Chores into Engaging Projects

Once you've mastered the basics, you can move on to more advanced ways of gamifying chores, which tap into different aspects of the ADHD brain's needs.

The "Co-op Cleaning" Game

For the ADHD brain, social interaction and accountability are powerful motivators. The concept of **body doubling** is a cornerstone of this strategy. You can invite a friend or family member to help you clean, or even just have them on a video call while you both do chores in your respective homes. The presence of another person provides a subtle form of accountability and an external anchor for your focus. It turns a solitary, boring task into a shared, social experience. You're no longer alone with your thoughts; you're part of a team, and the shared experience makes the time pass more quickly and enjoyably.

The "Deep Dive Challenge"

Connect this to the concept of **hyperfocus**. Instead of dreading a tedious task, turn it into a deep-focus project. This works best with a chore that has a clear end point and allows for a sense of mastery. For example:

- **"The Closet Overhaul":** Can you categorize and organize your entire closet in a series of timed sprints? The challenge and the clear goal make the task more appealing.
- **"The Pantry Pro":** See if you can organize your pantry to look like a professional grocery store aisle. This uses visual interest and a sense of creative challenge to engage your brain.

The "Task Bingo" or "Randomizer"

Monotony is the enemy of the ADHD brain. To combat this, use a simple randomizer to pick which chore to do next. Create a list of small chores and use a simple app or a bingo card to pick one. This introduces an element of **novelty and unpredictability**, which the brain finds highly engaging. It breaks the monotony of a fixed routine and makes the process of doing chores feel less like a repetitive obligation and more like a playful surprise.

The "Power of Transformation"

The ADHD brain is highly visual. You can use this to your advantage by framing cleaning as an act of **transformation**. Before you start a chore, take a picture of a messy space. After you've cleaned it, take another picture. The visual contrast is a powerful, dopamine-releasing reward. You have tangible proof of your effort and a clear record of your accomplishment. This visual reward is often more impactful than a simple mental acknowledgment and can be used to motivate you for future projects.

The Final Philosophy: Working with Your Brain, Not Against It

The goal of all these games and strategies is not to trick your brain, but to work with it. You are respecting your brain's need for novelty, urgency, and reward, and you are building a system that is supportive rather than restrictive. By reframing chores as games, you are changing your mindset from one of dread to one of possibility. You are building a sustainable system that allows you to live in a clean and organized home, not through willpower and grit, but through clever, intentional strategies that align with your unique neurodiversity. The end result is a cleaner home and a less stressed mind, and that is a win worth playing for.

CHAPTER 4

DELEGATE, AUTOMATE, OUTSOURCE: CLEANING STRATEGIES WHEN YOU CAN'T DO IT ALL.

The myth that you have to do everything yourself is a major source of burnout and frustration, especially for individuals with ADHD. The human brain, regardless of neurotype, has a limited capacity for executive functions, the mental skills that include planning, organizing, and managing tasks. For those with ADHD, this capacity is often more easily depleted. Trying to manage every single task, from paying bills to doing laundry to cleaning the entire house, is a recipe for overwhelm. This chapter is about recognizing that it's okay to ask for help, and that delegating, automating, and outsourcing are not signs of failure; they are strategic choices for success and for creating a more sustainable, peaceful life. These strategies are proactive ways to conserve your limited mental energy and redirect it toward what you do best and what you genuinely enjoy.

Delegating with a Purpose: The Shared Mental Load

If you live with a partner, family, or roommates, delegation is key. The issue is not just about getting help; it's about addressing the **shared mental load** of running a household. The mental load refers to all the invisible labor involved in managing a household: the planning, the remembering, and the organizing of tasks. For a neurodiverse person, this can be an enormous, unseen source of stress.

Instead of simply asking for help, which can often lead to frustration and miscommunication, create a clear, shared system. The goal is to move from a place of unspoken assumptions to a system of clear, explicit agreements.

- **Use a Whiteboard or a Shared App:** A whiteboard in a central location, a shared to-do list app like Trello or Asana, or even a simple calendar can act as your external brain. This system provides a single source of truth for all household tasks. It externalizes the mental load, so you don't have to be the one constantly remembering who needs to do what.
- **Be Specific About What "Done" Means:** Avoid vague requests like "clean the kitchen." Instead, be specific. "Wipe down the counters, wash all the dishes in the sink, and sweep the floor." This removes ambiguity and reduces the likelihood of misunderstandings. The ADHD brain thrives on clear instructions and defined end points.
- **Play to Your Strengths:** Delegate tasks based on interest and skill. If your partner enjoys cooking but you hate doing dishes, make a deal. If you're great at organizing the pantry but they prefer taking out the trash, that's a win-win. This approach makes the tasks feel less like a chore and more like a contribution to the household team.

By delegating with a purpose, you're sharing the mental load, which is a powerful act of self-care and a cornerstone of a healthy shared living space.

Automating for Simplicity: The Set-and-Forget Strategy

Automation is a powerful tool for the ADHD brain. It's the ultimate "set-and-forget" strategy that removes the need for a decision, a reminder, or a mental effort. Every automated task is a small victory over the chaos of daily life. The neurobiological benefit is that you are essentially offloading a routine task from your brain's already strained executive functions to a reliable, external system.

- **Automatic Bill Pay:** Automate as many of your bills as possible to prevent late fees and anxiety. A forgotten bill is a classic consequence of time blindness and can be a major source of stress. By setting up automatic payments, you are completely removing the task from your mental to-do list. The effort to set it up once is far less than the cumulative effort and anxiety of remembering to pay every bill every month.
- **Subscription Boxes:** Use subscription services for things like meal kits, cleaning supplies, or even groceries. This reduces the mental effort of planning, shopping, and decision-making. Meal kits, for example, solve the triple problem of "what to cook," "what to buy," and "how to prepare it." This is a perfect example of a system that works with the ADHD brain, providing novelty and variety without the overwhelming effort of planning.
- **Automated Calendar Reminders:** Use your phone's calendar app to set up recurring reminders for chores like taking out the trash or watering plants. These are tasks that are easy to forget but have a significant impact when they're not done. A simple, recurring alert that says "Take out the trash" is an invaluable external cue that prevents you from having to rely on your unreliable working memory.

Outsourcing for Peace of Mind: A Strategic Investment

The idea of outsourcing certain tasks can feel like a luxury, but it's more accurately a **strategic investment in your mental health and well-being.** If a task consistently causes you stress, anxiety, or burnout, and you have the means, consider outsourcing it. The mental space you gain from outsourcing a task is often more valuable than the money you spend on it.

- **A Cleaning Service:** If cleaning your home consistently feels overwhelming and you have the financial means, hiring a cleaning service, even for just a few hours a month, can be a game-changer. The mental relief of knowing a major task is being handled is immense. It allows you to focus on the things you enjoy and reduces the shame and guilt that can accompany a messy home.
- **A Laundry Service:** For some, laundry is a multi-step, overwhelming task that is never truly finished. Outsourcing this to a service that handles washing, drying, and folding can be a profound source of peace.

- **A Virtual Assistant (VA):** For managing your digital life—organizing your email, scheduling appointments, or managing your digital files—a VA can be an invaluable tool. This is a perfect example of outsourcing a task that requires a high level of executive function and consistent attention, which are areas where the ADHD brain can struggle.

By delegating, automating, and outsourcing, you're creating a support system that frees up your energy for the things that you are uniquely good at and that bring you joy. You are not failing by asking for help; you are succeeding by building a sustainable system that allows you to thrive. You are making an intentional choice to live a life with less friction and more peace. This is the ultimate goal of organization: not to create a perfect home, but to create a life that feels more manageable, more joyful, and more authentically your own.

CHAPTER 5

APPS THAT KEEP YOU MOVING: DIGITAL TOOLS TO SIMPLIFY YOUR ROUTINES AND REMINDERS.

Technology can be both a blessing and a curse for the ADHD brain. While a phone can be a source of endless distraction, a portal to social media scrolls and impulsive online shopping, it can also be a powerful tool for managing your life. This chapter explores how to use apps and technology to create a supportive, external system that helps you stay on track. The goal is to turn a potential source of chaos into a reliable **"digital scaffold,"** a framework that supports your daily life and compensates for the internal challenges of memory, attention, and time management.

The key to using technology effectively is to be intentional. Don't let your technology become another source of clutter and overwhelm. When used strategically, technology can be a powerful ally in building an organized and less chaotic life.

Your External Brain for Your Internal Thoughts

For the ADHD brain, which struggles with working memory, a simple thought can be a fleeting ghost that vanishes before you can act on it. A phone can act as a powerful "external brain" for all the things you need to remember. This is the digital version of a **brain dump**—a reliable, always-on system for capturing your mental fragments so your internal brain is free to focus on the task at hand.

To-Do List Apps: From Chaos to Clarity

To-do list apps are far more than just digital sticky notes. They are a place to capture all the tasks from your "brain dump" and organize them into manageable, actionable lists. The power of these apps lies in their ability to take a large, overwhelming project and break it down into smaller, more manageable steps, a process that is critical for overcoming task paralysis.

- **Simple vs. Complex:** For some, a simple notes app like Apple Notes or Google Keep is enough. You can use it to create quick checklists. For others, a more robust app like **Todoist** or **Trello** is a game-changer. These apps allow you to create subtasks, assign due dates, set priorities, and even link to other files. This turns a vague task like "clean the garage" into a series of actionable steps: "take out trash," "sort tools," "create a donation pile."
- **The Power of Visualization:** Many to-do list apps use visual cues. **Trello**, for example, uses a **Kanban board** system with cards that can be moved from "To Do" to "Doing" to "Done." This visual progression provides a powerful, tangible sense of accomplishment, which releases dopamine and reinforces the positive behavior. It makes your progress visible, which is incredibly motivating.

Calendar Apps: Making Time Tangible

Time blindness makes it difficult to perceive the passage of time, but a digital calendar makes time a tangible, visual entity. Using a digital calendar with color-coding is a highly effective external brain strategy.

- **Color-Coding Your Life:** Assign different colors to different areas of your life (e.g., green for personal appointments, blue for work, yellow for self-care). When you look at your schedule, you can immediately see a visual breakdown of your week. This reduces the mental effort of trying to figure out what's on your plate.

- **The Power of Reminders:** Don't just use your calendar for appointments. Use it to block off your **"focus sprints"** and **"deep dives."** Set up recurring reminders for chores like taking out the trash or watering plants. The reminder acts as a non-judgmental nudge that bypasses your working memory and prompts you to act. The trick is to treat these calendar blocks like a real appointment—a commitment you've made to yourself.

Timers and Habit Trackers: Gamifying Your Routine

The ADHD brain is motivated by novelty, challenge, and reward. Timers and habit trackers are a way to gamify your daily life and turn mundane tasks into engaging, rewarding activities.

- **The Pomodoro Technique:** The Pomodoro Technique is a time-management method that uses a timer to break down work into intervals, traditionally 25 minutes in length, separated by short breaks. There are countless apps dedicated to this method, from simple timers to more elaborate ones that track your progress and provide stats. The timer acts as a constant external anchor for your attention, and the visual countdown helps make time a concrete, perceivable entity.
- **Habit Trackers:** Apps like **Streaks** or **Habitica** can be powerful motivators. The visual representation of your progress, seeing a chain of completed days, provides a powerful dopamine hit and a strong incentive not to break the chain. **Habitica** takes this a step further by turning your life into a role-playing game. You earn "experience points" and "gold" for completing tasks, which you can use to buy in-game items. This harnesses your brain's natural desire for a challenge and a reward in a fun, engaging way.

Automation and Focus: Technology as a Partner

Beyond simple organization, technology can automate tasks and create a more focused environment.

Automation Apps: Reducing Micro-Decisions

Automation is a key strategy for the ADHD brain. It removes the need for a decision, which conserves valuable executive function energy. While there are advanced automation platforms like **Zapier** and **IFTTT** (If This Then That), even your phone's built-in features can be used.

- **Scheduled "Do Not Disturb" Mode:** Set your phone to automatically switch to "Do Not Disturb" mode during your focus sprints or at night. This prevents notifications from hijacking your attention and ensures you have dedicated periods of uninterrupted work or rest.
- **Location-Based Reminders:** Use your phone's built-in reminders to get a notification when you arrive at a specific location. For example, a reminder that says "buy milk" that pops up when you get to the grocery store. This external cue connects the task to the time and place where it can be completed, bypassing your internal memory.

Mindfulness and Focus Apps: Quieting the Noise

For many with ADHD, the internal monologue is a constant source of distraction. The brain is like a crowded, noisy room. Mindfulness and focus apps can act as a way to turn down the volume.

- **Meditation Apps:** Apps like **Headspace** or **Calm** provide guided meditations that can help you practice quieting your mind and returning your focus to the present moment. Even a five-minute session can have a profound impact on your ability to concentrate.
- **White Noise and Ambient Sound Apps:** For some, absolute silence is a distraction. A low, constant sound can help to "fill in the gaps" and prevent the brain from seeking out other, more distracting stimuli. Apps that provide white noise, ambient sounds, or even binaural beats can be an effective way to create a more focused environment.

The Final Word: Curation and Intentionality

The sheer volume of apps available can be a source of overwhelm in itself. The key is to curate your technology. Choose one or two apps for each category, one for your to-do list, one for your calendar, and maybe a timer app. Don't fall into the trap of constantly searching for the "perfect" app. The best app is the one you actually use.

The goal isn't to become a tech wizard; it's to create a small, manageable, and highly effective system. When used strategically, your phone and technology can move from being a source of chaos to being a powerful ally, a trusted partner in your journey toward a more organized and less chaotic life. You are not fighting against your brain's nature; you are building a supportive, external system that allows your unique neurodiversity to shine.

CHAPTER 6

SEASONAL ROUTINES: ADAPTING HABITS WITH THE CALENDAR

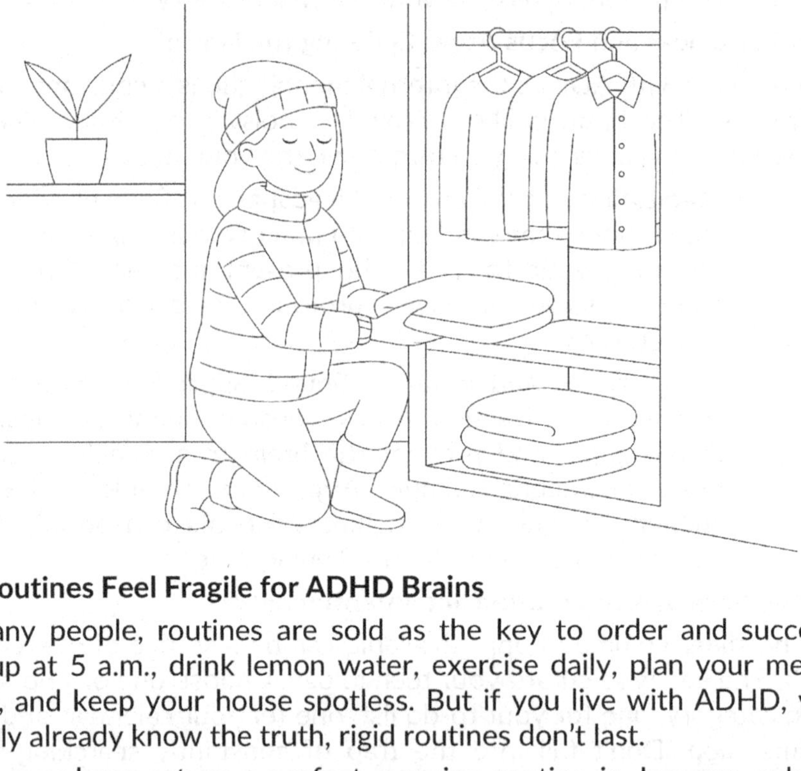

Why Routines Feel Fragile for ADHD Brains

For many people, routines are sold as the key to order and success: wake up at 5 a.m., drink lemon water, exercise daily, plan your meals, journal, and keep your house spotless. But if you live with ADHD, you probably already know the truth, rigid routines don't last.

You may have set up a perfect morning routine in January, only to see it unravel by February. Or maybe you've tried the same evening checklist a dozen times, each time thinking *this will stick*, only to watch it fall apart after a stressful week or schedule change.

Here's why: ADHD brains are wired for **novelty, flexibility, and adaptation**. They resist monotony and crumble under rigidity. That doesn't mean routines are impossible. It means routines must be **living, breathing structures**, not concrete slabs.

This is where **seasonal routines** come in. By syncing habits to natural cycles, seasons, months, or transitional periods, you create systems that evolve with you instead of breaking when life shifts.

The Seasons as Natural ADHD Anchors

One of the most frustrating parts of ADHD is how time feels slippery. Days blur together. Weeks pass without warning. A month can vanish before you've caught your breath. Seasonal routines solve this by anchoring your habits to the natural markers of the year.

Think of the seasons as built-in **reset buttons**:

- **Spring:** Renewal, decluttering, new projects.
- **Summer:** Activity, lightness, movement.
- **Fall:** Structure, routines, preparation.
- **Winter:** Rest, reflection, coziness.

Instead of fighting the ADHD relationship with time, seasonal routines work with it. They create natural opportunities for refresh and restart, which ADHD brains crave.

Why Seasonal Flexibility Works

Rigid routines fail because they assume life is constant. But ADHDers live in flux, our energy, focus, and motivation rise and fall. Seasonal shifts mirror this ebb and flow, and by adapting routines to them, we create systems that:

1. **Feel new** every few months (satisfying the ADHD need for novelty).
2. **Allow for flexibility** when energy dips or rises.
3. **Break the cycle of shame** by building resets directly into the year.

When you know your routines are *supposed to* change with the season, you stop feeling like a failure when the January plan doesn't work in June. Instead, you adjust. That's not failure, that's design.

Step 1: Identify Seasonal Energy Patterns

The first step is noticing how your energy, focus, and habits shift during the year.

- Do you feel more energized in spring?
- Do summers throw you off with travel and disrupted schedules?
- Does fall feel like a natural time for structure?
- Do winters drain you or invite rest?

Write down your patterns (mentally or on paper). These aren't rules, they're observations. Your unique rhythms will guide how you shape seasonal routines.

Step 2: Anchor Core Habits to Each Season

Every season can hold specific routines that align with its natural energy.

Spring: Renewal & Decluttering

- Open windows for fresh air while cleaning.
- Do a light declutter (a drawer, a closet) to match the "fresh start" energy.
- Rotate clothes and linens (winter away, spring/summer out).
- Use increased daylight to reset wake-up cues.

Spring is ADHD-friendly because it feels new. Lean into that momentum.

Summer: Light & Playful

- Shorter routines to leave room for fun and flexibility.
- Cleaning sprints instead of deep cleans.
- Use outdoor time as natural resets (watering plants, sweeping porches).
- Hydration and sunscreen routines as new anchors.

Summer routines should feel breezy and low-pressure, or they'll collapse.

Fall: Structure & Stability

- Ideal for reintroducing planner use or calendars.
- Weekly resets become anchors as school and work cycles restart.
- Focus on meal prep and cozy home routines.
- Decluttering surfaces and "resetting" spaces before the holiday season.

Fall brings structure naturally: this is the ADHD-friendly time to build frameworks.

Winter: Rest & Reflection

- Simplify routines to bare minimums.
- Use cozy rituals as anchors (tea before bed, lighting candles, soft blankets).

- Short cleaning routines to avoid overwhelm during darker days.
- Annual reset rituals (organizing papers, reviewing budgets, planning the year).

Winter is not about high productivity, it's about sustainable maintenance and recovery.

Step 3: Build Seasonal Reset Rituals

Every season is an invitation to reset. These don't have to be big, they can be simple traditions that signal change.

- **Spring reset:** Swap linens, open windows, donate one bag of clutter.
- **Summer reset:** Pack away school or work clutter, refresh your calendar for lighter weeks.
- **Fall reset:** Buy new notebooks, reset your planner, clear out summer clutter.
- **Winter reset:** Reflect on the year, declutter digital spaces, prepare cozy corners.

These resets act as bookmarks in your year, giving your ADHD brain tangible markers for time and change.

Step 4: Use Seasonal Cues for Motivation

ADHD brains respond to cues. Seasonal shifts bring natural cues you can harness:

- **Smells:** Fall candles, spring flowers, winter spices.
- **Light:** Adjust wake-up routines with changing daylight.
- **Temperature:** Use cozy blankets as evening reset cues, or summer breezes for morning resets.
- **Holidays:** Anchor routines to annual events (Thanksgiving cleaning reset, New Year paper purge).

Instead of resisting these cues, fold them into your systems.

Step 5: Plan for Seasonal ADHD Challenges

Each season brings hurdles. Preparing ahead makes them manageable.

- **Spring:** Overcommitting to too many "fresh start" projects. → Solution: Pick one main focus.
- **Summer:** Disrupted routines due to travel or kids at home. → Solution: Shrink routines to "bare minimums."

- **Fall:** Pressure to be hyper-productive. → Solution: Focus on sustainable systems, not overload.
- **Winter:** Seasonal depression and low motivation. → Solution: Prioritize cozy, minimal routines.

Anticipating challenges makes them less overwhelming when they arrive.

Step 6: Rotate Tools and Systems

Novelty is fuel for ADHD brains. Seasonal routines give permission to swap tools.

- **Spring:** Try a new planner or wall calendar.
- **Summer:** Use sticky notes or digital reminders for short-term goals.
- **Fall:** Reintroduce structured planners or bullet journals.
- **Winter:** Switch to simple to-do lists or cozy routine checklists.

Changing tools seasonally prevents boredom without guilt.

Step 7: Layer Seasonal Habits With Existing Anchors

Anchor seasonal routines to habits you already do.

- In winter, drink tea every night → add "wipe kitchen counter" before pouring.
- In summer, water plants → add "pick up clutter in living room."
- In fall, prep school/work bag nightly → add "10-minute tidy."
- In spring, open windows → add "dust shelves."

Layering keeps routines simple and sustainable.

Step 8: Seasonal Routines for Home Organization

Each season naturally lends itself to different organization projects.

- **Spring:** Closets, wardrobes, storage refresh.
- **Summer:** Outdoor spaces, patios, garages.
- **Fall:** Paperwork, calendars, family command centers.
- **Winter:** Digital files, finances, cozy spaces.

Breaking projects into seasonal chunks prevents overwhelm and creates natural cycles of progress.

Step 9: Family and Household Seasonal Routines

If you live with others, seasonal routines can create shared rhythms.

- **Spring:** Family declutter day (one room together).
- **Summer:** Weekly outdoor cleanup with music.

- **Fall:** Calendar sync and schedule reset.
- **Winter:** Cozy cleanup with hot cocoa afterward.

Shared rituals reduce shame, build teamwork, and make routines feel communal rather than isolating.

Step 10: Seasonal Self-Compassion

Perhaps the most important element of seasonal routines is compassion. ADHD lives are full of ups and downs. Instead of demanding perfection year-round, seasonal routines give you permission to ebb and flow.

- Low energy in winter? That's expected. Simplify.
- Bursting with energy in spring? Ride the wave.
- Distracted in summer? Shrink routines and embrace flexibility.
- Focused in fall? Build structures to carry you through.

When you see yourself as part of a cycle instead of a failure, routines stop being punishments and start being supports.

Case Study 1: Hannah and the Winter Collapse

Hannah always set big January goals: gym five days a week, meal prepping, cleaning routines. By February, she'd burn out and spiral into shame.

When she learned about seasonal routines, she shifted her expectations. Winter became her "maintenance" season. Instead of new goals, she set a cozy evening reset (tidy dishes, light a candle, tea). By spring, she felt refreshed and ready to add bigger habits. Her routines stopped collapsing because they were designed to flex.

Case Study 2: Marcus and the Summer Chaos

Marcus, a teacher with ADHD, loved the structure of the school year but crashed in summer. Without a schedule, his home fell apart.

He adopted summer-specific routines: short 5-minute resets twice a day, paired with outdoor habits (watering plants, sweeping porch). He simplified meal planning to salads and grilled dinners. By embracing seasonal lightness instead of fighting for strict routines, Marcus enjoyed summer without losing control of his space.

Step 11: Seasonal Rituals as ADHD-Friendly Motivation

Rituals are moments of meaning. Seasonal rituals add novelty and joy to routines.

- Spring cleaning day with windows open and favorite playlist.
- Summer reset with iced drinks and 10-minute tidy before heading outside.
- Fall "planner refresh" with new pens and cozy blankets.
- Winter "digital detox day" with cocoa and phone declutter.

These rituals anchor time, add fun, and make routines feel like celebrations.

Closing Thought

ADHD brains are not broken because routines slip. They are wired for movement, novelty, and adaptation. Seasonal routines honor that truth. They turn failure into flexibility, collapse into cycles, and shame into compassion.

Instead of trying to force the same routine year-round, embrace the rhythm of the seasons. Let your routines breathe, bend, and evolve with the calendar. You don't have to fight your brain or the year, you can design systems that work with both.

When you sync your life to the seasons, routines stop being fragile. They become flexible. They stop being punishments. They become support. And that shift changes everything.

CHAPTER 7

EMERGENCY ROUTINES QUICK SYSTEMS FOR CHAOTIC DAYS

Why We Need Emergency Routines

If there's one truth about ADHD life, it's this: some days simply fall apart. The alarm doesn't go off. The kids are melting down. You forgot about the deadline. You're already late, and your house looks like a tornado hit it.

In those moments, standard routines feel impossible. A "perfect morning checklist" is laughable when you're rushing out the door without breakfast. An elaborate evening reset won't happen after a day that leaves you drained and fried.

This is where **emergency routines** save the day. Think of them as the fire extinguishers of daily life: small, fast, bare-minimum systems you pull out when chaos strikes. They aren't glamorous, and they aren't about doing everything "right." They're about keeping life afloat with the least effort possible.

For ADHDers, this matters even more. Without emergency routines, chaotic days spiral into shame spirals: "I failed again. I'll never get this together." With emergency routines, chaotic days become survivable. You have a fallback. You don't need to collapse into guilt.

The Power of "Bare Minimum"

Many ADHDers operate in all-or-nothing mode. Either we clean the entire kitchen top-to-bottom, or we let dishes pile until they're overwhelming. Either we follow our routine perfectly, or we abandon it completely.

Emergency routines break this cycle. They ask: **What's the smallest action that will make life livable today?**

- Instead of "deep clean the kitchen," it's "throw dishes into the sink and rinse."
- Instead of "cook a balanced dinner," it's "order takeout or make a sandwich."
- Instead of "reset the whole house," it's "clear one surface."

By lowering the bar, you still move forward. And forward, even if small, is what breaks the cycle of chaos.

Step 1: The "Three Non-Negotiables"

On the worst days, focus on three things only:

1. **Eat something.** It doesn't have to be healthy or elaborate—just fuel your body.
2. **Hydrate.** ADHD brains forget water, but dehydration makes chaos worse.
3. **Meds (if prescribed).** These are your foundation.

Everything else, laundry, cleaning, emails, comes after. When you strip it down to survival needs, you give yourself grace.

Step 2: Morning Emergency Routine

Mornings can make or break a chaotic day. An emergency morning routine is **fast, minimal, and grounding**.

Example:

- Brush teeth (2 minutes).
- Drink water (30 seconds).
- Dress in something clean and comfortable (5 minutes).
- Grab one food item (banana, granola bar, toast).

That's it. Not a full workout, not journaling, not a perfect breakfast. Just the minimum to leave the house fed, dressed, and semi-functional.

Step 3: Evening Emergency Routine

Evenings are another danger zone. ADHDers often collapse into exhaustion, then wake up to chaos the next morning. An emergency evening routine prevents this spiral.

Example:

- Do a 5-minute "surface sweep" (clear counters or put dishes in sink).
- Plug in devices (phone, laptop).
- Set out clothes for tomorrow.
- Collapse into bed.

Even if the rest of the house is messy, these few actions make tomorrow less overwhelming.

Step 4: Cleaning Emergency Routine

Some days the house feels like it exploded. Instead of thinking *"I have to clean everything,"* use an emergency cleaning system.

The 5-Minute Tidy:

- Set a timer.
- Pick one small area (couch, entryway, kitchen counter).
- Put away only what fits in your hands.
- Stop when timer ends.

The "One Surface Rule":

- Choose one surface (desk, table, counter).
- Clear it completely.
- Celebrate the visible difference.

The Laundry Quick Fix:

- Gather all dirty laundry into one basket.
- Toss one load into washer.
- Don't worry about folding yet.

Cleaning emergencies are about visibility and relief, not perfection.

Step 5: Food Emergency Routine

ADHD brains often forget to eat, or eat chaotically. When life is messy, meals should be **automatic and low-effort**.

- Keep a stash of emergency foods: granola bars, instant noodles, frozen meals, cheese sticks, fruit.
- Use "assembly meals": sandwiches, wraps, quesadillas.
- Order takeout guilt-free when needed.

The goal is not gourmet, it's nourishment. A fed brain is a functioning brain.

Step 6: Work/School Emergency Routine

When deadlines crash and focus is gone, an emergency system keeps you from drowning.

The 15-Minute Start:

- Set a timer.
- Open the assignment or task.
- Work for 15 minutes, no pressure.

Often, starting breaks the paralysis. If it doesn't, you've still done 15 minutes more than nothing.

The "One Thing List":

- Write down the one most urgent task.
- Ignore everything else until it's done.

The Quick Reset:

- Step outside.
- Breathe deeply.
- Return with a clear head.

These routines cut through overwhelm and reduce procrastination spirals.

Step 7: Family and Household Emergency Routines

If you live with others, chaotic days affect everyone. Emergency routines can be communal.

- **Family 10-Minute Cleanup:** Everyone picks one zone. Blast music, clean for 10 minutes, stop.
- **Kid Survival Routines:** Snacks, water, screens for 30 minutes while you reset.

- **Partner Divide-and-Conquer:** One handles food, one handles tidying.

When everyone knows the emergency system, chaos doesn't fall on one person's shoulders.

Step 8: Travel and Out-of-Routine Emergencies

Vacations, holidays, or unexpected events often wreck ADHD systems. Emergency routines keep the basics intact.

- **Travel Bag Anchors:** Pack snacks, meds, chargers, water bottle.
- **Hotel Reset:** Keep clothes in one spot, charge devices in same outlet.
- **Holiday Chaos Plan:** Prioritize food, hydration, and one daily tidy.

Instead of expecting perfect structure, expect disruption, and plan small anchors to survive it.

Step 9: The "Reset in 5" System

Sometimes the whole day has collapsed, and you need a restart. The Reset in 5 is a quick rescue:

1. Drink water.
2. Wash your face or hands.
3. Pick up five items.
4. Open a window or step outside.
5. Write down one next task.

In less than five minutes, you feel fresher, the space looks better, and your brain has direction.

Step 10: Emergency Emotional Routine

Chaotic days aren't just messy, they're emotional. ADHD brains default to guilt and shame when routines collapse. That only makes things harder.

An emotional emergency routine calms the storm:

- Take three deep breaths.
- Say out loud: *"This is temporary. I'm not a failure."*
- Text a supportive friend, or use body doubling.
- Put on a calming or uplifting song.

Soothing yourself is part of survival.

Case Study 1: Maya and the Overloaded Morning

Maya often overslept, then spiraled into panic: she'd skip breakfast, forget her meds, and arrive at work frazzled. Her emergency morning routine became: brush teeth, drink water, grab a granola bar, take meds. Four steps, five minutes. Even on disaster days, she felt grounded.

Case Study 2: Andre and the End-of-Day Crash

Andre came home exhausted from work and collapsed on the couch. Dishes piled up, laundry sat in heaps, and mornings felt unbearable. He adopted an evening emergency routine: put dishes in sink, plug in phone, set out clothes. Ten minutes, then bed. His mornings became calmer, and the house stopped spiraling out of control.

Step 11: Building an Emergency Routine Menu

One of the best ADHD strategies is having a **menu of emergency options**. Instead of relying on memory in crisis, you already know what to do.

Sample Menu:

- Morning: brush teeth, water, clothes, food.
- Evening: 5-minute tidy, plug in devices, clothes out.
- Cleaning: one surface or 5-minute timer.
- Work: one urgent task or 15-minute start.
- Food: granola bar, sandwich, frozen meal.

Print it, post it, or keep it on your phone. When chaos hits, you grab the menu instead of spiraling.

Step 12: Normalize Using Emergency Routines

Emergency routines are not failures. They are **success strategies**. Everyone has days that collapse. The difference is whether you drown in guilt or float with systems.

Think of emergency routines like first aid: you don't use them every day, but when you need them, they save you. And the more you use them, the more you trust yourself to bounce back.

Closing Thought

ADHD life is unpredictable. Routines will fail. Days will collapse. Chaos will come. But chaos doesn't have to mean disaster.

Emergency routines are your life rafts. They are proof that survival doesn't require perfection, just small, simple, compassionate steps. They keep you afloat until calm returns.

And that is the point: you don't have to conquer every day. You only have to rescue it.

Reflection Questions:

- *Book 4 introduced the idea of creating a simple cleaning toolkit and using time-management hacks. Think about your current cleaning routine. What is one item you could add to your cleaning toolkit to make tasks easier, or what is one time-blocking or gamification technique you could try this week to make a specific chore more manageable?*
- *We also discussed delegating, automating, and outsourcing tasks. Is there a recurring chore or mental task that consistently causes you stress (e.g., paying bills, doing laundry)? What is one way you could either automate that task or ask for support to reduce your mental load?*
- *This book presented **"time blindness"** as a common challenge. Is there a specific, recurring task you consistently underestimate the time it will take to complete? What is a small change you could make this week to more accurately schedule that task, either with a timer or a calendar block?*
- *Think about the concept of **dopamine stacking** and making chores fun. What is one of your favorite high-dopamine activities (e.g., listening to a specific podcast, a new snack)? How could you intentionally pair that activity with a low-interest chore this week to make the task more appealing?*
- *We discussed the role of technology as an **"external brain."** What is one recurring thought or reminder that you constantly have to hold in your head (e.g., "I need to buy milk," "I need to call the doctor")? How could you use a simple digital tool, a reminder app, a calendar event, to offload that thought and free up your mental energy?*

BOOK FIVE

STAYING CONSISTENT AND BOUNCING BACK

CHAPTER 1

DON'T BREAK THE CHAIN: VISUAL MOMENTUM TRICKS TO KEEP YOU GOING.

Consistency is the ultimate goal, but for the ADHD brain, it can feel like the most elusive. The "Don't Break the Chain" method is a simple, visual, and highly effective tool for building and maintaining momentum on a new habit. It's a way to gamify consistency and get your brain to focus on a streak, not a single performance. This strategy directly addresses the challenges of **task initiation** and **inconsistency**, which are common symptoms of executive dysfunction. By turning a long-term goal into a short-term, daily challenge, you make consistency a tangible, rewarding experience.

How it Works

The method is simple: get a calendar, a whiteboard, or a simple habit-tracking app. For every day that you successfully perform a new habit—whether it's the "10-minute tidy" or the "evening reset", you place a checkmark or an "X" on that day. The goal is to build a chain of these marks, day after day. The visual representation of the unbroken chain becomes a powerful motivator.

This system works because it makes an abstract concept (**consistency**) concrete and visible. The chain is a physical record of your progress, and it provides a powerful dopamine hit every time you add a new link. It's a non-negotiable, visible cue that serves as a reminder and a reward all in one. The beauty of this method is its simplicity; it doesn't require complex planning or a rigid schedule. It only requires a single, small action each day.

The Psychology Behind It

This method works for the ADHD brain because it taps into several key psychological and neurobiological principles:

- **Visual Cue:** The chain provides a clear, tangible representation of your progress. It's a **dopamine hit** every time you add a new link. The brain is highly motivated by positive reinforcement, and a visual symbol of success provides that immediate reward. For a brain that struggles with working memory, a visual cue is a far more reliable source of motivation than an abstract promise of a "cleaner home someday."
- **Loss Aversion:** This is a powerful cognitive bias where we are more motivated to avoid losing something we have than to gain something we don't. The fear of "breaking the chain" can be a powerful driver to complete the task, even on a day when you don't feel like it. The chain is a visual representation of your effort, and the thought of losing that streak can be a stronger motivator than the initial effort required to start the task.
- **Small, Manageable Task:** The "chain" is not about the monumental task of organizing the entire house. It's about the small, daily action that builds the chain. This keeps the task from feeling overwhelming. By focusing on a single, low-effort habit, you are lowering the activation energy required to start. You are not saying, "I have to clean the whole house"; you are saying, "I just have to do the 10-minute tidy to keep my chain going." This shift in focus is a critical strategy for the ADHD brain.
- **The Power of Habit Stacking:** The "Don't Break the Chain" method is an excellent way to implement **habit stacking**, a strategy where you pair a new habit with an existing, well-established one. For example, if you already have a habit of making your morning coffee, you can "stack" a new habit on top of it. "After I make my coffee, I will do my 10-minute tidy and then check off my chain." This ties the new habit to an existing routine, making it more likely to stick.

The All-or-Nothing Trap and the "Don't Break the Chain" Method

One of the greatest challenges for the ADHD brain is **all-or-nothing thinking.** A single missed day can be interpreted as a complete failure, leading to the abandonment of the habit altogether. The "Don't Break the Chain" method helps to mitigate this. While the goal is an unbroken chain, a single missed day doesn't have to be the end of the world. It's a chance to learn, to adjust, and to start a new chain.

- **Compassionate Re-framing:** If you miss a day, instead of beating yourself up, try to understand why it happened. Was the task too big? Was the time unrealistic? This is a moment for self-compassion and problem-solving, not self-criticism.
- **The "Two-Day Rule":** A helpful rule of thumb is to allow yourself a single missed day, but never two in a row. This prevents a single slip-up from turning into a complete abandonment of the habit. It keeps you focused on the long-term goal without demanding a level of perfection that is unsustainable.

Practical Application: Starting Your First Chain

1. **Choose a Single, Simple Habit:** Don't try to build three new habits at once. Choose one, such as the "10-minute tidy," and commit to it. Make it as easy and low-effort as possible.
2. **Choose Your Tracker:** Find a visual tracker that works for you. A wall calendar is great because it's a constant visual reminder. A simple app is great because it's always with you.
3. **Start with a Small Goal:** Aim for a seven-day chain. The first week is often the hardest, but once you've completed a full week, the momentum is a powerful force.
4. **Celebrate Your Wins:** When you hit a milestone—a full week, a full month—take a moment to celebrate. This provides a crucial dopamine hit and reinforces the positive behavior.

The "Don't Break the Chain" method is not about perfection. It's about showing up, even when it's hard. It's about building a habit one day at a time, and celebrating the visual proof of your consistency. It's a strategy that respects your brain's unique wiring and turns the frustrating pursuit of consistency into a rewarding and achievable game. By using this method, you are building more than just a clean home; you are building a new, more supportive relationship with yourself.

CHAPTER 2

LIFE HAPPENS – HERE'S THE REBOUND PLAN HOW TO RECOVER QUICKLY AFTER A SLIP.

No matter how good your systems are, no matter how carefully you plan, life will inevitably get in the way. There will be sick days, travel, busy weeks, and moments when you just fall off the wagon. For the ADHD brain, a slip-up can feel like a total, catastrophic failure, leading to a downward spiral of shame and inaction. The brain's tendency for **all-or-nothing thinking** can turn a single missed day of a routine into a complete abandonment of the habit. This chapter is about learning the art of the rebound, getting back on track without judgment, and understanding that the ability to recover is far more important than the ability to be perfect.

The Myth of "Total Failure"

The myth of "total failure" is a dangerous one. It's the voice in your head that says, "Well, I missed my routine yesterday, so the whole week is a bust. I'll just start again next Monday." This line of thinking is a classic cognitive distortion that prevents progress. It's the idea that if a system isn't perfect, it's worthless.

A missed day is not a total failure. A missed week is not a total failure. It's simply a pause. The most important part of building a routine isn't the ability to never fall off; it's the ability to get back on quickly and without shame. The neurobiological reality is that the prefrontal cortex, which is responsible for self-regulation and long-term planning, is less active in the ADHD brain. When a habit is broken, this part of the brain doesn't have the "go-get-em" energy to say, "That's okay, let's try again." Instead, the emotional centers of the brain can take over, leading to feelings of guilt and shame, which are powerful demotivators. The key to the rebound is to interrupt this cycle before it can take hold.

Think of it like a diet or a workout plan. If you miss one day at the gym, you don't decide that the entire year is a failure. You simply go the next day. The stakes with a chore routine feel different, but the principle is the same. The art of the rebound is a critical skill for building a sustainable, organized life. It's the difference between a temporary slip-up and a permanent derailment.

The "Rebound Rule": Your Non-Negotiable Lifeline

The **"Rebound Rule"** is a simple, non-negotiable principle: **start again tomorrow.** No matter what happened today, no matter what you missed, tomorrow is a new day. You don't have to make up for the missed time or beat yourself up about it. Just wake up and start your routine again, one small step at a time.

This rule is a powerful counter to perfectionism and all-or-nothing thinking. It gives you a clear, simple instruction that doesn't require a complex mental calculus. It's a low-effort way to get back on track.

How to Implement the "Rebound Rule":

1. **Acknowledge, Don't Judge:** The moment you realize you've missed a habit, briefly acknowledge it. Don't get stuck in a shame spiral. A simple mental note like, "I missed my 10-minute tidy today," is enough.
2. **Put it on Tomorrow's List:** Immediately put the habit back on your schedule for the next day. This moves the decision-making from an emotional, in-the-moment choice to a planned,

scheduled action. You are making a commitment to your future self.

3. **Make it Tiny:** On the day you rebound, make the first task incredibly small and low-effort. For a "10-minute tidy," maybe you only commit to one minute. The goal isn't to be perfect; the goal is to get started. The act of starting, no matter how small, is a win.

This process works because it bypasses the emotional roadblocks and directly addresses the issue of **task initiation** by making the first step as easy as possible.

Self-Compassion is Key: Quieting the Inner Critic

The journey to an organized life is often derailed not by a lack of ability, but by a lack of **self-compassion**. The inner critic, that voice that tells you you're not good enough or that you're a failure, is a powerful force. This voice is often louder and more persistent for those with ADHD, fueled by a lifetime of perceived shortcomings.

Self-compassion is not an excuse for laziness. It's a deliberate choice to treat yourself with the same kindness and understanding you would offer a friend. Instead of saying, "I should have done better," try, "I did my best today, and tomorrow is another chance to show up for myself." The more compassionate you are with yourself, the easier it is to get back on track. This practice can lower cortisol levels, reduce stress, and create a more conducive mental state for action.

Concrete Examples of Self-Compassion:

- **Instead of:** "I'm so lazy, I didn't even do the dishes."
- **Try:** "I was feeling overwhelmed today, and that's okay. I'll load one dish into the dishwasher now and do the rest in the morning."
- **Instead of:** "I always mess up my routines."
- **Try:** "I'm learning what works for me. My routine didn't fit my energy level today, so I'll try a different approach tomorrow."

This reframing turns a moment of failure into a moment of learning, which is a far more productive and sustainable path.

The "Rebound Toolkit": Specific Strategies for Getting Back on Track

When you find yourself in a slump, a few simple, pre-planned tools can make the rebound process much easier.

- **The Five-Minute Reset:** This is a low-effort, high-impact strategy. Set a timer for five minutes and do a simple task to get a quick win. This could be putting away five items, wiping down a counter, or taking out the trash. The goal is to build momentum, not to complete a major project.
- **The "What I Learned" Journal:** Instead of focusing on what you did wrong, take a moment to reflect on what happened. Was there an external factor, like a lack of sleep? Was the task too big? Write down a short, non-judgmental note about what you learned. This turns a moment of frustration into a moment of data collection, which is invaluable for refining your systems.
- **Body Doubling:** As we discussed in Book 4, the presence of another person, even a virtual one, can provide a powerful anchor for your focus. When you're struggling to get back on track, reach out to a friend or a partner and ask them to "body double" with you. You can both do chores in the same room or on a video call. The social element provides a gentle accountability and a sense of shared purpose that can help you overcome the activation barrier.
- **The "Clean Slate" Method:** When a space becomes so overwhelming that you don't know where to start, try the "clean slate" method. Put everything on a surface into a single box or basket. This gets the visual clutter out of the way immediately. Then, deal with the items in the box one by one. This simple act of containment can provide an immense sense of relief and a clear starting point.

The art of the rebound is a critical skill for building a sustainable, organized life. It's the difference between a temporary slip-up and a permanent derailment. It's about building resilience and a supportive relationship with yourself. By learning to rebound with self-compassion and without judgment, you are building a life that is not only more organized but also more forgiving and more authentically your own.

CHAPTER 3

YOUR SUPPORT SQUAD: BUILDING ACCOUNTABILITY THAT ACTUALLY WORKS FOR ADHD.

Trying to build new habits in a vacuum can feel isolating and nearly impossible. The ADHD brain thrives on **external motivation** and support. This is a neurobiological reality. The brain's internal reward and motivation systems, driven by dopamine, are often less consistent. Therefore, an external system, like a friend checking in or a shared goal, can provide the necessary stimulus to initiate and maintain a habit. This chapter is about building a personal "team" of accountability partners and support systems that can help you stay on track, celebrate your wins, and get back up when you fall.

Find an Accountability Partner

An **accountability partner** is someone you check in with regularly to share your goals and your progress. This isn't about judgment; it's about mutual support and gentle pressure. The simple act of telling someone what you're going to do increases your likelihood of doing it. This is a well-documented psychological phenomenon. By externalizing your intentions, you create a social contract that is often a stronger motivator than a personal one.

How to find and work with an accountability partner:

- **Choose Wisely:** Find someone who is supportive, not critical. This could be a friend, a family member, or a fellow ADHD-er. Ideally, you should both be working on a similar goal, as this makes the relationship feel more reciprocal and less one-sided.
- **Establish a Routine:** Schedule a quick 10-minute call or text exchange once a week to share your wins and challenges. Consistency is key here. The routine of the check-in itself becomes a part of the habit.
- **Be Specific:** Instead of saying, "I'm going to be better this week," say, "I am going to do a 10-minute tidy every day after dinner." This gives both of you a clear, measurable goal to discuss.
- **Focus on Progress, Not Perfection:** The purpose of the check-in is not to report a perfect week. It's to be honest about your struggles. An accountability partner is there to help you problem-solve, not to shame you for a slip-up. They can help you brainstorm solutions when your routine isn't working for you.

Body Doubling: The Power of Presence

Body doubling is a specific and highly effective form of accountability. It's the practice of working on a task in the presence of another person, even if they aren't helping. The presence of another person provides a subtle form of accountability and an external anchor for your focus. It helps to regulate your attention and can make a tedious task feel less isolating.

- **In-Person Body Doubling:** This is the most effective form. Ask a friend or partner to work on their own project in the same room while you do your chores. The social element provides a gentle pressure and a sense of shared purpose that can help you overcome the activation barrier.

- **Virtual Body Doubling:** If an in-person partner isn't available, a virtual one can be just as effective. A quick video call with a friend where you both work silently on separate tasks can provide a similar sense of presence and accountability. There are even apps and online communities specifically for this purpose.

The science behind body doubling is fascinating. It's believed that the presence of another person doing a similar task helps to stimulate the **mirror neurons** in our brain. These neurons fire both when we perform an action and when we observe someone else performing the same action, creating a sense of shared purpose and a gentle push toward action.

Leverage Your Support System

Your support system is the community of people who love and care about you: your partner, your family, your close friends. Don't be afraid to lean on them. This is not a sign of weakness; it's a sign of maturity and self-awareness.

- **Communicate Your Needs:** The people who love you want to support you, but they can't read your mind. Explain to your loved ones what you're working on and how they can best support you. This could be as simple as, "I'm trying to be better about my morning routine. Could you remind me to put my keys on the launchpad at night?"
- **Make it a Team Effort:** Frame your organizational journey as a team effort. Instead of saying, "Could you help me clean the kitchen?" say, "Could we work together to get the kitchen clean so we can both relax for the rest of the night?" This shared language of "we" and "our" makes it a collaborative effort rather than a one-sided favor.
- **Ask for Specific, Actionable Help:** Avoid vague requests. Instead of saying, "Help me get organized," ask for specific, actionable help. "Could you spend an hour with me this Saturday to help me go through my closet using the 'Keep, Toss, Donate' method?" This gives your support system a clear, defined way to help you, which makes them more likely to agree.

Professional Support: Therapists and ADHD Coaches

For some, an organized life is a long and winding road that may require professional support. Working with an ADHD coach or a therapist can be a game-changer. These professionals are trained to understand the unique challenges of the ADHD brain and can provide invaluable, personalized strategies.

- **ADHD Coaches:** An ADHD coach specializes in helping individuals develop systems and strategies for managing their symptoms in daily life. They act as a highly specialized accountability partner, helping you set realistic goals, break down tasks, and build sustainable habits. They don't just tell you what to do; they help you find what works for you.
- **Therapists:** A therapist, particularly one who specializes in ADHD, can help you work through the underlying emotional challenges that often accompany ADHD, such as shame, anxiety, and a low sense of self-worth. They can help you reframe your relationship with your brain and develop self-compassion, which is the foundation for all lasting change.

The Power of Community

In addition to one-on-one support, finding a community of people who understand your struggles can be incredibly powerful. Online forums, local support groups, or even social media groups dedicated to ADHD and organization can provide a sense of belonging and a space to share your wins and challenges without judgment. This community can be a source of new ideas, motivation, and the powerful reminder that you are not alone in your journey.

The Final Word: You Are Not a Lone Wolf

Building a support system isn't a sign of weakness; it's a sign of strength. It's a recognition that you don't have to do it all alone and that a team approach is the most effective way to build a sustainable, organized life. By leaning on your accountability partners, your support system, and, if needed, professional help, you are creating a safety net that catches you when you fall and a launchpad that propels you forward when you succeed. The goal isn't to be perfect, but to build a life that is so well-supported that you can thrive, not just survive.

CHAPTER 4

CELEBRATE EVERY WIN
HOW SMALL VICTORIES KEEP YOUR BRAIN MOTIVATED.

For the ADHD brain, the "end of the road" reward, a perfectly organized home, a completely clean garage, can feel so far away that it loses its motivational power. This is because our brains are hardwired to prioritize immediate rewards. This isn't a flaw; it's a feature. The problem with tasks like deep cleaning is that the reward is often abstract and delayed. This is why it's so important to build a system of immediate, smaller rewards. This chapter is about acknowledging and celebrating your wins, no matter how small they are, to keep your brain engaged and motivated.

Think of it like a video game. You don't have to beat the final boss to get a reward. Every small enemy you defeat, every coin you collect, every level you complete gives you a small, immediate win that encourages you to keep going. We are going to apply that same principle to the tasks in your home.

The Neurobiology of Celebration: The Dopamine Feedback Loop

The ADHD brain is driven by **dopamine**, a neurotransmitter that plays a crucial role in motivation, reward, and pleasure. When we complete a task and immediately celebrate that win, we are giving our brain a dose of that feel-good chemical. This creates a powerful **positive feedback loop**:

1. You start a task.
2. You complete a small part of it.
3. You immediately celebrate the win.
4. Your brain releases dopamine, which makes you feel good.
5. This positive feeling is then associated with the task, making it more likely that you will want to do it again.

This is a deliberate, neurobiologically-informed strategy. By celebrating a win, you're not just being self-indulgent; you're actively reinforcing the neural pathways for the new habit, making it easier and more automatic over time. You are training your brain to see these tasks not as tedious chores, but as opportunities for a reward.

The Power of Immediate Gratification

The key to this system is making the reward immediate and aligned with the effort. The reward should be a low-effort, high-impact experience that provides an immediate dopamine hit.

Verbal Acknowledgment: The Power of Self-Praise

Verbal acknowledgment is the simplest, most immediate form of celebration. When you finish a task, say out loud, "I did it!" This simple act of self-praise reinforces the positive behavior. It's an external cue that acknowledges your effort and makes your achievement concrete.

- **Make it a Habit:** The moment you finish putting away the last dish, say, "Done!" or "Boom! Another win." This simple verbal tag reinforces the feeling of accomplishment.
- **The Power of Framing:** Instead of just acknowledging the task, acknowledge your effort. Say, "I did a great job sticking to my 10-minute tidy today," or "I really showed up for myself by getting that done." This builds a positive self-narrative that is more motivating than a negative one.

This may feel silly at first, but it is a powerful way to train your brain. It is the verbal equivalent of a checkmark on a to-do list.

Small, Tangible Rewards: A Guilt-Free Treat

After a small win, a small, tangible reward can be a powerful motivator. The key here is to make the reward immediate, easy to access, and not so big that it becomes a distraction.

- **After a 15-minute cleaning sprint:**
  - Enjoy a piece of your favorite dark chocolate.
  - Watch one episode of a show you're currently watching.
  - Spend a few minutes playing a video game you enjoy.
  - Sit down for a few minutes with a special cup of tea or coffee.
- **After a "deep dive" project:**
  - Treat yourself to a movie night.
  - Order your favorite takeout for dinner.
  - Take a long, hot bath with a podcast playing.
  - Go for a walk in a place you love.

The reward should be **guilt-free**. It is not a sign of laziness; it is a strategic investment in your future motivation. You're giving your brain the encouragement it needs to keep going. It's a way of saying, "Thank you for the hard work, here's a little something for you."

Visual Proof: The Motivation You Can See

For the ADHD brain, which is often highly visual, seeing your progress is a powerful motivator. The chain on a habit tracker, a clean counter, or a tidied room provides a dopamine hit that can be revisited when you're feeling unmotivated.

- **Before-and-After Photos:** Take a picture of a messy space before you start a project and another one after you're done. The visual contrast is a powerful, tangible record of your accomplishment. Look at these pictures when you're feeling a lack of motivation.
- **The Habit Tracker:** As we discussed in Book 5, the visual chain of "X's" on a calendar is a powerful reward in itself. The longer the chain gets, the more motivated you are to keep it from breaking. This visual proof of your consistency is a testament to your hard work.
- **A "Trophy" Shelf:** For a project you're particularly proud of, put a small item, a toy, a piece of art, on a designated "trophy shelf." This is a physical, visual reminder of your ability to complete a task.

These visual cues bypass the need for memory and self-motivation by providing an immediate, powerful reminder of your success.

Advanced Celebration Strategies

Once you've mastered the basics, you can build on them with more advanced strategies.

The "Win of the Day" Ritual

At the end of each day, take just one minute to reflect on a single "win." It doesn't have to be a major accomplishment. It could be something as simple as, "I remembered to put the keys on the launchpad," or "I successfully completed my 10-minute tidy." This ritual of reflection is a powerful way to reframe your day from a series of perceived failures to a series of small wins. It trains your brain to look for the positive, which can have a profound impact on your overall mindset.

Connect Wins to Values: The "Why" of the Win

For a deeper sense of motivation, try connecting a small win to a larger value. This adds a layer of meaning that can be incredibly powerful.

- **Instead of:** "I did the dishes."
- **Try:** "I did the dishes, which is an act of self-care and helps create a more peaceful, beautiful home for myself."
- **Instead of:** "I paid that bill on time."
- **Try:** "I paid that bill on time, which is a great way to show responsibility and reduce future anxiety."

This reframing moves the task from a simple chore to an action that is aligned with your deeper values, which can be a more sustainable source of motivation.

The Celebration Calendar

Create a simple calendar that is separate from your chore list. On this calendar, mark down every win, big or small. This calendar becomes a visual record of your successes, not just your obligations. It's a powerful reminder that your life is a series of wins, not just a series of challenges.

The All-or-Nothing Trap and the "Rebound"

The all-or-nothing trap is the voice that says, "I didn't get all the dishes done, so it doesn't count." This is the enemy of progress. Celebration is the perfect counter. Celebrate the fact that you did *some* of the dishes. Celebrate the fact that you started. The act of celebrating is a signal to your brain that effort is the important part, not perfection.

This ties back to the **"Rebound Rule"** from Chapter 2. When you do fall off the wagon, you can use celebration as a tool to get back on. Celebrate the fact that you're choosing to rebound. The act of returning to a habit after a slip-up is a huge win, and it deserves to be celebrated.

The Final Word: You Are Worthy of Celebration

Celebrating your wins isn't about being self-indulgent; it's about being strategic. You're giving your brain the encouragement it needs to keep going. You are not fighting against your brain's nature; you are working with it, using its need for immediate gratification to build long-term, sustainable habits. By building a system of immediate, tangible rewards, you are training your brain to see your tasks not as obstacles, but as opportunities for a win. You are building a new, more supportive relationship with yourself, and that is a reward in itself.

CHAPTER 5

YOUR ORGANIZED FUTURE: CREATING A HOME AND LIFE THAT STAYS MANAGEABLE FOR THE LONG HAUL.

As we reach the end of this journey, it's important to remember that organization is not a destination. It's a continuous practice of building systems, being flexible, and showing yourself compassion. This book has given you a toolkit, but you are the architect. Your organized future is not a perfectly clean home; it's a home that feels peaceful, functional, and supportive of your unique brain.

Redefining Your Relationship with Organization

For many people, the word "organization" conjures images of pristine, minimalist spaces, color-coded shelves, and an impossibly tidy aesthetic. For the ADHD brain, this vision can be a source of shame and overwhelm. It sets an unrealistic standard that is often based on the neurotypical brain's capacity for routine and sustained attention. The first step toward your organized future is to let go of this myth.

Your organized future isn't about perfection; it's about **functionality**. It's about a system that works for you, not against you. Your home is not a museum to be admired; it's a launchpad for your life. The goal is to reduce the friction in your daily existence so that your limited mental energy can be directed toward what truly matters: your relationships, your career, your passions, and your well-being. This is an identity shift. You are moving from a person who *struggles* with organization to a person who *maintains* systems that support your life.

The Functional Home: A Sanctuary for Your Brain

What does a functional home actually look like for someone with ADHD? It's a home that is designed with your specific neurobiology in mind. It's a home that understands your need for visual calm, your challenges with working memory, and your brain's craving for novelty and reward.

The "Visual Calm" of a Low-Friction System

One of the most powerful concepts in this book is the idea of a **low-friction system**. A low-friction system is one that requires minimal mental energy to use. Think of the "launchpad" for your keys and wallet. The friction of hunting for them is gone. Your organized future is a home filled with these low-friction systems.

- **Open-Face Storage:** For many with ADHD, "out of sight, out of mind" is a constant reality. Closed cabinets and opaque boxes can be a death sentence for organization. Your functional home will likely use more open-face storage, like clear bins or open shelves, so that you can see what you have. This externalizes the need to remember where things are.
- **The "One-Touch Rule":** This is a simple principle to live by. When you bring an item into your home, it should only be touched once before it is put in its proper place. This is a difficult habit to build, but it's the cornerstone of a functional home. It prevents the pile-up of mail, clothes, and other items that create a "chaos hotspot."
- **Zones of Function:** Your organized future doesn't have perfectly clean rooms; it has functional **zones**. Your entryway is the "launchpad" zone. Your kitchen counter is the "prep zone." Your desk is the "focus zone." By defining these zones, you are giving each space a clear purpose, which reduces the mental effort required to know what to do in that space.

Your functional home is a sanctuary, not because it is perfectly tidy, but because it is designed to support you. It's a space where you are in control, not overwhelmed by the demands of a chaotic environment.

The Journey from Shame to Self-Compassion

Perhaps the most significant journey you will take is the one from shame to self-compassion. Many people with ADHD have spent a lifetime internalizing a narrative of "failure." You've been told you're lazy, unmotivated, or just not trying hard enough. This book has hopefully shown you that these are not character flaws, but symptoms of a unique neurotype.

Your organized future is a life where you have replaced shame with **self-compassion**. A slip-up is just a slip-up, not a total failure. The "Rebound Rule" is not just a scheduling hack; it's a profound act of self-forgiveness. It's the moment you say to yourself, "I am a human being, I did my best today, and tomorrow is another chance to show up for myself."

- **Acknowledge the Pain:** The first step to self-compassion is acknowledging the pain of past struggles. It's okay to recognize that it has been a hard journey. Acknowledging this pain is not a sign of weakness; it's a sign of strength and a necessary step toward healing.
- **Reframe the Narrative:** Instead of seeing past struggles as a sign of personal failure, reframe them as moments of learning. The messy closet wasn't a sign that you are a bad person; it was a sign that the system you were using wasn't working for you. Your organized future is built on these lessons, not on a foundation of guilt.
- **Forgive Yourself:** Practice forgiving yourself for the times you fell off the wagon. You were doing the best you could with the tools you had. Now you have a new toolkit, and with it comes a new chance to build a better future.

This journey of self-compassion is the emotional engine that will power your long-term success. It's the difference between a system that is a source of anxiety and one that is a source of peace.

Your Personal Playbook: The Art of the Architect

This book is a collection of blueprints, not a finished house. You are the architect. The "Don't Break the Chain" method, the "Beat the Clock" game, the cleaning caddy—these are all tools. Your job is to experiment, iterate, and build a personalized system that works for your unique brain.

- **Start Small and Iterate:** Don't try to implement every strategy at once. Pick one small, low-effort habit, like the "One-Song Tidy," and try it for a week. If it works, great. If not, try another one. This is a process of scientific discovery, not a race to perfection.
- **Listen to Your Brain:** Pay attention to what works and what doesn't. When a system fails, don't blame yourself. Ask, "What did I learn from this?" The answer might be, "I learned that I hate doing dishes, so maybe I should look into outsourcing that." Or, "I learned that visual timers are more effective for me than my phone timer."
- **The "Maintenance Mindset":** The most powerful identity shift you can make is to stop thinking of organization as a one-time event and start thinking of it as a continuous practice. You are not "getting organized"; you are "maintaining my systems." The 10-minute tidy isn't a chore; it's the daily maintenance of your system. This small shift in language can have a profound impact on your motivation and consistency.

This is a powerful and empowering vision. You are not a passive victim of your neurodiversity; you are an active agent, a designer, a problem-solver. You are building a life that is tailored to your unique strengths and needs.

The Universal Message: A Call to Action

While this book has been a guide for men with adult ADHD, its lessons are universal. They are for anyone who has ever felt overwhelmed by a chaotic world, for anyone who has ever felt shame for not living up to an impossible standard.

This book is a call to action: to stop fighting your brain and start working with it. Embrace your neurodiversity, celebrate your unique gifts, and continue to build the extraordinary life you are capable of living. Your organized future is not a destination to be reached; it is a journey to be enjoyed, one small, compassionate step at a time. It is a life where your home is a source of peace, not stress, and where you have the mental space to focus on the things that make you feel alive.

CHAPTER 6

MOMENTUM BUILDERS
RESTARTING AFTER FALLING OFF TRACK

Why ADHD Makes Consistency Hard

If you live with ADHD, you already know the story: you start something with excitement, energy, and hope. A new planner, a new exercise routine, a new cleaning system: it feels like *this time, it's going to stick.* For a while, it works. Then life happens. You get sick, your schedule changes, your interest wanes, or something stressful throws you off course. Suddenly, the habit is gone.

Here's the painful part: ADHD brains often don't just stop the habit, they pile guilt and shame on top. "I ruined it. I'll never be consistent. I'm broken." The shame becomes heavier than the original task.

But here's the truth: **falling off track isn't failure—it's inevitable.** Everyone, ADHD or not, falls off routines. The difference is that neurotypical brains tend to slip back more easily, while ADHD brains get caught in the restart trap. We interpret a break as the end. Restarting feels like climbing Mount Everest in flip-flops.

That's why this chapter matters. Momentum isn't about never stopping. It's about learning to **restart quickly, gently, and without shame.**

The Myth of "Forever Consistency"

One reason ADHDers get stuck is the myth that "real consistency" means *never missing a day*. That's not realistic for anyone. Athletes miss workouts. Writers miss writing days. Parents miss routines. Life happens.

What matters is not perfection, but **returning.** Consistency is the art of coming back. And for ADHDers, this means designing momentum builders, small, powerful tools to restart without shame spirals.

Why Restarting Feels Impossible for ADHD

Before we dive into solutions, let's break down why restarting is so hard:

1. **Time blindness.** A "two-day break" might feel like two months. It's easy to believe too much time has passed to restart.
2. **Perfectionism.** If you can't restart "perfectly," it doesn't feel worth trying at all.
3. **Shame spiral.** Falling off track feels like failure, which makes action harder.
4. **Boredom/novelty seeking.** Restarting feels dull compared to starting something new.
5. **Task initiation difficulty.** Restarting is essentially starting again—and starting is the hardest part with ADHD.

Recognizing these barriers isn't about blame, it's about clarity. When you know the obstacles, you can design momentum builders to overcome them.

Momentum Builder #1: The Tiny Restart

When restarting feels overwhelming, shrink the restart step until it feels laughably small.

- Haven't cleaned in weeks? Pick up **one item.**
- Haven't worked out? Do **one stretch.**
- Haven't journaled? Write **one sentence.**
- Haven't studied? Open the book for **one minute.**

Tiny restarts break through the wall of initiation. The brain shifts from *"I can't do this"* to *"Well, that wasn't so bad."* Often, the small action snowballs. But even if it doesn't, you've restarted, and that's momentum.

Momentum Builder #2: The Fresh Start Ritual

ADHD thrives on novelty. Instead of trying to drag yourself back into the old habit, create a ritual that marks a new beginning.

- Light a candle before restarting your evening routine.
- Put on a favorite playlist before tackling the kitchen.
- Buy a new pen before reopening your planner.
- Declare out loud: *"I'm starting again."*

Rituals shift the restart from punishment to celebration. They remind your brain that starting again is renewal.

Momentum Builder #3: Lower the Bar Permanently

One reason we fall off track is that the habit was too ambitious to begin with. The restart then feels impossible. Lowering the bar ensures the habit is resilient.

- Instead of daily workouts, aim for two per week.
- Instead of cleaning the whole kitchen nightly, aim for clearing one counter.
- Instead of journaling a page, aim for one line.

When the bar is lower, the restart doesn't feel like climbing Everest. It feels like stepping back onto a sidewalk.

Momentum Builder #4: The "Restart Menu"

In chaos, ADHD brains forget options. A restart menu is a pre-made list of tiny, easy actions you can choose from.

Example Restart Menu:

- Drink a glass of water.
- Put laundry in basket.
- Write one to-do.
- Wipe one surface.
- Take meds.

Keep your menu on the fridge, in your phone, or taped to your desk. On restart days, don't overthink, just pick one and begin.

Momentum Builder #5: Gamify the Restart

ADHD brains crave dopamine. Restarting feels boring, so inject novelty and fun.

- Set a timer: "Can I clean for 3 minutes?"
- Race yourself: "Can I beat yesterday's restart?"
- Use apps that track streaks, but count restarts as wins.
- Reward yourself for restarting, not for perfect streaks.

The goal is to make restarting stimulating instead of shameful.

Momentum Builder #6: The "Future Me" Perspective

ADHD brains live in the now. Restarting feels pointless because the payoff is delayed. Reframe it as a gift to your **future self.**

- *"Future me will thank me for putting this load of laundry in."*
- *"Future me will feel better if I restart this planner."*
- *"Future me will be calmer if I wipe this counter."*

Speaking directly to the future makes the action more immediate and motivating.

Momentum Builder #7: Body Doubling

Restarting alone feels daunting. With another person, even virtually, it becomes manageable.

- Ask a friend to body double on video while you restart.
- Join a study-with-me stream.
- Sit near a family member while doing your task.

Accountability transforms restart energy. Suddenly, you're not alone, you're supported.

Momentum Builder #8: Reset the Environment

Physical environment cues mental restart.

- Open windows for fresh air.
- Clear one surface.
- Change your workspace location.
- Put on a new outfit.

Environmental resets signal to your brain: *something has shifted, it's time to begin again.*

Momentum Builder #9: "Forgiveness First"

The heaviest barrier to restarting is shame. Before taking action, pause and forgive yourself.

Say out loud:

- *"I'm not broken. Everyone falls off."*
- *"Restarting is progress."*
- *"I don't have to earn permission to try again."*

Forgiveness clears the emotional clutter so action feels possible.

Momentum Builder #10: Seasonal Restarts

Instead of expecting habits to run nonstop, build restarts into seasonal cycles.

- Spring: refresh routines with new energy.
- Summer: simplify to light, minimal routines.
- Fall: rebuild structure with calendars and planners.
- Winter: reduce to bare minimums, focus on rest.

When restart is scheduled, it's no longer a failure, it's design.

Case Study 1: Lila and the Exercise Spiral

Lila joined a gym in January, went three times a week, then stopped when work got stressful. Months passed. She felt guilty, avoided the gym, and told herself she was a failure.

Then she used the **tiny restart**: one five-minute walk. That one walk became two. Then a class. Soon she was moving again. The key was lowering the restart barrier.

Case Study 2: Daniel and the Planner Shame

Daniel bought a beautiful planner, used it for three weeks, then stopped. Months later, he looked at it and thought, *I wasted my money. I can't stick to anything.*

Instead of throwing it away, he used the **fresh start ritual**: he bought a new pen, decorated one page, and wrote just one task. Suddenly the planner wasn't a symbol of failure, it was alive again.

Momentum Builder #11: Celebrate the Restart, Not the Streak

Traditional advice praises streaks. But streaks set ADHDers up for heartbreak, miss one day, and the streak is "ruined." Instead, celebrate restarts.

- Missed five days? Restarted today. That's a win.
- Restarted laundry after a month? Win.
- Restarted journaling after six months? Win.

Consistency is not how many days you never miss, it's how many times you restart.

Momentum Builder #12: Visual Progress Anchors

ADHD brains thrive on visual cues. Use them to make restarts satisfying.

- A calendar with restart days marked in bright colors.
- A jar where you drop a marble every time you restart.
- Before-and-after photos of small resets.

Visual proof creates momentum when your brain forgets progress.

Momentum Builder #13: Pair Restarts With Dopamine

Link restarts with pleasure to make them stick.

- Restarting cleaning? Play your favorite upbeat song.
- Restarting a workout? Pair with your best podcast.
- Restarting a planner? Use colorful pens and stickers.

When restarts feel enjoyable, your brain seeks them instead of avoiding them.

Momentum Builder #14: Emergency Restart Routine

Sometimes life implodes, and you need a one-size-fits-all rescue plan.

The 5-Step Emergency Restart:

1. Drink water.
2. Pick up 5 things.
3. Do one tiny self-care task (wash face, meds, snack).
4. Write one next step.
5. Celebrate restarting.

This sequence can be used anytime you feel stuck in paralysis.

Momentum Builder #15: Build "Restart Resilience"

The more you practice restarting, the easier it becomes. Instead of fearing the next fall, expect it, and trust your restart system.

- Miss a day? Restart tomorrow.
- Miss a week? Restart next week.
- Miss a month? Restart next month.

Restarting isn't failure. It's resilience.

Deep Dive: The Psychology of Restarting

Let's zoom in on why these momentum builders work.

- **Dopamine regulation:** ADHD brains struggle with dopamine. Novelty, gamification, and rewards make restarting engaging.
- **Task initiation:** Shrinking tasks lowers the activation barrier.
- **Time blindness:** Visual cues and seasonal resets anchor the sense of time.
- **Emotional regulation:** Forgiveness and rituals reduce shame, making action easier.
- **Executive function:** Menus, body doubling, and environmental resets scaffold weak executive skills.

Restarting becomes less about willpower and more about designing systems that bypass ADHD roadblocks.

Case Study 3: Sofia and the Cleaning Collapse

Sofia's home would swing between spotless and disaster. After a busy week, the mess piled up. Instead of restarting, she'd spiral into shame, avoid cleaning, and the house worsened.

She built a **restart menu**: pick up 5 things, wipe one surface, start laundry. Every time she fell off, she chose one menu item. Slowly, her home stopped collapsing into chaos. Restarts became her momentum.

Case Study 4: Malik and the Writing Project

Malik wanted to write a book. He wrote daily for a month, then stopped. For six months, he avoided it, convinced he'd failed.

Then he tried the **tiny restart**: write one sentence. That sentence became a paragraph. Weeks later, he was writing regularly again. The book didn't die, it paused, then restarted.

Closing Thought

Consistency isn't the absence of failure. It isn't never missing a day. For ADHDers, consistency is the **courage to restart, again and again.**

Momentum isn't about flawless streaks. It's about building resilience into your systems so falling off doesn't mean the end. It means a pause. A cycle. A chance to begin again.

Every time you restart, you prove something powerful: You are not broken. You are adaptable. You are resilient.

And in the end, resilience, not perfection, is what keeps momentum alive.

CHAPTER 7

CONSISTENCY THROUGH VARIETY: CHANGING SYSTEMS WITHOUT QUITTING

The ADHD Struggle With Consistency

If there's one thing that makes ADHD brains grind against traditional advice, it's the idea that consistency means doing the **same thing, the same way, every day, forever.**

You've probably heard it before: *Pick a planner and stick to it. Find a cleaning system and never change it. Pick a workout routine and do it religiously.*

But here's the truth: ADHD brains are wired for **novelty, stimulation, and change.** What feels like security to a neurotypical brain often feels like suffocation to an ADHD brain. Doing the same routine every day, with no variation, quickly becomes dull. Once the dopamine wears off, the system collapses.

That doesn't mean consistency is impossible. It means we need a new definition:

For ADHD, consistency doesn't mean sameness. It means continuity - showing up again and again, even if the *form* of the system changes.

This is the heart of **consistency through variety.** Instead of trying to force one rigid system forever, you design flexible systems that evolve with your brain's needs.

Redefining Consistency

Before we dive into strategies, let's shift the definition. Traditional consistency = "Do the same task the same way daily, no excuses."

ADHD consistency = "Keep coming back to the goal, even if the method shifts."

- If you journal using a notebook one month, a phone app the next, and voice memos after that, you're still journaling consistently.
- If you exercise with yoga for two weeks, then walk for three weeks, then dance for a month, you're still consistently moving your body.
- If you clean your house using a checklist one season, a visual reset system the next, and a timer method after that, you're still consistently maintaining your home.

Consistency is not about the **tool.** It's about the **direction.**

Why Variety Works for ADHD Brains

Variety isn't a weakness, it's a superpower when channeled intentionally. Here's why it works:

1. **Novelty fuels dopamine.** New systems feel exciting, which motivates action.
2. **Flexibility prevents collapse.** When one system feels stale, variety gives you alternatives instead of total abandonment.
3. **Prevents all-or-nothing spirals.** Instead of quitting, you pivot.
4. **Builds resilience.** By using different methods, you discover multiple ways to reach the same goal.
5. **Honors energy cycles.** Different seasons of life (and seasons of the year) require different systems.

By embracing variety, you stop fighting your ADHD wiring and start working with it.

The Danger of Variety Without Intention

Of course, there's a flip side. ADHDers often chase novelty endlessly, abandoning systems as soon as the shine wears off. This leads to clutter (five unused planners, three apps), wasted money, and a sense of failure.

The difference between **chaotic variety** and **intentional variety** is one key rule:

- Chaotic variety = quitting and starting over every time.
- Intentional variety = rotating tools and methods while staying anchored to the same underlying goal.

This chapter is about building intentional variety, consistency through change.

Strategy 1: Anchor to the Core Habit, Not the Tool

Instead of tying consistency to one tool, anchor it to the outcome.

- The core habit is **movement.** Tools may be yoga, walking, dancing.
- The core habit is **planning.** Tools may be a notebook, an app, a whiteboard.
- The core habit is **cleaning.** Tools may be checklists, sprints, or visual resets.

By defining the habit broadly, you give yourself freedom to rotate tools without guilt.

Strategy 2: Create a Rotation System

Think of your systems like a wardrobe. You don't wear one outfit forever, you rotate based on weather, season, and mood. Systems can work the same way.

- **Planners:** Paper journal in winter, digital app in summer.
- **Exercise:** Indoor routines in cold months, outdoor walks in warm months.
- **Cleaning:** Deep cleaning bursts in spring, quick maintenance resets in busy fall.

Rotation prevents burnout and keeps habits alive.

Strategy 3: Build "Novelty Days" Into Routines

Instead of abandoning a system when it feels stale, schedule novelty into it.

- Use themed cleaning days (Music Monday, Timer Tuesday, Flash-Clean Friday).
- Try new recipes once a week while keeping regular meals the rest of the time.
- Rotate pens, colors, or stickers in your planner for visual novelty.
- Once a month, completely change the setting for your work (coffee shop, park, library).

Novelty days refresh the brain without dismantling the system.

Strategy 4: Use Parallel Systems

Some ADHDers thrive with multiple options running at once.

Example: Planning systems.

- Daily tasks go in a paper notebook.
- Weekly overview on a whiteboard.
- Long-term appointments in Google Calendar.

This layered approach provides variety while ensuring you always have a system running. If one tool fails, another catches you.

Strategy 5: Seasonal System Swaps

ADHD thrives on cycles. Just as seasons change, your systems can too.

- **Spring:** Energizing routines, fresh starts.
- **Summer:** Light, flexible systems.
- **Fall:** Structured planners, stability.
- **Winter:** Simplified, cozy routines.

Design seasonal swaps so change is expected, not shameful.

Strategy 6: The "Toolkit Approach"

Think of your routines as a **toolkit, not a prison.**

Your cleaning toolkit might include:

- 5-minute sprints
- One-surface resets
- Checklists
- Body doubling

You don't have to use all at once. On any given day, pick the tool that fits your energy. Consistency comes from showing up, not from using the same hammer every time.

Strategy 7: Differentiate "Healthy Variety" From Avoidance

Sometimes switching systems is a healthy adaptation. Other times it's avoidance. How to tell the difference?

- **Healthy variety** keeps you moving toward the goal. (Switching from yoga to walking, still moving your body.)
- **Avoidance variety** abandons the goal completely. (Stopping workouts and calling it a "system change.")

Ask yourself: *Am I still moving toward the same outcome, or am I abandoning it entirely?*

Strategy 8: Reframe Abandoned Systems as "Chapters"

When a system no longer works, instead of calling it failure, call it a chapter.

- *"That planner worked for me in Fall 2023. That chapter is closed. Now it's Winter 2024, and I'm writing a new chapter."*

This language shifts the narrative from shame to evolution. Systems aren't wasted—they served their season.

Strategy 9: Gamify Variety

Turn system shifts into a game instead of guilt.

- Rate your current system on a scale of 1–10.
- When it dips below 5, swap to a new one.
- Keep a "variety log" of all the systems you've tried. Celebrate the creativity.

The goal is not to lock yourself into one method, but to see how many creative ways you can move toward the same outcome.

Case Study 1: Emma and the Planner Pile

Emma had six half-used planners on her shelf. Each time she abandoned one, she felt guilty and told herself she was a failure.

When she reframed consistency as continuity, she realized each planner was part of her journey. She started rotating between a bullet journal and Google Calendar, depending on her energy. Instead of guilt, she saw variety as strategy.

Case Study 2: Jordan and Exercise Burnout

Jordan joined a gym and followed a strict weightlifting program. After three weeks, he quit, bored out of his mind.

With the **consistency through variety** approach, he designed a rotation: dancing on Mondays, yoga on Wednesdays, hiking on weekends. He never stuck to one workout for long, but he consistently moved his body year-round.

Strategy 10: Visualize Consistency as a Spiral, Not a Line

Neurotypical consistency is imagined as a straight line: same step, every day. ADHD consistency works better as a spiral. You circle around the same goal again and again, sometimes closer, sometimes further, but always returning.

This spiral view reframes restarts as part of the design, not failure.

Strategy 11: Celebrate "Consistency of Return"

Instead of measuring how long you did something without stopping, measure how many times you came back.

- Journaling for 3 months, stopping, then returning a year later? That's consistency of return.
- Cleaning your house in bursts every season? That's consistency of return.
- Using five different planners in five years? That's consistency of return.

What matters is not the gap, it's the return.

Strategy 12: Build Variety Into Rewards

Rewards fuel ADHD motivation. Instead of one static reward, rotate them.

- After cleaning: sometimes a favorite show, sometimes a snack, sometimes a call with a friend.
- After workouts: new music one week, a smoothie the next.
- After journaling: stickers, colored pens, or sharing with a friend.

Changing rewards keeps systems fresh.

Strategy 13: Social Variety

ADHDers thrive on interaction. Bring variety through people.

- Clean alone some days, with a friend others.
- Join a coworking group once a week.
- Share progress with different accountability buddies.

Different people bring different energy, keeping routines lively.

Strategy 14: Use "System Audits"

Every month or season, do a quick audit:

- What's working?
- What feels stale?
- What needs a swap?

Instead of waiting for burnout, you proactively refresh systems.

Case Study 3: Leah and Cleaning Resets

Leah tried a strict "clean the kitchen every night" rule. It lasted two weeks, then collapsed. Instead of giving up, she created a variety system:

- Mondays = 10-minute kitchen sprint.
- Wednesdays = clean one surface.
- Fridays = family reset.

The variation kept her engaged, and the kitchen stayed consistently manageable.

Strategy 15: The "Playlist Effect"

Think of routines like playlists. You don't listen to one song on repeat forever. You rotate songs, shuffle, add new ones. But the playlist is still yours.

Your routines can be playlists too: rotating methods, refreshing with new tools, but always anchored to the same beat.

Deep Dive: The Neuroscience of Variety

ADHD brains have lower baseline dopamine and higher novelty-seeking behavior. That's why:

- New planners feel thrilling.
- New workouts feel exciting.
- New apps feel irresistible.

But once novelty fades, motivation crashes. Intentional variety prevents the crash by supplying novelty in controlled doses. Instead of abandoning systems, you rotate them to sustain dopamine long-term.

Case Study 4: Carlos and Study Routines

Carlos was a college student with ADHD. He tried flashcards, quit. Tried apps, quit. Tried study groups, quit.

Once he reframed consistency, he realized he wasn't failing, he was building a **study toolkit.** Some weeks he used flashcards, others study groups, others apps. He passed his exams not because he stuck to one system, but because he rotated systems and kept returning to the goal.

Closing Thought

ADHD consistency will never look like rigid repetition. And it doesn't need to.

Consistency for us means returning again and again, even if the path shifts. It means designing routines that breathe, flex, and evolve with our brains. It means variety not as avoidance, but as strategy.

When you embrace consistency through variety, you stop seeing yourself as broken for "not sticking with it." You see yourself as creative, resilient, and adaptive.

You are not failing when you change systems—you are succeeding when you keep showing up.

And that's the truth: **Consistency isn't sameness. Consistency is return.**

Reflection Questions:

- *The "Don't Break the Chain" method and the "Art of the Rebound" are two sides of the same coin when it comes to consistency. What is one small habit you want to start building, and how will you use both a visual "chain" and a self-compassionate "rebound rule" to ensure a slip-up doesn't derail your progress?*
- *This final book is about building a supportive, sustainable life. Who is one person in your life you can enlist as an accountability partner or support system for your new organizational goals? What is a small win you've had recently that you will take a moment to celebrate?*
- *This book presented a vision of your organized future as one of functionality, not perfection. In what specific area of your life could you let go of a perfectionistic ideal and instead focus on creating a system that is simply good enough and functional for your brain?*

- *Think about the concept of a "functional home." What is one small change you could make to a "chaos hotspot" in your home (e.g., your entryway, kitchen counter, or desk) to make it a more supportive and low-friction space for your daily life?*
- *What is one core takeaway from this book that you will commit to remembering when a moment of frustration or self-doubt arises? How can this new understanding help you reframe that moment with self-compassion?*

CONCLUSION

You have reached the end of this volume, but the journey toward a more organized and peaceful life is just beginning. Throughout these pages, we've explored a new approach, one that rejects rigid rules and embraces the unique wiring of the ADHD brain. We've learned that organization is not about achieving a flawless, static state, but about building flexible, compassionate systems that support your life as it actually is.

You've built a new mental toolkit. You now have a framework for shifting your mindset from overwhelm to empowerment. You have strategies for creating routines that work with your energy, not against it. You've learned how to turn tedious chores into manageable games and how to use technology as an ally. Most importantly, you've learned the art of self-compassion and the power of the rebound—the most critical skills for long-term consistency.

The goal is not to eliminate all chaos, but to manage it in a way that frees up your mental energy for the things that truly matter: your passions, your relationships, and your well-being. Your organized future is not a destination; it's a continuous practice of showing up for yourself, one small, imperfect step at a time. Embrace your neurodiversity as the superpower it is, and continue to build a life that is not just organized, but also authentic and joyful.

The Mindset Shift: From Overwhelm to Empowerment

The most significant change you've made is not in your home, but in your mind. Before this journey, you may have viewed your struggles with organization as a personal failure. Now, you understand them as a challenge that can be overcome with the right tools and a compassionate perspective. This is a fundamental shift from a mindset of **overwhelm** to one of **empowerment**.

Embrace "Functional Chaos"

The idea of a perfectly tidy, minimalist home is often an impossible and ultimately demotivating goal. Instead of striving for perfection, embrace the concept of **"functional chaos."** This means accepting that your life will not always be Pinterest-perfect, but that the systems you have in place will allow you to quickly find what you need and reset your space when necessary. Your home doesn't need to be tidy 24/7; it just needs to be functional. A system of "chaos containers", a designated basket for miscellaneous items on a countertop, for example can contain the mess until you have the energy to deal with it. This is not laziness; it's a strategic, low-friction solution to the reality of daily life.

The "Good Enough" Principle

For the ADHD brain, the pursuit of perfection can be a powerful inhibitor. The thought, "If I can't do this perfectly, I shouldn't do it at all," is a common trigger for **task paralysis**. You've now learned to counter this with the **"Good Enough" principle**. This is the understanding that a 10-minute tidy is far better than a two-hour tidy that never happens. It's about accepting that progress, not perfection, is the goal. When you find yourself getting stuck, ask yourself, "What is the smallest, easiest version of this task that I can do right now?" The answer is always "good enough."

Externalizing the Brain: The Physical-Digital Hybrid

This book has shown you how to use external tools to compensate for internal challenges. You've learned to build a **physical-digital hybrid system** that works for you. This system combines the tactile satisfaction of physical tools with the reliability of digital ones.

Tips for your hybrid system:

- **The Physical "Launchpad":** Create a dedicated physical space near your front door for keys, wallet, and phone. This simple, visible location externalizes the task of remembering where you put your most important items.
- **The Digital "Brain Dump":** Use a single notes or to-do list app as a catch-all for every thought, task, and idea that pops into your head. Don't worry about organizing it immediately. Just get it out of your head and into a trusted system.
- **The "Sensory" System:** Use visual timers for time-blocking, color-coding for calendars, and tactile cues like a small, physical "done" box to make your progress tangible and perceivable.

Advanced Strategies for Sustained Momentum

As you continue your journey, you can build on the foundational principles from this book with more advanced strategies. These are tools for sustained momentum, designed to keep your systems running smoothly over the long haul.

Tip: The Weekly Reset

A **"Weekly Reset"** is a dedicated 30-60 minute ritual at the end of each week (e.g., Sunday night) to prepare for the week ahead. This ritual is a strategic investment in your future peace of mind.

How to do a Weekly Reset:

1. **Clear the Clutter:** Spend 15 minutes clearing the main chaos hotspots: your kitchen counter, your desk, and your entryway. This doesn't have to be a deep clean, just a quick tidy to create a blank slate.
2. **Plan Your Week:** Review your calendar and your digital to-do list. Block out time for important appointments, but also block out time for your "focus sprints" and "10-minute tidies."
3. **Future-Self Prep:** Do one small thing that will make your future week easier. Lay out your clothes for Monday, pack your gym bag, or prepare your lunch. This simple act of foresight is an act of self-compassion.

This weekly ritual provides a powerful sense of closure for the past week and a feeling of control for the week to come, which can significantly reduce Sunday-night anxiety.

Tip: The "Future You" Method

The "Future You" method is about recognizing that your current self is in a position to make your future self's life easier. It's a powerful framework for building habits. Every time you finish a task, ask yourself, "What is the one small thing I can do right now that will make tomorrow easier for me?"

Examples:

- **After dinner:** Instead of leaving the dishes for the morning, load them into the dishwasher. Future You will thank you for not having to face a messy kitchen first thing.
- **Before bed:** Put your phone on the charger in a different room. Future You will get a better night's sleep and won't be tempted to scroll in the morning.
- **After getting the mail:** Instead of leaving the pile on the counter, throw away the junk mail and place the important mail in a designated spot to be dealt with later.

This simple mental prompt reframes a task from a chore to an act of kindness toward yourself, which is a powerful motivator.

Tip: The "Two-Minute Rule" for Everything

You've learned to break down large tasks, but what about the small ones that pile up? The **"Two-Minute Rule"** is a simple and effective hack: If a task takes less than two minutes to complete, do it immediately. This rule is perfect for the ADHD brain's need for a quick win and a sense of accomplishment.

Examples of Two-Minute Tasks:

- Taking out the trash.
- Putting a dish in the dishwasher.
- Putting a shirt on a hanger.
- Sending a quick email.
- Taking your vitamins.

This rule prevents the small, manageable tasks from accumulating into a larger, overwhelming pile.

Tip: Habit Stacking, a Deeper Look

We've touched on **habit stacking**, but it's worth a deeper look. This is a strategy where you "stack" a new habit on top of an existing, well-established one. The cue for the new habit is the completion of the old one. This leverages the brain's existing neural pathways, making it easier to adopt a new behavior.

Tips for effective habit stacking:

- **Identify Your Existing Habits:** What are the things you do every single day without fail? (e.g., making coffee, brushing your teeth, sitting down to watch TV).
- **Choose a Simple New Habit:** Pick one small habit to stack on top. For example, "After I make my morning coffee, I will take out the trash."
- **Be Specific:** The new habit should be a clear, simple action. Avoid vague statements like "After I watch TV, I will be more productive." Instead, say, "After I watch the first 15 minutes of my show, I will get up and put away three things."

The Role of Self-Compassion in Your Daily Practice

This journey is not just about building systems; it's about building a better relationship with yourself. The **art of the rebound** is the most critical skill you have learned. It is the understanding that a moment of imperfection is not a sign of failure, but a part of a human journey.

Reframe Your Self-Talk

The voice in your head is a powerful force. You have to actively choose to replace negative, judgmental self-talk with compassionate, supportive language.

- **Instead of:** "I'm so lazy, I just couldn't get started."
- **Try:** "My energy was low today, and that's okay. I'll make a plan to start again tomorrow."
- **Instead of:** "I always mess things up."
- **Try:** "I'm still learning. My system didn't work perfectly today, so I'll adjust it for next time."

This practice of reframing is a habit in itself, and it is the foundation for all other habits. It's the difference between a slip-up that derails you for a week and one that derails you for a day.

Rest is Not Laziness

For the ADHD brain, which is often in a state of hyper-arousal, rest is not a luxury; it is a necessity. The urge to constantly "do" and the guilt that comes from "not doing" are powerful forces. You've now learned to treat rest as a strategic part of your routine. The built-in breaks in the Pomodoro Technique, the guilt-free rewards—these are all tools for giving your brain the rest and dopamine it needs to function. A tired brain is an unmotivated brain. You are not lazy for taking a break; you are being strategic.

Your Team, Your Toolkit, Your Future

You are not alone in this journey. This book has empowered you to build a team and a toolkit that supports your life.

- **Your Accountability Partner:** This person is a trusted ally who provides external motivation and helps you problem-solve.
- **Your Support System:** This is your community of loved ones who celebrate your wins and help you get back on track.
- **Your Professional Support:** If needed, an ADHD coach or a therapist can be an invaluable part of your team, providing expert guidance and a safe space to process your feelings.

These are not crutches; they are **scaffolds**. They are temporary structures that help you build something strong and stable. As your habits become more ingrained and your systems become more automated, you may find that you need less external support. The goal is to build a self-sustaining system, and your team is the launchpad for that.

The Final Word: Embracing Your Neurodiversity

This book has shown you that ADHD is not a deficit; it is a unique wiring with its own set of challenges and gifts. Your brain's ability to **hyperfocus**, your creative and divergent thinking, your unique energy are all superpowers. Your organized future is a life that is not just free from chaos, but also free to express these gifts.

By building systems that manage the day-to-day, you are freeing up your mental energy to focus on what you do best. You are building a life that is not just organized, but also authentic and joyful. The journey is not over. It is a continuous practice of showing up for yourself, one small, imperfect step at a time. Embrace your journey, celebrate your progress, and continue to build a life that is not just manageable, but extraordinary.

REFLECTION QUESTIONS

Welcome to the reflection section of this volume. You've just completed a journey through new concepts and practical tools designed to help you build a more organized and peaceful life. This is not the end of the road; in fact, it's the most important part of the process.

Information alone doesn't create change. It's only through thoughtful reflection that information becomes knowledge, and knowledge becomes action. The purpose of these questions is to help you process what you've learned and start applying these ideas to your unique life. Think of this as your personal workshop, a space to pause, consider, and begin building your own personalized toolkit.

Don't feel the need to answer every question at once. Pick the one that resonates with you most right now and give it your full attention. Grab a journal, open a note on your phone, or simply take a walk and think about it. The act of reflection is a powerful way to solidify new ideas and turn them into sustainable habits. Your organized future is waiting, and it begins with these first, intentional steps.

Book 1: The Foundations of a Flexible Routine

Reflection Question: Which of the core principles, redefining your relationship with clutter, embracing a "good enough" mindset, or the power of small wins, resonates with you the most, and why?

This question is designed to help you identify the single most impactful mindset shift from the first book. The journey toward an organized life isn't just about cleaning; it's about fundamentally changing how you think about your home and your abilities. For the ADHD brain, which can easily get bogged down in perfectionism and all-or-nothing thinking, this first step is a critical one. You must first change your internal operating system before you can effectively change your external environment.

Exercise: The Mindset Pivot

This exercise is designed to help you dive deeper into your chosen principle and make it a concrete part of your daily life.

Step 1: Identify Your Core Challenge. First, reflect on which of the three principles feels like the most powerful counter to your biggest current challenge.

- **Redefining Clutter:** Does clutter feel like a personal failing? Do you get overwhelmed by the visual noise of your home? If so, this is your principle.
- **Embracing "Good Enough":** Do you often get stuck, paralyzed by the thought that a task must be done perfectly? Do you find yourself avoiding a task entirely because you don't have the time or energy to do it "right"? If so, this is your principle.
- **The Power of Small Wins:** Does the end goal of a clean home feel so far away that it loses all motivation? Do you struggle with task initiation, feeling like your efforts won't make a difference? If so, this is your principle.

Step 2: Journal Your "Why." Now, take a few minutes to write about why this particular principle resonates so deeply with you. What specific past experiences or feelings come to mind when you think about it?

- *If you chose **Redefining Clutter**:* Write about a time a messy space caused you shame. Now, reframe that memory from the perspective of "functional chaos." What was the space trying to do for you? (e.g., "My kitchen counter was a landing zone for everything I needed, but it looked messy.") How can you create a system that meets that need without the shame?
- *If you chose **Embracing "Good Enough":** Write about a task you've been avoiding because you can't do it perfectly. Now, write down a "good enough" version of that task. (e.g., "Instead of cleaning the entire garage, I will spend 10 minutes throwing away the trash.") The goal is to get a small win, not a perfect result.
- *If you chose **The Power of Small Wins**:* Write about a time you felt unmotivated. Now, identify a small win that would have given you a dopamine hit in that moment. (e.g., "I could have simply put away three items on the counter.") The goal is to train your brain to seek out these small, immediate rewards.

Step 3: Create a Mantra. Distill your reflection into a simple, memorable mantra that you can repeat to yourself when you feel overwhelmed. This mantra will be your compass, a single thought that can pull you out of a negative thought spiral.

- **For Redefining Clutter:** "My home is a tool for my life, not a showcase."
- **For Embracing "Good Enough":** "Progress, not perfection."

- **For The Power of Small Wins:** "One small thing is better than nothing."

Your ability to reframe your thinking is the ultimate skill. This exercise isn't about finding the "right" answer; it's about choosing a mindset that empowers you to take action.

Book 2: Mastering Routines and Habit Formation

Reflection Question: Which of the routines, the morning reset, the evening routine, or the weekend deep dive, do you think would have the most immediate positive impact on your life? What is one specific, tiny action you can take this week to begin implementing it?

Routines are not meant to be rigid, but to serve as supportive scaffolding for your life. For the ADHD brain, which struggles with time management and task initiation, a solid routine is a lifeline. This question pushes you to think about which part of your day is most in need of this support. By choosing one routine to focus on, you avoid the overwhelm of trying to fix everything at once. The key is to start with a single, tiny, non-negotiable action to build momentum.

Exercise: The Micro-Habit Blueprint

This exercise guides you to build a single, tiny habit that will serve as the foundation for a larger routine.

Step 1: Identify Your "Biggest Pain Point" Time. Think about your typical week. At which point do you consistently feel the most stress or chaos?

- **The Morning:** Do you feel rushed, forget things, and start the day feeling behind? If so, the **morning reset** is for you.
- **The Evening:** Does the end of your day feel like a sudden crash, with clutter accumulating and a lack of preparation for the next day? If so, the **evening routine** is for you.
- **The Weekend:** Do you feel a sense of dread about the deep cleaning that needs to be done, leading to inaction and a feeling of being overwhelmed? If so, the **weekend deep dive** is for you.

Step 2: Design Your Micro-Habit. Now, come up with one tiny, almost comically easy action that you can perform in your chosen routine. The action should take no more than two minutes.

- *For the* ***Morning Reset***: Instead of, "I will make my bed and get ready," try, "I will drink a glass of water." Or, "I will put my phone on its charger." The goal is to start a chain reaction with an easy win.
- *For the* ***Evening Routine***: Instead of, "I will clean the entire kitchen," try, "I will put one dish in the dishwasher." Or, "I will put my keys on the launchpad." The goal is to signal to your brain that the day is ending and the next day is being prepared for.
- *For the* ***Weekend Deep Dive***: Instead of, "I will clean the whole garage," try, "I will spend five minutes throwing away the trash in the garage." Or, "I will put on a timer and a podcast and commit to working for a single song."

Step 3: Stack It. To make your micro-habit stick, you're going to use **habit stacking**. This means you'll pair your new, tiny habit with an existing habit you already perform daily.

- **Example for the Morning Reset:** "After I turn off my alarm, I will drink a glass of water."
- **Example for the Evening Routine:** "After I close my laptop, I will put my keys on the launchpad."
- **Example for the Weekend Deep Dive:** "After I make my morning coffee on Saturday, I will put on a podcast and do a single 'One-Song Tidy' in the garage."

By intentionally connecting a new, tiny action to a deeply ingrained habit, you are leveraging your brain's existing neural pathways to create a new, effortless routine.

Book 3: Decluttering and Organizing Made Easy

Reflection Question: Which of the "chaos hotspots" in your own home feels the most overwhelming to you, and what is one small, manageable change you can make this week to begin a "Keep, Toss, Donate" session?

Decluttering can feel like a monumental task, especially when you have a strong emotional attachment to your belongings or when the sheer volume of items is overwhelming. This question is designed to help you identify the area that causes you the most mental distress and give you a simple, actionable strategy to begin tackling it. By starting with one small area, you can build confidence and momentum without getting stuck in overwhelm.

Exercise: The Micro-Declutter Blueprint

This exercise takes the "Keep, Toss, Donate" method and applies it in a way that is sensitive to the challenges of the ADHD brain.

Step 1: Identify Your Hottest Hotspot. Walk through your home and identify the single space that makes you feel the most defeated. This is your "chaos hotspot."

- Is it the **kitchen counter** where mail, keys, and random items accumulate?
- Is it your **desk** where papers and half-finished projects pile up?
- Is it the **chair in your bedroom** that has become a clothes rack?
- Is it a **drawer** you haven't opened in years?

Step 2: Introduce a "Chaos Container." The first step is not to get rid of anything. The first step is to contain the chaos. Find a simple, non-judgmental container—a basket, a box, a bag—and place it next to your hotspot. The container's purpose is to act as a temporary holding zone. All the items that don't belong in that space will be placed in the container. This simple act of containment provides immediate visual relief and a sense of control.

Step 3: Schedule a "One-Song Session." Now, schedule a single, low-pressure session this week to deal with the contents of that container. Put on one of your favorite high-dopamine songs and commit to working only for the duration of that song.

- **Keep:** For each item, ask yourself: "Does this item serve a clear purpose, and do I have a home for it?" If yes, find its home immediately.
- **Toss:** If the item is clearly trash, toss it.
- **Donate:** If the item is something you no longer need but is in good condition, place it in a designated donation box.

Tip: The key is to be ruthless in your decisions. If an item doesn't have a clear home, or if you can't remember the last time you used it, it's likely a candidate for the Toss or Donate pile. The goal of this session is not to get rid of everything, but to make a few decisions that will get the ball rolling.

Step 4: Celebrate! After the song ends, stop immediately, regardless of whether you're finished. You've completed your task. Take a moment to look at your now-clearer hotspot and give yourself a verbal acknowledgment. "I did it!" or "Boom! I've started the process." This small act of celebration reinforces the positive behavior and gives you the dopamine hit you need to feel motivated to do it again.

Book 4: The Cleaning Toolkit and Time Management

Reflection Question: What is one time-blocking or gamification technique you could try this week to make a specific chore more manageable?

For the ADHD brain, a chore is often a tedious, unrewarding task that is easy to put off. The long-term reward of a clean home is often not enough to motivate action in the moment. This question asks you to think strategically about how to make a chore more appealing by either making it a time-bound challenge or a rewarding game. This is a direct application of the principle of **dopamine stacking**, where you pair a low-interest task with a high-interest one.

Exercise: The Chore-Game Blueprint

This exercise helps you turn a chore you dread into a game you can win.

Step 1: Identify Your Most Dreaded Chore. Think about the one recurring chore that you consistently avoid. This is your target.

- Is it **doing the dishes**?
- Is it **taking out the trash**?
- Is it **folding laundry**?
- Is it **wiping down the bathroom counter**?

Step 2: Choose Your Game. Now, choose a game that will make the chore feel more engaging.

- **The "Beat the Clock" Game:** Set a timer for 10 minutes and challenge yourself to see how much of the chore you can get done in that time. The ticking clock provides a sense of urgency and a finish line, which is highly motivating.
- **The "One-Song Tidy" Game:** Put on a favorite song and commit to working only for the duration of that song. The music provides a rhythmic anchor for your focus, and the song's end provides a clear finish line.
- **The "Power Hour" Game:** For a larger task, break it into 15-minute intervals. Do a 15-minute sprint, take a 5-minute break, do another 15-minute sprint, and so on. This uses the principles of the Pomodoro Technique to make a large task feel manageable.

- **The "Dopamine Stacking" Game:** Pair the chore with something you genuinely enjoy. For example, listen to a specific podcast or audiobook *only while* you are doing that chore. This makes the chore the price of admission for a high-dopamine activity.

Step 3: Prep Your "Game" Station. Before you start the game, make sure your "game station" is ready.

- *For a time-based game:* Have your timer or phone ready.
- *For a music-based game:* Have your playlist or headphones ready.
- *For a dopamine-stacking game:* Have your podcast or audiobook ready to go.

Tip: The goal is to make the start of the game as effortless as possible. The less friction there is, the more likely you are to play.

Step 4: Celebrate! After the game is over, you win! The reward is immediate. Whether you got the chore done or just made a dent in it, the act of playing the game and the dopamine hit from your reward are the real wins.

Book 5: Staying Consistent and Bouncing Back

Reflection Question: What is one small habit you want to start building, and how will you use both a visual "chain" and a self-compassionate "rebound rule" to ensure a slip-up doesn't derail your progress?

Consistency is the ultimate goal, but for the ADHD brain, it is also the most challenging. This final question brings together the two most important concepts from this book: the proactive motivation of building a streak and the compassionate forgiveness of a slip-up. This is the art of building a sustainable, long-term practice. By combining these two principles, you are building a system that is both motivating and forgiving, which is the key to lasting change.

Exercise: The Resilience Blueprint

This exercise helps you design a habit that is built not on a foundation of perfection, but on a foundation of resilience.

Step 1: Choose a "Chainable" Habit. Pick one simple, low-effort habit that you want to perform every day.

- **Make it Simple:** The habit should take no more than 5-10 minutes. (e.g., a "10-minute tidy," a "journaling session," or a "5-minute meditation.")

- **Make it Specific:** The habit should have a clear beginning and end. (e.g., "I will put away three items from the kitchen counter," rather than "I will organize the kitchen.")
- **Make it "Stackable":** As you learned, stack this new habit on top of an existing one. (e.g., "After I brush my teeth, I will put away three items from the kitchen counter.")

Step 2: Choose Your "Chain" Tracker. Find a visual tracker that you will use every day.

- A simple wall calendar with a pen.
- A habit-tracking app on your phone.
- A small whiteboard in a central location.

The tracker's purpose is to provide a visible, tangible representation of your streak. The visual chain is a powerful, non-judgmental source of motivation.

Step 3: Design Your "Rebound Rule." Now, prepare for the inevitable slip-up. Write down your personal "Rebound Rule" and put it somewhere you can see it, such as on your tracker.

- "If I miss a day, I will not let it become two days."
- "A slip-up is a learning opportunity, not a failure."
- "No matter what happened yesterday, today is a new chance to show up for myself."

Tip: The purpose of this rule is to preemptively counter the shame and all-or-nothing thinking that often accompanies a missed day. You are preparing for imperfection.

Step 4: Put It into Practice. Now, start your chain. For every day you complete the habit, put a mark on your tracker. If you miss a day, do not beat yourself up. Acknowledge it, refer to your "Rebound Rule," and simply start again tomorrow. The true victory is not in the unbroken chain, but in your ability to get back up after you fall. This is the skill of resilience, and it is the key to a sustainable, organized life.

RESOURCE SECTION

You've now completed the five volumes of this guide and have built a comprehensive toolkit of concepts and strategies. As we know, knowledge is only the first step. The true power lies in action. This resource section is designed to be a bridge from theory to practice, providing you with a set of tangible, immediate resources to begin your journey.

Think of this as your personal command center. Whether you're looking for a quick-start guide, a flexible routine template, or a physical worksheet to get you going, you'll find it here. These resources are not rigid rules; they are scaffolding. They are designed to support you as you build your own sustainable, personalized systems.

The Quick-Start Checklist: Your First 7 Days

The first week of any new habit is the most critical. This checklist is your blueprint for getting started without feeling overwhelmed. The goal is to build momentum with low-friction, high-impact actions. Pick one item from each section and make it your mission for the day.

Day 1: Mindset and Mission

- **Acknowledge Your Wins:** Take a moment to write down one small accomplishment from the past 24 hours. It could be as simple as putting a dish in the dishwasher.
- **Embrace "Good Enough":** Identify one task you've been avoiding due to perfectionism. Write down the "good enough" version of that task.
- **Reframe Your Self-Talk:** When a negative thought about your organization arises, immediately counter it with a compassionate thought. (e.g., "I'm not lazy, my brain just needs a different approach.")

Day 2: The Physical Foundation

- **Create Your Launchpad:** Choose a specific, dedicated spot near your front door for your keys, wallet, and phone. Make it a rule to put them there every single time you come home.
- **Identify Your Chaos Hotspot:** Pick the one area in your home that causes you the most stress. This is your target for later.

- **Assemble Your Cleaning Caddy:** Fill a small caddy or basket with a few essential cleaning supplies (all-purpose cleaner, a rag, and a trash bag). Place it in a central, easy-to-access location.

Day 3: Harnessing Motivation

- **Schedule a "One-Song Tidy":** Pick one high-energy song and commit to tidying for its duration. Do not continue after the song ends.
- **Gamify a Chore:** Pick one chore you dread (e.g., doing dishes) and find a podcast or audiobook you will only listen to while doing it.
- **Choose a Visual Timer:** Use a visual timer, like a kitchen timer or a sand hourglass, for your tasks. The visual countdown provides a clear finish line that is highly motivating.

Day 4: Building a Support System

- **Find Your Accountability Partner:** Identify one person (a friend, partner, or fellow ADHD-er) you can check in with once this week.
- **Draft Your "Rebound Rule":** Write down a simple, compassionate phrase to use when you have a slip-up. (e.g., "A slip-up is not a failure. Today is a new day.")
- **Ask for Help:** Ask a partner or family member for help with one specific, low-effort task. (e.g., "Could you remind me to put the trash out on Tuesday morning?")

Day 5: Your First Routine

- **Implement a Micro-Habit:** Choose one of the routines (Morning, Evening, or Weekend) and commit to a single, tiny action for the next three days. For example, "Every evening, I will put one dish in the dishwasher."
- **Use a Habit Tracker:** Draw a simple calendar on a notepad or a whiteboard and mark an 'X' for every time you complete your micro-habit.
- **Celebrate a Win:** After you complete your micro-habit, give yourself a verbal acknowledgment or a small, tangible reward.

Printable Templates and Routines

These templates are designed to be used as a starting point. Feel free to copy them, print them, or adapt them to your own needs. The key is to make them personal, functional, and forgiving.

Sample Routine Templates

Use this template as a guide to building your own Morning, Evening, and Weekend routines. Fill in the sections with actions that make sense for your life.

Routine	Time	Habit Stack
Morning Reset	15 mins	After I **[make coffee]**, I will **[drink a glass of water]**.
		After I **[drink my coffee]**, I will **[do a 10-minute tidy]**.
		Before I **[leave the house]**, I will **[grab my keys from the launchpad]**.
		After I **[leave the house]**, I will **[listen to a podcast]**.
Evening Routine	30 mins	After I **[finish dinner]**, I will **[put one dish in the dishwasher]**.
		After I **[brush my teeth]**, I will **[do a 5-minute tidy in the bathroom]**.
		After I **[get into bed]**, I will **[read one page of a book]**.
Weekend Deep Dive	1-2 hours	On **[Saturday morning]**, I will **[put on a podcast]** and **[clean out one drawer]**.
		On **[Sunday afternoon]**, I will **[do a 30-minute weekly reset]** and **[plan my week]**.

The "Don't Break the Chain" Habit Tracker

This is a simple, visual template to track your progress. The goal is to build a long chain of successes. A slip-up is just a single broken link; it is not a permanent derailment. Use this tracker to visually represent your dedication to a new habit.

Habit: ____

My Rebound Rule: ____________________________________

Monthly Tracker: _____________________________________

Week 1	**Mon**	**Tues**	**Wed**	**Thurs**	**Fri**	**Sat**	**Sun**
	[ ]	[ ]	[ ]	[ ]	[ ]	[ ]	[ ]
Week 2	**Mon**	**Tues**	**Wed**	**Thurs**	**Fri**	**Sat**	**Sun**
	[ ]	[ ]	[ ]	[ ]	[ ]	[ ]	[ ]
Week 3	**Mon**	**Tues**	**Wed**	**Thurs**	**Fri**	**Sat**	**Sun**
	[ ]	[ ]	[ ]	[ ]	[ ]	[ ]	[ ]
Week 4	**Mon**	**Tues**	**Wed**	**Thurs**	**Fri**	**Sat**	**Sun**
	[ ]	[ ]	[ ]	[ ]	[ ]	[ ]	[ ]

Chaos Hotspot Worksheet

Use this worksheet to make your decluttering session more structured and less overwhelming. Focus on just one hotspot at a time. The goal is to make a few decisions, not to finish the entire space.

My Chaos Hotspot: _________________________________

My "One-Song Tidy" Song: ___________________________

I am a winner because I: ____________________________

This resource section is your first, tangible step toward a more organized life. Remember that this journey is not a sprint; it's a marathon of small, intentional steps. Use these resources as a guide, but always listen to your brain. Your organized future is waiting, and it begins with these first, intentional actions.

This section is not required reading, but it's here to serve you if you want to go deeper. Think of it as a **toolkit of prompts and templates** you can return to whenever you feel stuck, overwhelmed, or in need of a reset. You don't need to complete every exercise. Instead, flip through, find what resonates, and let these pages meet you exactly where you are.

1. Journaling Prompts for Deeper Insight

Sometimes clarity comes not from solving problems, but from asking yourself the right questions. These prompts are designed to spark self-awareness and reveal hidden patterns.

- *What does "organized enough" look like for me—not for Pinterest, not for my neighbor, but for my real life?*
- *When I think about clutter, do I feel more shame or more relief? Why?*
- *What is one area of my home that already works for me? How can I use that success as a model elsewhere?*
- *What's the kindest story I can tell myself about why routines are hard for me?*
- *If I could wave a magic wand, which task would disappear forever—and what does that reveal about what drains me most?*

Tip: Don't rush your answers. Set a timer for 5 minutes per question and just write freely.

2. Mantra Builder Worksheet

Use this template to create your own personal mantras that interrupt shame spirals and get you back into action.

- **Trigger Thought:** "The house is such a mess, I don't even know where to start."
- **Reframed Mantra:** "One small step is enough to move me forward."

Now create three of your own:

1. Trigger: __________ Mantra: __________
2. Trigger: __________ Mantra: __________
3. Trigger: __________ Mantra: __________

Write these on sticky notes, put them on mirrors, fridge doors, or inside planners.

3. Chaos Hotspot Map

Draw a rough floor plan of your home (it doesn't need to be artistic). Mark with an or cross the areas that feel most overwhelming. Then answer:

- Which hotspot drains me the most daily?
- Which hotspot is small enough to tackle in one "one-song session"?
- Which hotspot could I outsource, delegate, or ignore for now without guilt?

This visual map helps ADHD brains see the problem spatially, making it easier to prioritize.

4. Micro-Habit Menu

Here's a ready-to-use menu of micro-habits you can pick from and stack into your routines. Cross out what doesn't fit and highlight what sparks energy.

Morning Reset Micro-Habits

- Drink one glass of water after turning off alarm.
- Put phone on charger while brushing teeth.
- Open blinds to let light in immediately.

Evening Routine Micro-Habits

- Place keys in launchpad spot after closing laptop.
- Put one dish in dishwasher before bed.
- Write tomorrow's top 1–2 tasks on a sticky note.

Weekend Reset Micro-Habits

- Throw away five items of obvious trash.
- Do a "one-song tidy" in the kitchen.
- Start laundry while making Saturday coffee.

ADHD tip: Don't try to adopt all of these. Circle ONE per category to experiment with this week.

5. Dopamine Stacking Planner

Sometimes boring chores just need a dopamine partner. Use this template to design your stack.

- **Task I Avoid:**
- **Fun Thing I Crave:**
- **Stack Plan:** "I will only [fun thing] while I [boring task]."

Examples:

- I will only listen to my favorite podcast while folding laundry.
- I will only watch my comfort TV show while decluttering papers.
- I will only drink my fancy coffee while cleaning the bathroom.

This way, the chore becomes the **price of admission** to dopamine.

6. Chain Tracker Template

Draw a simple 30-day grid on paper or use a calendar. Every day you complete your habit, mark an X, star, or symbol.

- Habit I'm tracking:
- My Rebound Rule:
- My Reward After 30 Days:

Tip: ADHD brains love visual progress. Don't underestimate how motivating a simple chain of Xs can be.

7. "Emergency Routine" Cue Card

Life gets chaotic. Instead of spiraling, create a **bare-minimum backup plan** you can pull out of your pocket. Write it on a card or your phone.

- **Morning Emergency Routine:** Brush teeth, drink water, meds.
- **Evening Emergency Routine:** Put dishes in sink, plug in phone, lights off.
- **Weekend Emergency Routine:** Clear one surface, take out trash.

These routines are not about thriving, they're about **surviving without shame.**

8. Reflection Through Movement

Reflection doesn't always need to be sitting still with a journal. ADHD brains often do their best thinking in motion. Try these alternatives:

- Record a voice memo while walking.
- Talk through prompts with a friend during a drive.
- Use sticky notes on a wall, rearranging them until patterns emerge.

The goal is to make reflection **fit your brain, not fight it.**

Closing Thoughts

This additional content is here to remind you: you don't have to rely on memory, willpower, or shame to create change. You can externalize reflection, track progress visually, and gamify the process until it feels lighter.

You now have more than questions, you have **tools.** And every tool you pick up and try is another step toward building the life you want: flexible, functional, and filled with self-compassion.

QUIZ SECTION

YOUR ADHD ORGANIZATION AND CLEANING PROFILE

Welcome to the quiz section of this book. Think of this as a self-discovery tool rather than a test. There are no failing grades here, only insights that can help you tailor the strategies you've learned to your unique ADHD brain.

This quiz is meant to function as a mirror. Just like a mirror doesn't judge you but simply reflects back what's already there, the following questions are designed to reflect your current habits, challenges, and strengths. Too often, ADHDers have been told that they are "failing" or "falling short" when it comes to organization, consistency, or routines. That's not the case here. This space is different. Here, every answer, whether it reveals a struggle or a strength, is valuable information.

By answering honestly, you are gathering data about yourself. Think of it like running a gentle experiment. If you score lower in one area, it doesn't mean you're broken or incapable; it simply means that part of your life could benefit from a little extra support, creativity, or structure. If you score higher in another area, that's something to celebrate, it means you've already developed strategies or mindsets that work for you. This information isn't about labeling; it's about identifying patterns so you can move forward with more awareness.

How to Approach the Quiz When answering the questions, resist the temptation to choose what you think is the "right" or "ideal" answer. ADHD brains often have a strong sense of how things *should* be done, and perfectionism can sneak in and distort self-assessment. Instead, aim to answer based on what actually happens most of the time in your real life.

If, for example, a question asks about evening routines and you wish you had one but rarely follow through, the honest answer is closer to a 1 or 2. If you sometimes succeed and sometimes don't, a 3 may be more accurate. If you've managed to build consistency and it works for you most days, you might choose 4 or 5.

There's no benefit in inflating your answers to match what you think they "should" be, because the goal isn't to measure up to an outside standard. The goal is to uncover your personal baseline. From there, you can apply the tools from this book in ways that feel meaningful and sustainable for you.

The Scale: 1 to 5 Each question in the quiz will use a simple five-point scale. This scale is intentionally broad and flexible to accommodate the fluctuations that come with ADHD. No one is a perfect 5 all the time, just as no one is locked into a permanent 1. You may notice that your answers change depending on the season of life you're in, your stress levels, or even your energy on a given day. That's normal and expected.

Here's a guide to keep in mind as you rate yourself:

- **1 = Never true for me.** This statement does not reflect my experience at all.
- **2 = Rarely true.** I occasionally experience this, but it's uncommon.
- **3 = Sometimes true.** This applies to me inconsistently. It comes and goes.
- **4 = Often true.** This happens more often than not in my daily life.
- **5 = Almost always true.** This is a consistent part of my reality.

Why Honesty Matters The value of this quiz lies not in perfection, but in clarity. When you give yourself permission to be honest, without shame, without judgment, you are reclaiming agency over your story. Many people with ADHD have internalized years of criticism around organization and productivity. This exercise offers the opposite: a compassionate lens through which to see yourself.

Consider this quiz an act of self-compassion as much as self-reflection. By identifying where you struggle, you are not admitting defeat; you are opening a doorway to solutions that fit *you*. By naming your strengths, you are creating a foundation to build on.

The Big Picture When you complete this quiz, you won't just have numbers on a page. You'll have a profile that highlights your unique combination of challenges and resources. Think of it as a map. Some areas of the map may feel like rough terrain; other areas may be smooth and easy to travel. Knowing where those landscapes exist allows you to prepare better, plan routes that make sense, and pack the right tools for the journey.

Ultimately, this quiz is less about measuring who you are and more about illuminating what you need. With this knowledge, you'll be able to apply the strategies from the book with greater precision, building systems that aren't generic, but personalized, crafted for your brain, your home, and your life.

So take a deep breath, grab a pen, and dive in. Each answer is a stepping stone toward greater self-understanding and more sustainable progress.

Section One: Mindset & Foundations

This section measures your relationship with clutter, perfectionism, and the idea of progress.

1. When I see clutter in my home, I immediately feel like I've failed.
2. I often avoid starting tasks because I don't think I can do them "the right way."
3. I believe a small action (like putting away one item) is still progress toward my goals.
4. I replay past mistakes around organization in my head, which keeps me stuck.
5. I'm able to reframe clutter as a neutral signal rather than a shameful sign.
6. Perfectionism often stops me from trying at all.
7. I can acknowledge and celebrate small wins, even if the bigger project is unfinished.
8. I often compare my home or habits to other people's and feel discouraged.
9. I can remind myself that "good enough" is better than "not at all."
10. I'm beginning to shift from seeing my home as a test of character to seeing it as a tool for living.

Scoring for Section One:

- 10–20: Your mindset may be working against you more than with you. Focus on mantras, reframing, and self-compassion exercises from Book 1.
- 21–35: You are in the middle of a mindset shift. You sometimes catch yourself in shame spirals, but you are building awareness. Keep leaning on the "progress not perfection" tools.
- 36–50: You have a strong foundation of flexible thinking. You're learning to treat clutter and routines without moral judgment, which gives you more freedom to act.

Section Two: Routines & Habits

This section explores how you build and sustain daily, weekly, and seasonal rhythms.

1. My mornings often feel chaotic and rushed.
2. I have a consistent evening wind-down process that helps me transition into rest.
3. I feel like weekends are my biggest opportunity to reset, but I rarely use them well.
4. When I try to create routines, I tend to overcomplicate them.
5. I've experimented with micro-habits (very small steps that stack into larger routines).
6. I sometimes abandon routines because they feel boring or restrictive.
7. I have at least one daily anchor (like coffee, brushing teeth, or taking meds) that I build habits around.
8. I struggle with task initiation more than task completion.
9. I've used habit stacking successfully at least once in the past.
10. My routines feel flexible enough to adapt to different seasons or phases of life.
11. I can identify my "pain point times" of day and know where routines would help most.
12. I often try to change too many habits at once and end up burning out.

Scoring for Section Two:

- 12–24: Routines feel like a mystery to you. You might need to focus on just one micro-habit to build trust with yourself.
- 25–40: You're experimenting, but consistency is shaky. Try focusing on one routine anchor (like morning reset) and let it stabilize before adding others.
- 41–60: You're building strong ADHD-friendly routines. The key for you is to prevent boredom by cycling in variety and seasonal resets.

Section Three: Decluttering & Organization

This section looks at how you approach stuff—your systems, hotspots, and emotional attachments.

1. I feel overwhelmed when I think about decluttering my home.
2. I have at least one "chaos hotspot" that drains my energy daily.
3. I use the "Keep, Toss, Donate" method (or something similar) when I declutter.
4. I struggle with decision fatigue when deciding what to keep or toss.
5. I've tried using a container or basket to temporarily manage chaos.
6. Decluttering feels emotionally heavy because of guilt or attachment to items.
7. I find it easier to declutter when I set a short time limit (like one song).
8. My home has zones that actually function well and bring me calm.
9. I can celebrate progress after even a small decluttering session.
10. I sometimes avoid decluttering altogether because the job feels endless.

Scoring for Section Three:

- 10–20: Decluttering currently feels like an impossible mountain. Start with chaos containers and one-song sessions to create quick relief.
- 21–35: You've dabbled with decluttering but struggle with follow-through or guilt. Focus on neutralizing hotspots and practicing decision-making.
- 36–50: You're making progress in creating functional systems. Keep building momentum by tackling one zone at a time.

Section Four: Cleaning & Time Management

This section measures how you handle chores, cleaning, and time-based systems.

1. I often procrastinate on chores until they feel like emergencies.
2. Time-blocking or scheduling chores works well for me.
3. I've used gamification (timers, songs, challenges) to make chores easier.
4. I avoid certain cleaning tasks because they feel boring or endless.
5. I often underestimate how long cleaning will take.
6. I sometimes lose track of time while doing chores and either hyperfocus or avoid them.
7. I've tried pairing chores with enjoyable activities (like music or podcasts).
8. I feel satisfied when I complete even a partial version of a chore.
9. I know which chores are most critical to my daily functioning.
10. I sometimes overcommit to cleaning binges that leave me burned out.
11. I've experimented with "emergency routines" for chaotic days.
12. I find that visual cues (like a checklist or tracker) help me stay on task.

Scoring for Section Four:

- 12–24: Cleaning feels mostly reactive for you. Start with small gamified systems to reduce dread.
- 25–40: You've begun experimenting with tools but need more structure. Time-blocking or "beat the clock" games could help you.
- 41–60: You're integrating ADHD-friendly tools. To sustain progress, balance efficiency with rest.

Section Five: Consistency & Resilience

This section explores how you maintain progress and bounce back after setbacks.

1. I get discouraged easily when I miss a day or fall off track.
2. I've tried visual chain trackers (like calendars or apps).
3. I often give up on habits after a slip-up.
4. I can remind myself that every day is a new chance to restart.
5. I've written or used a "rebound rule" for myself.
6. I sometimes push too hard and end up burning out.
7. I can identify at least one habit I've been consistent with over time.
8. I feel motivated when I see visible progress.
9. I sometimes switch systems too often and lose consistency.
10. I've celebrated a restart after falling off track.
11. My routines feel sustainable because they are flexible.
12. I can separate my identity from my slip-ups (missing a task doesn't mean I'm a failure).

Scoring for Section Five:

- 12–24: Consistency feels fragile. Focus on resilience by building compassionate rebound rules.
- 25–40: You're practicing consistency but struggle with shame spirals. Emphasize visual tracking and self-forgiveness.
- 41–60: You're cultivating sustainable resilience. Keep embracing flexibility so you don't fall into all-or-nothing traps.

Interpreting Your Results

After you've completed all five sections, reflect on your scores. Which areas scored the lowest? That's where you may want to focus your energy first. Which areas scored the highest? These are your strengths—celebrate them, and use them as leverage in the areas where you struggle.

This quiz is not about labeling you as "good" or "bad" at organization. It's about shining a light on your unique ADHD profile so that you can work with your brain, not against it.

- High **Mindset** scores suggest you're building compassion and perspective.
- High **Routines** scores suggest you have functional anchors to build upon.
- High **Decluttering** scores suggest you're learning to manage chaos zones effectively.
- High **Cleaning & Time Management** scores suggest you're using gamification well.
- High **Consistency** scores suggest you're resilient and flexible in your progress.

If you scored low in any area, treat it not as failure, but as information. This simply shows you where more support, tools, or creative strategies could help.

Next Steps After the Quiz

1. **Choose one focus area.** Don't try to fix everything at once. ADHD brains thrive on focus.
2. **Revisit the corresponding book section.** Align your weakest area with the book that addresses it most.
3. **Pick one tool.** Don't overhaul your life—choose a single exercise (like one-song decluttering or a visual chain tracker).
4. **Track progress for two weeks.** Use a simple tracker, sticky note, or journal entry to monitor your efforts.
5. **Reflect and adjust.** If it doesn't stick, adjust the tool—not yourself.

Closing the Quiz Section

You've just completed a comprehensive self-assessment. You now have a personalized map of how ADHD interacts with your organization and cleaning systems. Remember, this quiz is not about passing or failing, it's about understanding yourself better and choosing the right tools for your brain.

Change starts with self-awareness. You've taken that step. Now, you have the power to act with intention, flexibility, and compassion.

If you enjoyed this book, I'd greatly appreciate a review on Amazon because it helps me to create more books that people want. It would mean a lot to hear from you.

To leave a review:

1. Open your camera app.
2. Point your mobile device at the QR code.
3. The review page will appear in your web browser.

Thanks for your support!

HERE'S ANOTHER BOOK BY VIVIAN WHITMORE THAT YOU MIGHT LIKE

Made in United States
Orlando, FL
04 November 2026

90201509R00226